Prospero and Caliban

O. MANNONI

Prospero
and Caliban

THE PSYCHOLOGY OF COLONIZATION

Translated by
PAMELA POWESLAND
With a New Foreword by
MAURICE BLOCH

Ann Arbor Paperbacks
THE UNIVERSITY OF MICHIGAN PRESS

First edition as an Ann Arbor Paperback 1990
New Foreword copyright © by the University of Michigan 1990
All rights reserved
Published in the United States of America by
The University of Michigan Press
Manufactured in the United States of America

1993 1992 1991 1990   4 3 2 1

First published in 1950 by Editions du Seuil, Paris,
under the title *Psychologie de la Colonisation*

LIBRARY OF CONGRESS CATALOGING-IN-PUBLICATION DATA

Mannoni, Octave.
    [Psychologie de la colonisation. English]
    Ann Arbor, MI : University of Michigan Press, 1990. — 1st ed. as
an Ann Arbor pbk.
      p. cm. — (Ann Arbor paperbacks)
    Translation of : Psychologie de la colonisation.
    Includes bibliographical references (p.) and index.
    ISBN 0-472-09430-0 (cloth). — ISBN 0-472-06430-4 (paper)
    1. Ethnology—Madagascar. 2. Ethnopsychology—Madagascar.
3. France—Colonies—Africa. 4. Colonies—Psychological aspects.
5. Dependency (Psychology) I. Title. II. Series.
DT469. M276M3613 1990
155.8′9691—dc20   90-11270
                                            CIP

NEW FOREWORD
by Maurice Bloch

Prospero and Caliban is the translation of a book originally written in 1948 in Madagascar, during and immediately after a revolt that led to one of the bloodiest episodes of colonial repression on the African continent. The book is an attempt to account for this anticolonial revolt and for the brutal subsequent behavior of the French army, which resulted in nearly 100,000 deaths.[1] Mannoni's attitude toward these events is ambiguous. It is clear that the book is written by someone who is opposed to colonial exploitation and racism and who foresees and wishes for the end of the colonial situation, but it is also clear that it is written by a Frenchman who became the head of the information services of the colony.

The original purpose of the book is often forgotten, especially in English-speaking countries. This is not surprising, for it seems that while Mannoni was writing the book, he became caught up in an irresistible current of thought that carried him further and further from his original rather specific aims, and eventually plunged him headlong into a vast theoretical enterprise. Hence we find Mannoni attempting to explain and to account for the mentality of colonization and racism in general, rather than confining himself to Madagascar in the twentieth century. On an even more ambitious scale, Mannoni attempts to sketch an evolutionary theory intended to be applicable to the whole of mankind as well as a universal theory of individual psychological development.

It is one feature of these general theories that has made the book famous, since it is chiefly remembered for the notion of the "dependency complex" which Mannoni constructs in it and which was subsequently extensively discussed in psychological and psychoanalytical writing. The fame of the book in these disciplines is also linked to Mannoni's close association with and subsequent influence on the famous French psychoanalyst Lacan.

The obvious enthusiasm, intellectual daring, and encyclopedic learning of the author remain attractive to his readers today, and these good qualities are always conveyed through an admirably lively style. What is more, *Prospero and Caliban* can be viewed as a book that is in many ways well ahead of its time.

First of all, Mannoni's idea that studies of traditional African societies and cultures have to make the colonial experience central, not discreetly sweep it under the carpet or peripheralize it in a chapter on "social change," came to be accepted only much later in academic disciplines such as anthropology. In the English-speaking world we had to wait for the collection on colonialism and anthropology edited by Talal Asad in 1973 to have the point made again as powerfully as it is in Mannoni's book.[2]

Second, Mannoni's work is unusual and praiseworthy for his realization that a study of the "psychology of colonization" requires that as much attention be paid to the behavior of the colonizers as to that of the colonized.

Third, *Prospero and Caliban* may be seen as an early example of "reflexive ethnography." Indeed, the author was later to present, in the Author's Note to the English translation, what may be seen as an early manifesto for this recent trend. *Prospero and Caliban* is a book in which the personality and emotions of the author are on display and are acknowledged to have fundamentally affected the account of the Malagasy presented to us. This is all to the good, although, as often happens, this emphasis on the personal also seems to function as an excuse for Mannoni's failure to pay sufficient attention to the implications of his ethnic, social, and administrative status for the production of the argument.

Although the book does range far and wide, its starting point remains the Malagasy and Mannoni's understanding of the Malagasy and of their behavior during the revolt. This means that if these are wrong, then the whole edifice of theory must be called into question; and for me, as an anthropologist with considerable experience of Madagascar, what Mannoni has to say about the country and its people is profoundly unsatisfactory. Therefore I shall suggest that, in spite of his good intentions and his engaging personality, Mannoni knew little about either the Malagasy in general or the causes of the revolt in particular. In fact, much of the elaborate theory we are presented with may be little more than an attempt to make up for this lack of comprehension by relying on psychoanalytic theories that supply facile motivational explanations for actions that at first sight are meaningless to the foreign observer. As often happens, these ad hoc explanations can themselves become excuses for not bothering to find more straightforward explanations, which would have required at least a minimum understanding of the culture concerned. Furthermore, I suggest that this dangerous way of going about things has implications for many other attempts to apply psychoanalytical theories to other cultures.

These failings cannot be divorced from the colonial power situation for which Mannoni, in the end and after a degree of hesitation, makes himself the apologist. It is not surprising that shortly after its publication, *Prospero and Caliban* received a very general but furious and largely deserved refutation in Fanon's book *Peau Noire, Masques Blancs,* in the chapter entitled "The Pretended Dependency Complex of Colonised People."[3]

Mannoni's lack of understanding of the revolt of 1947 is in part explicable by the fact that exactly what had happened remained for a long time very obscure, thanks, no doubt, to systematic disinformation by the French authorities. Nonetheless, Mannoni's acceptance of tendentious myths concerning the revolt, current at the time among the French, sent him off on the wrong track right from the first.

In the book Mannoni sees the revolt as an event fundamentally caused by motivations that are illogical and inexplicable in rational terms.[4] Subsequent research, however, has shown that the rebellion was similar to other anticolonial revolts occurring at the same time, for example in Indo-China, and that the causes were much more straightforward and more fundamental than he would have us believe.[5] Two particular misconceptions about the revolt are especially misleading to both Mannoni and his readers.

First, Mannoni believes that the revolt followed a *liberalization* of French policy that made things better politically and economically for the Malagasy. This is, at best, a gross oversimplification and, at worst, a self-serving dissimulation of the situation, one much encouraged by the French at the time. This belief is nevertheless crucial for Mannoni's argument because it gives him an excuse for ignoring rational causes for the revolt or, for that matter, what contemporary Malagasy nationalists were saying at the time and it justifies him in searching instead only for *unconscious* causes.

Second, in his book Mannoni confirms the image, again popular among the French at the time, that the revolt was led by "sorcerers" who persuaded their followers into the irrational and unscientific belief that, if they used certain "charms," the bullets of the French army would turn to water. In fact, far from being the wild "primitives" evoked by Mannoni, the leaders of the revolt were either extremely well educated politicians or, at a lower level of command, noncommissioned Malagasy officers recently demobilized from the French army. Furthermore, although there is no doubt that magical and religious beliefs had a role in the revolt and that these were used by the rebel leaders to build up their followers' courage, this was of only minor importance. In any case, all soldiers, European as well as African, carry charms, and religion has always been used to bolster the morale of the troops, whether in "civilized" or "primitive" armies. Mannoni's endorsement of the "sorcerer theory," however, means that, once again, he feels that what he has to explain is irrational and bizarre behavior that can only be accounted for by the prelogical (hence the many references to Lévi-Bruhl) or, better still, by the "unconscious."

The Argument

Mannoni's general evolutionary theory is reminiscent of both earlier theorizing by such writers as Durkheim and Tonnies and subsequent theorizing by authors such as Dumont. This is no accident, since what we are presented with is, under a thin new disguise, very much the "received" view of social evolution that became accepted in the earlier part of the twentieth century through the gradual osmosis into general currency of the theories of nineteenth-century anthropologists and social scientists. As was the case for many of these early writers, Mannoni's argument combines European history, ontogeny, and evolutionary anthropology. For him this general theory provides the basis for the concepts that ultimately "explain" the rebellion of 1947. Here is an outline of the argument.

The child first experiences life in a state of dependence on his parents. He[6] expects succor from them and does not consider himself their equal; this is a relationship of dependency and it is the basis of all the child's moral and intellectual judgments. This early experience, with which we all start, is Mannoni's famous "dependency complex." Among civilized people this tie of dependency gets broken, largely on the initiative of the child, who nonetheless experiences the break as "abandonment" by his parents. (Here Mannoni is borrowing heavily from Adler.) The result of this "abandonment" can be good or bad. It may lead to a free development of the individual personality and to a rational and empirical mentality, typical of all that is best in European culture, or it may result in an "inferiority complex" that leads the actor to want to dominate others who, if the truth be known, represent his own unconscious guilt caused by the memory of his desertion of his parents.

This history of the individual is also the history of Europe. Long ago, there existed in Europe a primitive state of society in which "dependence" somehow combined with egalitarianism. Then, during the feudal period, dependence obliterated all traces of egalitarianism and dependency reigned supreme. Then, after the (French) revolution came democracy and the republic, which meant that society as a whole turned its back on dependency and instead valued egalitarianism and individualism. This rejection of dependency sometimes led to the development of a national inferiority complex, but it also contained within itself the potential for "freedom," a "freedom" that, as Mannoni envisages it, seems to owe much to postwar French existentialism. This final stage in the history of Europe produced, among other things, the French colonials. They are an example of people who suffer from the "inferiority complex" variant of modernity and try to make up for it by dominating colonized peoples.

This history of Europe also explains the different types of cultures to be found in different parts of the world. The most primitive, peoples like the Africans, are in a state of dependency, but they still retain a certain degree of primitive egalitarianism; others, more evolved semicivilized peoples, are in a state of feudalism, and thus they suffer from the dependency complex with no trace of primitive egalitarianism or modern republican freedom. Mannoni assures us, however, that he does not mean to imply by this merging of individual and historical development that the subject people of the colonies are arrested children. They are adults, but they retain the state of dependency by inventing lifelong pseudo-parents in the form of elders and ancestors whom they worship.

The theory is then applied to Madagascar. The coastal peoples of Madagascar are primitives like the Africans. (Significantly, although unhappy with the term *primitive* Mannoni cannot do without it and merely isolates it in inverted commas.) These are illustrated in the book by references to Father Cotte's rather simple and short study of the Betsimisaraka.[7] The Merina, on the other hand, the group that dominated Madagascar until the coming of the French and from which most Malagasy professionals are drawn, are at the "feudal" stage and therefore deep into undiluted dependency.

Because of their "dependency complex," the Malagasy must have parent figures if they are not to go insane. Because of their "dependency complex," the Malagasy cannot have a democratic government since this is based on impersonal social relationships at odds with their type of society and personality. Because of their "dependency complex," they accept knowledge merely on the basis of the authority of a father figure and cannot develop scientific techniques and undertake experiments, and so they will always remain prey to charlatans who tell them such nonsense as that bullets cannot harm them.

These Malagasy with their dependency complex were, however, faced by colonization. Their reaction to this event was inevitably entirely contained within the logic of dependency. Having witnessed the failure of their own rulers, one kind of father figure, in the face of the French, the Malagasy merely transferred their dependence onto the colonials, who also became a kind of father figure on whom they entirely and uncritically relied. The colonials for their part had their own complexes to deal with. Having been psychologically abandoned by their parents, they had developed an "inferiority complex" and were in need of primitives to dominate.

The coming together of dependent Malagasy and secretly guilty Europeans is thus what creates "the psychology of colonization."

This meeting of psyches was, however, to be disturbed in the decade preceding the revolt. First of all, the colonials, these substitute parents, were shown to be weak, and in a way that the Malagasy, their substitute children, could not ignore. This happened when the Vichy French government of Madagascar, which had been set up by the colonial settlers at the outset of the Second World War, was defeated and humiliated by the Allies, who landed in Madagascar in 1942. The return of the Free French and the Allies led to a period of uncertainty. Partly in order to get the colonial peoples on their side, partly to placate their American allies whose rhetoric was going through one of its anticolonial phases, the French promised self-determination and the possibility of independence to their colonies after the war. Consequently, the immediate postwar French government attempted to give a degree of self-determination to the Malagasy. In fact the policy was a total muddle and the promise of liberalization was soon to be reversed as the French government moved to the right and as the Americans, seeing what was happening in Korea and Vietnam in particular, began to support the reassertion of colonial power. Furthermore, quite apart from the contradictory policy emanating from Paris, the old colonial settlers, having recovered from their defeat at the hands of the Allies and taking advantage of some new laws, began unofficially to increase their use of coerced Malagasy labor.

Mannoni, however, sees things more simply. As noted above, for him, the colonial government was making straightforward progress toward more democratic forms and the Malagasy were being given more free-dom. According to Mannoni, the problem arose rather because this generosity, following as it did on the earlier demonstration of the weak-ness of the parents/colonial power, was misunderstood and interpreted as "abandonment" by the Malagasy. Instead of being grateful, they felt lost. The Malagasy, unlike the modern young European reaching adoles-cence, were totally unable to cope with such a situation and so they acted irrationally and started the revolt. As for the Europeans, whose inferiority complexes the reader will recall were based on guilt over the adolescent rejection of their parents, the sight of the Malagasy uprising served to reactivate the drama suppressed within their own unconscious. Subconsciously fearing that their own psychic past was returning to threaten them, they reacted to the revolt with a ferocity as irrational as the behavior of the Malagasy. The rebellion is therefore for Mannoni the product of the congruence of two personality crises.[8]

Having explained the rebellion to his own satisfaction, Mannoni then goes on to suggest "what can be done." It is noticeable that in this he seems much less confident than in his explanation of the past. The problem he sees is that the Malagasy should be led toward self-govern-ment, because the trend is that way, but that this should not happen too suddenly lest another "abandonment" crisis be caused. In any case, this self-government ought not to lead toward a Western democratic system because the Malagasy are not yet sufficiently evolved to be able to cope. "The average Malagasy . . . does not decide for himself and has very little sense of responsibility" (175). The solution should therefore be a gradual and firmly guided move toward partial self-determination and a revival of the traditional Malagasy communal organic village councils, the *Fokon'olona*, which, so Mannoni believed, once decided things unanimously under the guidance of the elders and the ancestors. In this way a gradual passage from dependence to freedom could be achieved without the Malagasy having to undergo the traumas of abandonment.

What is very interesting about Mannoni's "solution" is that it is ex-actly the one attempted by the French administration after the revolt, though how far Mannoni's book was influential in this policy I do not know. In particular, the French attempted to govern via the revived *Fokon'olona*, which was also to be the forum for the organization of economic development.

The administration's enthusiasm for the "revival" of the *Fokon'olona* goes back to the very beginning of French administration in Madagascar and to its first governor, Gallienni. In fact, it is very doubtful whether the kind of councils imagined by Gallienni's advisers or Mannoni ever existed spontaneously.[9] The term *Fokon'olona* literally means "the people of the locality" and nothing more. In the nineteenth century the Malagasy kings delegated a number of administrative duties to such local communities as a way of doing the job on the cheap. When the French came, they saw the usefulness of such an approach and so attempted to use the *Fokon'olona* in much the same way. In this attempt they genuinely believed that they were reviving an ancient institution. This was in part due to their general ideas concerning the evolution of society, ideas strongly influenced by European nationalism, which often relied on the belief that all primitives were once organized into holistic and egalitarian self-regulating communities. This idea had also been strengthened by the supposed rediscovery of similar councils in Asia, especially in Indo-China, where many early French administrators in Madagascar had been trained.

The belief in the existence of this kind of ancient collective administration was attractive to liberal administrators for many reasons, but it was also attractive to Malagasy nationalists seeking to regain their dignity in a postwar world that apparently valued democracy above everything else. One such nationalist writer, Dama Ntsoha, was Mannoni's guide on the matter of the *Fokon'olona*. Dama Ntsoha was clearly inspired by Gandhi and, perhaps for this reason, argued not only for a revival of the *Fokon'olona* and its supposed egalitarian values but also for an Indic and Buddhist origin for the Malagasy. Thus, ironically, a notion that had started in Europe, been used for cost-cutting in Gallienni's colonial administration, and then been mistakenly adopted by the Malagasy as a nationalist argument, was ultimately given a new lease on life by the French, dressed up as something the Malagasy nationalists had taught them and for which, subsequently, they employed an anthropologist to guide them in this hypothetical return to tradition.[10]

In Mannoni's work, however, the future role of the *Fokon'olona* is not merely political but also psychological. The *Fokon'olona* was first to be revived as a way of reassuring those with a dependency complex that they were not being abandoned as they had feared in 1947, but then it was to be subtly transformed as a way of gradually weaning the Malagasy away from dependence and toward a truly "free" future.[11]

The Evidence

This, then, is Mannoni's argument, breathtaking in its boldness, scope, and logic. But what does it rest on? It rests on Mannoni's identification of the "inferiority complex" of the colonials in Madagascar and his identification of the "dependency complex" of the Malagasy. It is therefore surprising that, even by his own admission, his evidence for such psychological attitudes is weak. I do not believe that Mannoni had any real basis for his evaluation of the psyche either of the French colonials or of the Malagasy, and I shall argue that in the case of the latter his supposed knowledge is based on serious misunderstandings.

Mannoni's knowledge of the French colonial mind does not rest on any body of psychological work. To make good this deficiency, he refers to various literary works, paying special attention to Shakespeare's *Tempest* (hence the title of the translation) and to *Robinson Crusoe*. To these he adds thumbnail sketches of the childhoods of Descartes and Pascal. I leave it to the reader to decide whether such evidence can be convincing as a way of telling us much about twentieth-century French settlers in Madagascar.

At first sight, Mannoni's knowledge of the Malagasy psyche seems better documented than his knowledge of the French colonial psyche. He also seems to be more aware in the Malagasy case of the dangers of insufficient documentation. Unfortunately for his argument, however, Mannoni's apologies on this point reveal the extreme scantiness of his information. Although he had managed to obtain "some descriptions of dreams" and had had "sustained relations . . . with certain Malagasies," Mannoni makes it clear that he cannot speak Malagasy properly and finds "no hope of obtaining psychoanalyses of typical Malagasies: there never have been any, and it is extremely doubtful if there could be any" (41). This awareness of the weakness of his evidence does not, however, seem to hinder him from drawing on these dreams and "sustained relations" to develop a general theory about the Malagasy. In fact, he draws on three kinds of data which I shall consider in order. First, there is the information he obtains from his reading of the ethnography of Madagascar; second, the dreams; and third, Mannoni's "sustained relations."

Although *Prospero and Caliban*'s bibliography is fairly respectable, the sources on the Malagasy actually used to a major purpose by Mannoni are few and unreliable. In particular he is greatly influenced by Cailliet's earlier attempt to psychologize the Malagasy, which was itself based on the flimsiest of observations.[12] Intermingled with Cailliet's work are occasional references drawn from different parts of Madagascar. This in itself causes a major problem, since the peoples of Madagascar are extremely varied in terms of beliefs, social organization, and mode of life, as is indeed occasionally noted by Mannoni himself. The resulting amalgam is therefore not really about anywhere or anyone in particular. To make matters worse, Mannoni, armed with his evolutionary beliefs concerning the fundamental similarity of all primitive peoples, does not hesitate to supplement the picture with information from Africa or Melanesia. The resulting picture of the Malagasy is thus very inaccurate. It would be very tiresome to go through all of Mannoni's mistakes; it should suffice here to note a few that are of importance for his argument.

Mannoni, good psychoanalyst that he is, is very interested in the relation of children to parents. He demonstrates the authoritarian character of the Malagasy father by the fact that he "keeps tight hold of the purse-strings and controls economic life down to the smallest detail" (57). This is because he is "the natural interpreter of the will of the dead" (56). The child, in contrast, has a close physical tie to its mother. "He is hardly ever parted from the mother; she carries him everywhere with her on her back, wrapped in his *lamba*, head and all" (57). In fact, it is always women who, in Merina families, control money "down to the smallest detail." Women are also, more often than men, "interpreters of the will of the dead." The relationship of children to their own mother is looser in Madagascar than in any other part of the world I know. Any one of a whole group of women will carry a baby on her back for very long periods, and furthermore, it is very common for men, especially fathers, to carry babies on their back in the manner described by Mannoni and to behave toward babies in a manner that a European would think of as "maternal." Even more important and damaging for the argument is the fact that up to a quarter of Merina children are permanently separated from their parents when very young so that they can be brought up or adopted by relatives. Indeed, the traditional marriage contract specified that either the first or one child in three should be given to the mother's parents for adoption.[13]

Equally misleading is what Mannoni has to say about beliefs in the power of ancestors. The nature of ancestor worship in Madagascar is, in most places on the island, very different from what we find in Africa or from the picture of "ancestor worship" that used to be common in anthropology, yet this African model is the one Mannoni seems to have borrowed for constructing his Malagasy dependency complex. In particular, Merina ancestors are not guides to the everyday activities of the living. They are usually thought of as an undifferentiated mass with no individual volition. They normally exercise no direct control over the actions of the living. The ancestors are therefore quite unlike living parents or elders in terms of authority.[14]

So much for Mannoni's general knowledge of the Malagasy, but what about the psychoanalyst's supposed secret road to fundamental information via dreams? The dreams Mannoni refers to are very few in number and obtained in very indirect ways. They are to be found in the five-page epilogue to part 1. Six dreams are summarized and these are selected from an unspecified total "drawn from various sources, but in the main they have been collected in schools in the form of French homework." The fact that the dreams were written in a language foreign to the pupils does not stop Mannoni attaching great importance to the choice of words in the texts of these dreams. It is clear, however, that some of the odder phrases in the texts of the dreams analyzed are due to the difficulty of translation from Malagasy into French. Thus in one case we are told: "A point to note is the passage from the singular to the plural in the woman's reply" (90). However, in Malagasy plural and singular are not marked in nouns, and Malagasy with only an average knowledge of French have very great difficulty in handling number in French. It is probable that the switch noted by Mannoni is nothing more than a mistake caused by moving from one language to another with fundamentally different syntax.

Many of the interpretations given to the dreams seem to me totally arbitrary. Many dreams concern cattle, and although Mannoni remarks in a footnote on the significance of cattle symbolism to the Malagasy, it is only in order to dismiss this fact as being of no relevance. Instead there seems a calculated attempt to ignore the obvious. If we remember that these dreams were collected within months of the most brutal atrocities, committed largely by Senegalese troops of the French army, the following interpretation is perverse:

> He is being chased by (Senegalese) soldiers who "make a noise like galloping horses as they run" and "show their rifles in front of them." The dreamer escapes by becoming invisible; he climbs a stairway and finds the door to his home.
>
> The sexual significance of the rifles is obvious. The sound of galloping horses and the desire to be invisible are probably to be explained by the fact that the child has witnessed the sexual act: he has both *heard* and *seen*. It becomes clear . . . that it is in so far as he is felt to be an aggressor threatening the mother that the father is identified with all dangers. (90–91)

Mannoni's interpretation of what he calls his "sustained relations with

Malagasy" are even more misleading and also very revealing, as they suggest that his contacts with Malagasy must have been based on continual misunderstandings, which are then explained by Mannoni as being due to the Malagasy's primitive unconscious.

In point of fact only one such "relation" is discussed in any detail, but it plays a crucial role in his argument since his interpretation of this relationship supplies his basis for the "dependency complex." The person involved was his young Malagasy tennis coach, who, in the colonial context, was a kind of servant.

On hearing that the coach was sick with malaria, Mannoni went to the boy's house to give him antimalarial drugs. The events that followed were to be the basis of Mannoni's theory of dependence. Instead of the tennis coach showing the gratitude Mannoni expected after he had recovered from the attack, the boy instead continued to ask him for more small presents so that in the end, as Mannoni tells us, he had to show his disapproval of such behavior.

For Mannoni such behavior on the part of the coach is prima facie either objectionable or illogical. However, in a liberal fashion, Mannoni goes on to seek a reasonable explanation for the boy's actions. His solution to the problem is that, by having helped the boy in the first place, Mannoni had become a kind of father figure to the boy, who henceforth considered himself *dependent* on Mannoni for everything. This psychological "complex" explained the subsequent demands and was, so the author believes, an example of the way the Malagasy as a whole viewed their colonizers.

It is interesting to see what Mannoni does *not* do in reaching this conclusion. First of all, he does not consider that the preexisting master-servant relationship between him and the boy might affect the transactional relationship established by the gift of the drug. Second, he never considers discussing the matter with the boy or any other Malagasy. Third, he never thinks of observing how Malagasy interact among themselves. Instead, knowing practically nothing of what ordinary Malagasy life is like, he imagines a possible psychological scenario that could account for the boy's behavior and turns for help to such writers as Adler who, presumably, knew even less about Madagascar than himself. Inevitably he totally misunderstands the actions of the boy.

Any anthropologist faced by a situation such as this, not such an unusual one in many countries, before indulging in such wide-ranging speculation, would first try to understand the significance of such actions as gifts and demands in the context of Merina culture. Until this essential preliminary has been attempted, any speculation about an actor's motives, states of mind, or psychological complexes are, to say the least, premature.

The demands of the coach for such things as old tennis shoes and cigarette paper is interpreted by Mannoni as an example of dependent hierarchical behavior; in fact, it is the typical way in which Merina friends and relatives, standing in an egalitarian relationship, behave toward each other. If Mannoni had watched Merina of relatively equal status together, he would have seen them continually demanding things from each other, small presents such as tobacco or food. In such a situation the person asked is under an obligation to give what is asked if she possibly can, even though to comply with the request may be quite an imposition. In order to cope with the problem many Merina carry two tobacco containers with them, one empty, the other full; when asked for tobacco they then display with mock pathos the empty one to show they cannot fulfill the request. Occasionally, in a similar mode, a demand for something more important is made: for example, I have often been asked by friends in Merina villages to give them the shirt I was wearing. In such a case the demand has a certain element of tease, but the shirt must be handed over, although it may in fact be secretly returned later. Again, if a Merina passes the house of a friend or a relative she will shout to ask for food, although usually when invited in she will then say that she has not time to eat, or will make a joke about the quality of the food not deserving a halt. This behavior has therefore an element of joking, but the most important aspect is that it is, and should be, *reciprocal*. Mannoni seems quite unaware of this crucial fact. Demands are thus used to define a close relationship of equality: for the Merina, equals are people who, with a certain amount of humor, demand things from each other.

The full significance of the behavior underlying such demands can be grasped only when we contrast it with its opposite: the behavior of people who stand in a hierarchical position to each other. Merina hierarchical behavior, as it relates to transactions, is of two kinds, both of which involve unsolicited gifts.

First of all, the typical behavior of someone who is clearly superior is not to ask for things but to wait to have things offered to him. For example, when an important administrator enters the house of one of his subordinates during a round of duty he will, first of all, expect to be given a chair, alone in the northeast part of the house (the part associated with superiority), and then he will *wait* to be given food. This food will always be unprepared: if it is a chicken the chicken will be alive, if it is rice the rice will be unhusked. The point of this is that the superior is left to dispose of the gift as he wishes. He may take the food with him or he may order his host to kill, pluck, and cook the chicken or husk and cook the rice. Then, when the food is served, he will be free to invite his "host" to eat with him or not.

The second way of marking hierarchy is almost the opposite of the above and it occurs when an inferior visits someone he acknowledges as a superior. In such a case the inferior person will humbly go into the house and sit in the southwest corner (the inferior corner associated with slaves and where people eat normally), and there he will wait quietly to be offered food. The food he will receive will, in this case, be cooked, and the receiver will express fulsome gratitude.

The behavior of equals who demand things from each other is therefore part of a set of other forms of transactional behavior, which although easily grasped, cannot be understood without a certain amount of preliminary cultural knowledge. By and large, one can say that among the Merina reciprocal demands are characteristic of equals, while unsolicited gifts mark hierarchical relations.

With this small amount of background in Merina culture, the behavior of the coach and his understanding of Mannoni's own behavior becomes straightforward. The original gift of antimalarial drugs, although unconventional in Merina terms, was no doubt understood as it was meant, as an act of friendship and solidarity on Mannoni's part. And so the coach intended to continue the solidary relationship and therefore made minor demands while no doubt expecting similar demands to be made of him. Instead, Mannoni's reaction was what the coach probably feared from a European anyway, a refusal of egalitarian friendship and an insistence on the reassertion of hierarchy that would follow from the implicit demand for gratitude.

Mannoni of course did not see things in this way. He interpreted the behavior that was intended to mark solidary equality as the most extreme form of hierarchy: dependence.

The reason for this misunderstanding is simple; it is Mannoni's arrogance. It is not the racist arrogance of the white man, a type of behavior he genuinely avoids and despises in the colonials he saw around him in Madagascar. It is the arrogance of the psychoanalyst or anthropologist, who unthinkingly comes to indulge in the different but no less objectionable claim to superiority that his professional knowledge apparently gives him. The irony for someone like Mannoni is that it is the colonial situation in which he works that alone allows him to make his assumptions with impunity. In practice it means that working in a foreign country about which he knows little, he thinks he can fathom people's motives without making any real effort to understand the context of their lives or the surface meaning of what they are expressing. Ultimately, Mannoni disguises his ignorance of Malagasy motives only by substituting other motives deduced from theories originating in the highly specific intellectual tradition of his own culture.[15]

NOTES

1. The best general account of this revolt remains J. Tronchon, *L'Insurection Malgache de* 1947 (Paris: Maspero, 1974).

2. T. Asad, ed., *Anthropology and the Colonial Encounter* (New York: Humanities Press, 1973).

3. F. Fanon, *Peau Noire, Masques Blancs* (Paris: Seuil, 1952).

4. I believe Mannoni was later to become aware of his mistake (see n. 8).

5. Besides Tronchon, see P. Boiteau, *Contribution a l'Histoire de la Nation Malgache* (Paris: Editions Sociales, 1958); V. Thompson and R. Adloff, *The Malagasy Republic* (Stanford: Stanford University Press, 1965). Among the many accounts and analyses in Malagasy is J. Rakotomalala, *Zava-Miafin'ny* 29 *Marsa* 1947 (Antananarivo: Fanontam-Boky Malagasy, n.d.).

6. I retain the masculine *he* to reproduce Mannoni's usage.

7. V. Cotte, *Regardons Vivre une Tribu Malgache* (Paris: La Nouvelle Edition, 1947).

8. In a subsequent article Mannoni was to recognize that he had overestimated the importance of psychological causes in the buildup to the revolt. "The Decolonisation of Myself," originally published in *Race*, April, 1966, and reprinted in his book of essays *Clefs pour l'Imaginaire ou l'Autre Scène* (Paris: Seuil, 1969).

9. See M. Bloch, "Decision Making in Councils in Madagascar," in *Councils in Action,* edited by A. Richards and A. Kuper (Cambridge: Cambridge University Press, 1971).

10. The story of the attempt to revive the *Fokon'olona* is to be found in the book by the anthropologist G. Condominas, who was called in as an adviser: *Fokon'Olona et Collectivités Rurales en Imerina* (Paris: Berger-Levrault, 1960).

11. In his article "The Decolonisation of Myself" Mannoni was to recognize that reconciling the French and the Malagasy could not be achieved by simply curing both sides of their "complexes."

12. E. Cailliet, *Essai sur la Psychologie du Hova* (Paris: Presses Universitaires de France, 1926).
13. M. Bloch, *Placing the Dead* (London: Seminar Press, 1971).
14. Because of the variation there are some parts of Madagascar for which the picture evoked by Mannoni fits better. It is clear, however, that most of the time Mannoni means Merina when he says Malagasy and his "ancestor worship" is totally un-Merina.
15. A somewhat similar criticism of the use of psychology is to be found in A. Bouillon, *Madagascar: Le Colonisé et son "Ame"* (Paris: L'Harmathan, 1981), which devotes chapter 12 to a discussion of Mannoni's book and places it alongside many other attempts at "psychologizing" the Malagasy. However, I fear that Bouillon is so swept along by the vigor of his denunciation that he fails to place Mannoni's work in the specific context in which it was written. Also, Bouillon's general antiempiricism makes him appear to suggest that it is not reasonable to evaluate the accuracy, or otherwise, of Mannoni's contentions.

CONTENTS

AUTHOR'S NOTE

IN his foreword Philip Mason has, I think, said all that can be said to introduce this study to the English reader. I shall add a few words about one aspect of the question which only I am in a position to know, namely the conditions in which the book was written.

The present edition is, apart from a few unimportant modifications,[1] a faithful translation of a work which was completed at the end of 1948. This is a significant date in the history of Madagascar and incidentally in my own life.

For years I have been interested in everything I could find out about that country and its inhabitants, but for a long time I deliberately confined myself to ethnographical rather than psychological studies. However I realised, almost in spite of myself, that there was a background of more disturbing psychological problems behind the ethnographical ones. I found myself taking part either in imagination or in reality in a kind of community life that was quite new to me, and realised with surprise that my own essence was being gradually altered. If for instance I took part in ceremonies concerning the cult of the dead I tried to do it in the spirit of a good ethnographer with questionnaires, photographs, etc.; but I discovered that this cult in its Malagasy form had an equal significance for me, and one which I could not ignore, surround it as I might with the ethnographical bric-a-brac that I was collecting. I seemed to have unearthed that single root, from which, according to a Malagasy proverb, the branches of the human race divide off like the shoots on a pumpkin plant. At the same time, driven like everyone else by my own private devil, I carried out various strictly personal experiments which led me to further discoveries, and during my leave in Paris after the end of the war I began a training analysis in the hope of clarifying my ideas.

I had interrupted this analysis to make a further short stay in Madagascar when the 1947 rebellion broke out. A veil was torn aside

---

[1] The end of the Introduction from the bottom of page 33 to the bottom of page 34 has been rewritten for the English edition.

and for a brief moment a burst of dazzling light enabled one to verify the series of intuitions one had not dared to believe in. By good luck I was in a position to understand what I so unexpectedly saw. The difficulties which had inhibited and confused my former impressions had, as it were, melted away. As I wrote it seemed to me that the things I had just begun to understand I had really, after a fashion, known for a long time. Several people who later read what I wrote had the same impression.

At that particular time my own analysis had not got very far and I rashly employed certain theoretical concepts which needed more careful handling than I realised at the time. I must frankly admit that I am now disturbed by the obvious weaknesses of the book in this respect.

I might have attempted to amend it for translation but I realised that in doing so I ran the risk of losing a more important quality. This is that the significant points, such as they are, are shown just as they arose in the natural sequence of the discovery itself, and it is through this sequence that the reader is led. The reader makes a kind of voyage of psychological exploration and it does not matter very much if the maps are not absolutely accurate. On the whole, what I regret is not so much these weaknesses in my book as the fact that I have not produced a much more openly personal study.

Less explanation is needed as to why the date 1948 is of special significance in colonial history. That is obvious. I would add, however, because my book is rather silent on this point, that I do not think one can lay down clearly any natural laws about human behaviour. I have simply described a situation which existed at a particular time. It is now perhaps disappearing.

O. M.

Paris, 1956

Author's Note to the Second Edition

MANY changes have occurred during the past fifteen years that may justify my adding a few words about the way I see this book today. It now seems to me that it might serve as a preparation for another study, one that would surely be more difficult, which could be called *The Psychology of Decolonization*.

In Madagascar in 1948, when the colonialist cause at least temporarily had the upper hand, one could easily see that colonization no longer had a future. The powers to be vanquished still appeared strong and formidable—and that they were so in fact was soon borne out by the war in Algeria; but it was clear that the colonialist position was too unrealistic, too emotional—one might even say too neurotic—to last for very long, in spite of its enormous resources. We had the impression, then, that history was moving forward more quickly than even the most optimistic observers had calculated. Today, with our present perspective on these events, we can acknowledge that reflections like those I offered had no perceptible effect on an historical evolution that had already begun. On the contrary, one should consider them as replies to the obscure questions history posed at that time.

But the book was effective in another field. Ethnographers and sociologists wondered if they had not been wrong to regard colonial situations as bastardized and unworthy of their interest. What they had taken for the meeting point of *two* societies was, perhaps, a process of creating *one* society of a type that was worthy of study. Then too, their attitude of scientific objectivity, which forced them to keep their own personality outside the field of observation, disconcertingly began to appear as a White Privilege and seemed to be a source of difficulties—almost a symptom of their refusal to understand certain aspects of the situation. New preoccupations appeared in their research, in which my book played some part—although, as is always the case when some novelty appears, they criticized it as reckless and as contrary to the "rules" they followed.

From another aspect, the reactions to my book were more unpleasant. The administrators, military officers, and even missionaries who dealt with practical problems of colonial life adopted the book in order to exploit it, and extracted from it methods and gimmicks to use in the pursuit of their own ends—a development I might have forestalled had I expected it, but for which I was unprepared. And the Communists, most attentive to such potentialities, denounced the book as an obfuscation. Their misunderstanding of my purpose was related to the fact that the search for psychological solutions can all too often be an alibi for those who refuse to confront true political problems. Nevertheless, the French Marxists' hostility does not seem justifiable to me now. For the facts have demonstrated that it is not enough to denounce the colonial situation as one of economic exploitation—which of course it is. One must also be willing to examine, in all the minute particulars, the way economic inequality is expressed, how, one might say, it is embodied in struggles for prestige, in alienation, in bargaining positions and debts of gratitude, and in the invention of new myths and the creation of new personality types. The fact is that the French Communists did not know how to descend to this level and were entrenched on the abstract heights of economic theory, so that despite all their activity and all their devotion, they played only a negligible role in the process of decolonization, a process that is still far from completed.

As for the psychological concepts in my book, I said in my author's note of 1956 why and in what way I soon found them inadequate from a theoretical point of view. I wish I could say of myself, by way of an excuse, what Freud said to Pfister in August, 1909!

What I described as dependence (a badly chosen word) is a phenomenon that is strikingly noticeable in a colonial situation, yet, in more discreet form, one meets it everywhere, particularly on the analyst's couch. On the other hand, the perception of the place the dead occupy in the "primitive" personality—and the way the white man, without realizing it, came to occupy that place—seems to me an important discovery that invites further study.

I must add that those who read this book with the greatest interest, or who were most moved by it, were, by and large, those who had personally experienced colonial life. They recognized themselves in it immediately, as in a mirror—some with pleasure, others with resentment. Surely this was proof that I had accurately described something that really existed. But it may have been only a transitory thing. I fear, or perhaps I hope, that it will no longer mean the same for the younger generation.

O. M.

Paris
May, 1964

FOREWORD
by Philip Mason

Director of Studies in Race Relations at the
Royal Institute of International Affairs

THERE are books—not often met once thirty is past—which open entirely new worlds of thought, others—only less rare—which are no less stimulating because they set in order what had hovered unformulated on the fringe of consciousness and express in words what had been on the tip of one's tongue. Mannoni's *Psychologie de la Colonisation*, now appearing in English as *Prospero and Caliban*, for me falls into this second category.

When I first read it, I had spent some twenty years in India as an administrator, living rather than studying Race Relations, and had written novels about what I saw and heard. One of these tried to show how the English criminal law worked in the lives of individual Indian villagers, another how education in Western thought and in an alien language might affect a boy who came from superstitious peasant stock in the remote hills. But I had made no attempt to generalise on such subjects and I found a fascination and delight in M. Mannoni's psychological explanations of what he had observed in Madagascar.

Let me give one example in my own untechnical language. No one can have spent long among Europeans either in India before partition, or to-day, in East, Central or South Africa without hearing some such phrase as: 'The natives don't know what gratitude means.' 'There is no word for thanks in Urdu,' they would tell you, though I can think of three, and they will say the same of Swahili and Ci-Nyanja. M. Mannoni had taken a few lessons from a Malagasy tennis-coach; hearing this man was ill, he went to see him and gave him some quinine. When he was better, the young Malagasy expressed no thanks, but began to ask instead for small presents, a pair of tennis-shoes, cigarette-paper, and so on. Most people who have lived in what M. Mannoni calls a colonial situation can recall incidents of this kind. 'You have done something for me which you were under no obligation to do: therefore I am yours and you may command me but on the other hand I expect you to look after me,'—that is the attitude. A young Englishman would soon learn not to feed a stray dog in an Indian village because he found that it would follow him for ever; with people too it was as well to be a trifle wary about setting up this kind of relationship; in the end the newcomer would often feel obliged to put on the colonial mask and become 'unsympathetic'.

This need for caution does not arise if you do a trifling favour to someone who is part, like yourself, of a competitive society; he either repays you—by thanks or some favour in return—or is conscious of an unpaid debt, in which case he dislikes or avoids you. Why should this difference occur? Because, replies M. Mannoni, the structure of the personality is different in the two cases. In a static society,—so long as it stays truly static—the individual is safely dependent on a complicated social system which, in the case of the Malagasy, usually includes not only living members of the group but dead ancestors and unborn posterity. The arrival of even one representative of a competitive society—immune from local forms of magic, blessed with a new magic of his own—threatens the peace of this primitive but complicated structure; the dilemma is admirably expressed in the Victorian romances of the school of Rider Haggard, in which the white man among an unknown African people must either become king or be sacrificed to their god.[1] If he survives, he becomes, like Rajah Brooke, and a host of colonial administrators, the father and mother of his people. The phrase at first expressed on the level of consciousness a respectful affection; in India at least it came to stand as the symbol for a paternal, colonial system of administration, which has now long been regarded with just those mixed feelings of conscious respect merging into fear, of subconscious jealousy and dislike, that a Freudian would expect the word 'father' to arouse.[2]

[1] Since the writer is a man, it is often a white queen rather than a king who walks this perilous path. Jung quotes Rider Haggard, particularly in *She*, as a writer who exhibits with clarity the archetype of the *anima*. The white queen combines two myths, that of Robinson Crusoe or King of the Castle with La Princesse Lointaine. The Anglo-Saxon writer usually projects on to the imaginary tribe his own guilty consciousness that sexuality is less than divine; thus Kipling's 'Man who would be King' loses his crown and his life because he insists on taking a woman from his subjects. 'The slut's bit me!' he cries, as she demonstrates in public that he is flesh and blood. But Crusoes in real life do not seem to have found that the people of their island shared this view; on the contrary.

[2] In the early nineteenth century in India, Sleeman mentions objections to field-to-

In Madagascar, M. Mannoni tells us, the new rulers at first took the place—in certain contexts only—of the dead ancestors and were actually called by their name. In this stage so long as the static society is not disrupted, the ruled people are content. But as the old society begins to crack, there are detached a few individuals, like single floes from the pack-ice, whose first psychological need is to become dependent on something new,—on a regiment, on an officer, on a kind master. These are the strays who attach themselves to a passer-by for a few tablets of quinine. If the stray is allowed to become dependent and then harshly rejected, his dependence turns to a sharp animosity and his Oedipean instincts come to the surface. If the whole society feels itself similarly abandoned and betrayed, the same emotions will be aroused on a wider scale. It is lack of guidance, bewilderment in a strange world, the feeling of abandonment, that produces the 1947 revolt in Madagascar or Mau Mau in Kenya,[1] not 'the firm Hand' so much as the invitation to walk without it or perhaps merely its unaccustomed absence.

The need for something to depend on is, then, the first element in the structure of the Malagasy's personality as he emerges from the security of tribal life. He does not say thank you but attaches himself as a dependant. And this meets exactly the psychological need of the 'colonial' European. Everyone in a competitive society is, to some degree, the victim of an inferiority complex, which may be expressed in a manly determination to make good, in a desire for perfection—often for perfection in some minute and unimportant form of escapism such as stamp-collecting—in a tiresome aggressiveness, in a hundred other forms. To the spirit convinced of its own inferiority, the homage of a dependant is balm and honey and to surround oneself with dependants is perhaps the easiest way of appeasing an ego eager for reassurance. M. Mannoni suggests that the colonial administrator, the missionary and the pioneer show themselves, by choosing a colonial career, particularly prone to this weakness, of which the

---

field survey and mapping on the grounds that it amounted to incest; a ruler should not uncover his mother's nakedness. Land is the mother; the ruler is son to her, father to his people.

[1] Of course, it may be one individual or a small group who suffers this feeling of betrayal and infects the rest, in whom it is present only by a process of what Leibniz called representation. I should also add that not every colonial rebellion is of this nature. I had, however, formed the opinion, before reading Mannoni, that the Indian Mutiny was largely due to reactionary sentiment; I have not looked at the evidence again in the light of what Mannoni has taught me about myself.

germ is present in every member of a competitive society and flourishes with peculiar luxuriance in the warm broth of the colonial situation.

The settler mentality is not, then, created by the colonial situation. Shakespeare knew that it was there in human nature and drew the colonial type in Prospero, the escapist deeply reluctant to give up his magic, to leave his desert island and to return to the society of people who would argue with him. Prospero, you will remember, seldom speaks to Ariel, the good native, without reminding him of how grateful he ought to be because he was released from a cloven pine; Ariel reminds Prospero that he was promised self-government, and Prospero, who does not think he is ready for it, threatens to peg him inside the knotty entrails of an oak unless he will be obedient a little longer—but does not, as one might expect, offer him a knight-hood if he would. Prospero usually bullies Miranda; to Caliban, the bad native, he is consistently harsh and justifies his harshness by Caliban's attempt to violate Miranda. Caliban does not deny this; 'would it had been done', he says,—and yet, after reading Mannoni, one is inclined to wonder whether Prospero did not, by projecting his own desire on to Caliban, first put the thought into his head. Certainly Caliban provides a convincing picture of the mission boy who has not made good, of the degradation that results when the tribesman is prised away from his old background, transfers his dependence and then feels himself rejected. 'The island's mine. . .' he says; 'which thou tak'st from me. When thou camest first, thou strok'dst me and mad'st much of me. . . . Wouldst teach me how to name the bigger light and how the less. . . . And then I lov'd thee and show'd thee all the qualities of the isle. . . .' And he concludes: 'You taught me language, and my profit on't is, I know how to curse.'

Prospero at his best stands for many a man conscious of powers which he cannot exert to the full among his peers, a magnificent leader among people who give him unquestioning homage and do not compete with his greatness. Livingstone springs to the mind—but colonial history is full of them and none of us are quite free from the Prospero complex. I, at least, since I first read Mannoni, have caught myself again and again. And there are of course plenty of Prosperos who never cross the sea.

One phrase—'The natives are never grateful'—has led a long way. It would be easy to make a list of others on which Mannoni suggests stimulating comment. 'I never trust a servant who speaks English'—

'They just learn things like parrots; they don't really understand them',—'You mustn't think they're just black Englishmen',—these, and a dozen more to be heard every day in a colonial situation, are instances of observed data interpreted in the light of psychological factors of which the speakers are seldom aware.

M. Mannoni emphasizes the point that both the dependence complex and the inferiority complex are present in rudimentary forms in everyone; the difference is that most Europeans repress one and most Malagasies the other. He is careful to confine his comments as a rule to Madagascar, but much of what he says does apply, with many modifications, to circumstances so widely different as those of India in the nineteenth century and Africa in the twentieth. In this wider context, I feel that more stress is needed on the exceptions. There were Bantu kings whose behaviour, as recorded by the earliest explorers, displayed their conviction of their own inferiority, others who seem to have emerged from dependence, overcome inferiority, and achieved a balance. M. Mannoni stresses the difficulties experienced by the Malagasy educated in France—difficulties of the kind which impressed me profoundly in India in the case of boys from peasant stock or with uneducated mothers. But it does not sound as though he had met many of the second generation of the emancipated from dependence or was aware of the completeness of the emergence that can be achieved.

On the other side, there are people in Europe who want to be safe, who like a repetitive job which requires no thought, who like to be told what to do, who expect the state or the Trade Union or some other organization to look after them, just as the tribe did or the ancestors did. I was told in Africa of a skilled carpenter the door of whose house was dropping from its hinges, 'Mend it?' he said in surprise. 'But who would pay me?' This was related as a typical and inexplicable piece of African behaviour; a week after I was back in England the same tale was printed in a newspaper, but in this case it was an English carpenter living in a house built by a District Council. I do not know if either story is true; it may be that the stories reveal more about the newspaper and its readers, about my informant and myself, than about carpenters. But it seems to show that this kind of dependent behaviour is not unthinkable in modern Europe. And it may be that there is more dependence, less inferiority and competition, in England now than fifty years ago.

I think, then, that there are more people in either kind of society who are typical of the other than M. Mannoni found in his narrower field. And when he argues that 'our image of these peoples [non-Europeans] is simply a reflection of our own inner difficulties', it seems to me that he is overstating his case. The problems of which he writes are, it seems to me, real,—whatever that may mean—and do not proceed wholly from conflicts within Europeans or European civilization. What is true of these problems is that we distort them, because of our own conflicts. And 'fortunately', as M. Mannoni writes, 'what we need to know is why we perceive facts in a distorted fashion', and why we react in a way that to a person of detachment will sometimes seem absurd or extravagant. 'Few men', he writes, 'are capable, when at length they are obliged to acknowledge the existence of other people, of recognizing in themselves what they never suspected was there, without an outburst of the fear, hatred or harshness they had directed against an aspect of themselves which they had wanted to ignore.' This fear or dislike may be dealt with in several ways, according to the personality of the subject. One man will try to ignore the person on whom he projects the characteristics he dislikes and will make himself as different as possible from him,— becoming fastidiously neat and tidy, for example, if he lives among a people he regards as unmethodical and careless; another will give up the struggle and go native; a third will try to reform, to civilize and to evangelize in others what he believes he has overcome in himself; a fourth will resort to irrational brutality. In each of these cases, the colonial has identified with the 'native' something he dislikes in himself; this occurs because 'the colonial situation offers us expiatory victims at little cost'.

It is M. Mannoni's value that he makes his reader aware of the distortions with which it is almost inevitable that each party should regard a 'colonial situation'. For me, he illuminates almost every aspect of such a situation, in spite of the fact that I disagree with him when he deserts psychology for philosophy. 'Nature', he writes, 'is divided up into self-sufficient parts each of which in isolation reveals the working of the universal laws, so that the man with an inquiring, scientific spirit sees the human group divided up and himself as self-sufficient in his isolation and in harmony with the universal laws of reason without the intermediary of God or the ancestors and without acceptance of dependence on family, society or any sort of authority.' This is quite contrary to what I believe is the view of scientists about nature, and I can hardly attach any meaning to the thought of an individual 'self-sufficient' as against family, society, and God.

M. Mannoni's extreme individualism proceeds, I think, from a misunderstanding of the relation of part and whole, and from a habit of analysis so searching that at last even the individual disappears. He writes: 'there is an abstract concept of the individual who is considered to be unified by the metaphysical "I think".' But this is 'a purely theoretical unification', and nothing but 'an idealist construct—' and liable to be flouted by everyday facts. The implication is that the elements of the personality at a given moment are all that is 'real', a conclusion surely also at variance with everyday facts. But this existentialism does not affect the main argument of the book or its value as a guide to the understanding of colonial situations.

Prospero and Caliban is a book to be read as the opening speech of a debate, which best serves its purpose it if provokes an eagerness to continue the discussion. Specialists no doubt will assail minor points from the angle of their particular interest, but those whose concern is to exercise some influence on one of the most explosive elements in the world to-day will share my gratitude to M. Mannoni and join in congratulating him on his courage. There are men whose learning is so profound that a host of conflicting detail forces them to qualify every assertion until they find in the end that they cannot write at all; there are others too concerned with the exact nature of truth to venture into speculative fields or so specialized in their knowledge that they must leave it to an interpreter to relate it to human life. M. Mannoni is among the interpreters, and I believe there can be few colonial administrators, missionaries or settlers who would not find that his book started trains of thought of the most rewarding kind.

INTRODUCTION

Tsihy be lambanana ny ambanilanitra
Men form one great mat

Merina Proverb

THE colonial problem is one of the most urgent of those confronting the world to-day—and France in particular. But though it is my intention to try to throw some light on its psychological aspect, that is not because I hope or even wish to contribute either directly or indirectly to the search for a practical solution. On the contrary, I shall take pains to show how limited are the conclusions which may legitimately be drawn from a psychological study, and I shall explain why that is so.

My principal object, then, is rather different: it is to point out the human significance of colonial situations, because up to now it has not been sufficiently realized to what extent a study of them can enrich our general knowledge of mankind.

Such situations can, of course, be studied from very many different points of view—the economic, the political, ethical, historical, and so on. There are, in fact, as many possible approaches as there are disciplines among the moral sciences. Each is of interest in itself, and it would be wrong to suppose that I am attributing greater importance to the psychological than to other kinds of explanation. If there is any merit in a psychological study it is because whereas we are accustomed to seeing a colonial situation as a case of the rich dominating the poor, the weak being under the guardianship of the strong, of the systematic exploitation of a difference in standards of living and so forth, we are not in the habit of seeing it also as a case of the meeting of two entirely different types of personality and their reactions to each other, in consequence of which the native becomes 'colonized' and the European becomes a colonial. These reactions are no doubt familiar enough in themselves, but they have never been properly analysed.

It should not, therefore, be very difficult to distinguish between my purpose and that of ethnographers and sociologists who seek to penetrate what used to be called—the expression is now out of date— the 'primitive mentality'. What they try to do is to act simply as observers and not to overshadow, as it were, the field of observation, after the manner of the natural sciences. But that, they soon find, is impossible, for many of the traits of behaviour they study can be understood only if they are seen as the reactions of the observed in the presence of the observer. Once that is recognized, we are on the way not only towards better methods of study but also towards a clearer perception of the essential unity of mankind. The relationship between the investigator and the subject of his investigation is like that between a doctor and his patient—it is a special kind of social relationship, in which mutual influence and an exchange of views are possible. No observation which fails to take account of this relationship can be considered valid. But that is not all: there is another and much more obscure factor to be reckoned with, and that is the fact that the observer's description of the native's behaviour is necessarily an interpretation, and that this interpretation is also *a reaction*, that of the observer to the native before him—though the nature of the reaction is not immediately apparent. The reader will discover later on how and why it is that the presence of a man whom our unconscious takes to be a 'savage' can cause confused and disquieting feelings to be roused in us. He may even be able to guess the reasons from my analysis of dependent behaviour in Chapter I, which shows that it is in fact the observer's unconscious reaction which has prevented his understanding what he has chosen to call the primitives' lack of gratitude, although in reality there is nothing very difficult to understand in it.

In short, then, what I want the reader to realize is that a *colonial situation* is created, so to speak, the very instant a white man, even if he is alone, appears in the midst of a tribe, even if it is independent, so long as he is thought to be rich or powerful or merely immune to the local forces of magic, and so long as he derives from his position, even though only in his most secret self, a feeling of his own superiority. The man-in-the-street will say instinctively and without experience that if the white man who goes among the negroes avoids being eaten, he will become King. However consciously watchful we are, we can never entirely eradicate this assumption of superiority from our unconscious, and it must be included among the data of the problem if we are to avoid all risk of error. If the reader has been willing to go thus far with me, he will be prepared to admit the theoretical importance I would attach to a study of the colonial situation in its broader, human aspects.

The rest of this introduction will be devoted to clearing out of the way certain very common and widely-held ideas which, though not of great interest in themselves, might otherwise prevent the reader understanding questions I shall be taking up later on.

First, a word about human thought, and some reasons why its intelligibility has been doubted.

Baffled by the mixture of success and failure they have met with in their efforts to understand the natives' behaviour, Europeans have resorted, in their bewilderment, to one of two extreme and opposite attitudes, and these attitudes still prevail. Some simply give up the attempt to interpret and declare that thought is incommunicable. They draw a hard-and-fast demarcation line between the civilized and the non-civilized, and on the basis of some vague notion of racial inequality they conclude that the non-civilized are non-civilizable. The others, on the other hand, assume that all men are equally endowed with reason, and refuse to see differences which a less abstract psychology would immediately have brought to light. This attitude is undoubtedly more liberal at the outset, but it leads to an equal, if not greater misunderstanding in the end, for when at length these people come up against the real differences, they see them as offences against reason and feel an indignant urge to correct them in the name of common sense. Though this urge may remain moderate and humane enough in its expression, it is fundamentally a product of blindness and fanaticism. To use the language of psychology, the first group project upon the colonial peoples the obscurities of their own unconscious—obscurities they would rather not penetrate— and their interpretation of the natives' behaviour is repressed because it is associated with the dangers and temptations represented by the 'instincts'. This can in fact be proved without even leaving Europe; it is only necessary to remember how often the negro figures in the dreams of Europeans who have quite probably never even seen a negro. The attitude of the other group comes to much the same in the end, for they try to subject all humanity to the rule of their own super-ego. Thus these two attitudes, which at first sight seemed diametrically opposed to each other, finally coalesce in the single belief that the mentality of the native is incomprehensible, that there is therefore no point in wasting any time on it, and that since our way of thinking is the only right one we should impose it on the rest of the world in the interests of reason and morality.

I shall be referring later on to certain early sociological theories according to which there were mentalities not capable of assimilation one to the other—not that there is any point now in discussing their validity, for their very originators came in the end to modify them to the point of abandoning them altogether, but they are the product of the colonial situations which the observers entered into; they are an example of the reactions I have been speaking of. The observer is repelled by the thoughts he encounters in his own mind, and it *seems* to him that they are the thoughts of the people he is observing. In any such act of projection the subject's purpose is to recover his own innocence by accusing someone else of what he considers to be a fault in himself. Thus, in order to preserve our peace of mind, we are compelled to believe that people whose thoughts—as it seems to us— are the same as our own innermost thoughts, are inferior beings and have nothing in common with ourselves at all. These processes, it should be noted, were at work, not among the sociologists who propounded the theories, for they were simply using the records of travellers, but among the travellers themselves; they had not been trained for the task of observation and so brought to it their projections all ready-made. This I shall illustrate with examples later on.

The theorists, in point of fact, began at length to see that they were mistaken. In a lecture on the primitive mentality which he delivered in Oxford in 1931, Lévy-Bruhl said that in the mind of every human being, no matter what degree of intellectual development he had attained, there subsisted an irreducible core of primitive mentality. I would only say in passing that although sociology failed to do so, psychoanalysis has succeeded in reaching this core. Furthermore, in his lecture Lévy-Bruhl refers to it as if it were a sort of non-functional survival in civilized people—a blemish almost, a savage slumbering in every civilized person, dangerous if roused. We, of course, are in a better position to appreciate its real nature. We also know that 'intellectual development' actually plays little part in the matter. Nevertheless, Lévy-Bruhl's comment goes a good deal further than the text of the observations of the travellers whose records he made use of at first.

Another belief which in the past made the study of colonial peoples so difficult and hindered our understanding them was that of *primitivism*. Here, again, there is no question of our discussing the scientific value of the concept, for it has already been discarded. Its effect was to make people look for data of an elementary and primary kind; needless to say, they ran no risk of finding any. The belief has now been abandoned and the word 'primitive' can be used only between inverted commas, as if to show that we no longer really believe in it. But it is not enough to banish a word from the scientific language because 'experience has shown' that the thing does not exist; the real problem, surely, is to discover how the scholars could in the first place have believed in something which did not exist. In order to be sure of the answer, we must find out how the concept originated and what were the deep-seated reasons which led men to form it. These reasons will become clearer to the reader after he has read Part II, in which I discuss Crusoe and Prospero. The savage, as I have said, is identified in the unconscious with a certain image of the instincts—of the *id*, in analytical terminology. And civilized man is painfully divided between the desire to 'correct' the 'errors' of the savages and the desire to identify himself with them in his search for some lost paradise (a desire which at once casts doubt upon the merit of the very civilization he is trying to transmit to them) because of his unconscious and ambivalent attitude towards his memories of his own early childhood.[1] Literary critics have wondered why Baudelaire's 'green paradise of childhood loves' was further away than India and China. The answer is that Yvonne Pen-Moor, his childhood sweetheart, was a creole from Réunion Island ('Your crinkly hair, your dark mulatto's arms' he says in a sonnet in the *Poèmes divers* dedicated to her). But Baudelaire felt, as we all do, that savage countries and savage peoples were the nearest imitation he could find in the real world of that of his childhood—of paradise. We may go even further and say, with but slight exaggeration, that there would be no ethnographers, explorers, or colonials 'among the savages' if it were not for this *vocation*. I shall confine myself to a brief reference to it at this stage, but shall explain its psychological implications later on.[2] It accounts for our daydreams about the

---

[1] And this is also why the ethnographer is very often tempted to turn towards the *past* in all his studies, in spite of the barrenness of such an approach, and to neglect everything 'recent'.

[2] It can be illustrated by a much more striking example taken from the natural sciences. Observers have followed hordes of gorillas—at a discreet distance, of course

'pure', the 'primitive', and the 'primordial'. But the word 'primitive' is used by the psychoanalysts to mean archaic, infantile, or instinctual. This, again, is a rather unfortunate use and one which gives rise to misunderstandings, for we are inclined to superimpose the meaning formerly attached to the word in ethnography upon the meaning now attached to it in psychology. The reader will realize that this is a temptation which I believe should be resisted at all costs. For even if there are peoples of whom the ethnographers can say that they seem hardly to have been touched by the main currents of civilization, and even if, on the other hand, psychology can describe the least-developed psychical phenomena, as they occur in infantile thinking, in emotional disturbance, or in psychological regression, there is nothing whatever to justify our equating the one condition with the other, in spite of our natural tendency to do so. This tendency may teach us a good deal about ourselves but can tell us precious little about the 'primitives'!

I shall, however, use the word 'primitive'—always between inverted commas—because the alternatives, such as 'isolated', 'unevolved', 'archaic', 'stationary', and 'backward' are in fact no better; the idea of primitivism is still there, though veiled and hidden, and this concealment simply increases the chances of error. In any case it should be clear by now that the subject of this book is not 'primitive' thought—whatever meaning is attached to the word 'primitive' —but the phenomena which occur in a colonial situation and the way in which colonials as well as natives react to that situation. This is virtually an unexplored field of research.

It need hardly be said that in practice a colonial situation bears little relation to what is known abstractly as contact between two civilizations; it is an obvious over-simplification to think of two

---

—in order to study them in their natural surroundings. They have brought back an account which coincides remarkably with the idea psychoanalysis has formed of the 'primitive family'. But that idea was arrived at solely from an exploration of the unconscious of the 'civilized' man. The coincidence between what the naturalists observed through their binoculars and what the psychoanalysts have discovered in the unconscious is therefore suspect. It tends to suggest that the observation is influenced by the observer's unconscious and his complexes of infantile origin. (Otherwise we should have to admit that psychoanalysis is the best way of studying biology or pre-history, and even Jung would not go that far!) In any case it is interesting to consider why some naturalists have found it necessary to flee from their own families right to the heart of Africa simply in order to discover the gorilla family—and that in part imaginary. An inquiry of this kind would prepare the psychological ground for a truly objective study of the anthropoid hordes.

cultures as two vessels unequally filled and to suppose that they have only to be connected up for their contents to find a common level. Where does this idea come from? From our concept of charity, perhaps; we think it enough if the rich man who gives to the poor takes care to avoid those feelings of pride and vanity which are lying in wait for him. The poor man and his alms and his emotional reaction to generosity—all this, we believe, should be left to sort itself out as best it may without our bothering any more about it. This pious schema has, indeed, often served as the moral basis— sincere or otherwise—for colonial ventures. If we think of a man as naked, we cannot imagine him failing to accept the first garment offered him with the utmost joy and gratitude.

We are surprised, however, when we discover what parts of our civilization the colonial natives have more or less readily assimilated and what parts they have vigorously rejected. In general, it might be said that they accept everything in detail but refuse our civilization as a whole, and it is this attitude which gives Europeans the impression that the native is ready enough to mimic them but never succeeds in emulating them. The deeper reason for this impression, as we shall see later on, resides in a difference of personality-structure. Suffice it for the moment if we cast off the obscure and in part no doubt unconscious belief that we can bring 'the advantages (or, according to some, the disadvantages) of civilization' to people who, we say, have simply remained 'closer to nature'. This is nothing but primitivism in disguise and has no clear meaning. The social and mental state of a native is certainly not to be expressed as a fraction in which the numerator represents the proportion of Western civilization which he has already absorbed and the denominator the total amount we feel he ought to absorb. How far he has been colonized in reality depends on the way in which he, as he was, has reacted to ourselves as we are. His reaction, however, is very far from being a simple reflection of our action, but we frequently fail to see that it is something entirely new, especially if we are expecting a slavish imitation. It may well be that it is just because we look for a too faithful copy that we tend to see the actual result as grotesque mimicry.

'Civilization' is necessarily an abstraction. Contact is made, not between abstractions, but between real, live human beings, and the closest contact often occurs at the least desirable level. When a native chief meets a European leader the psychological impact is less than when native labourers work under the orders of a European foreman. The leaders are the refined specimens of the two cultures, but the value of their encounter is lost in the ceremonial niceties which appeal to what might be called the political imagination but do not help to bring about an adjustment at the level of the little every-day affairs where the real work of mutual adaptation must take place. The native's opinion of European culture usually rests on what he has learned of it from some mediocre European colonial, and that can easily be something very different from what we imagine. European civilization and its best representatives are not, for instance, responsible for colonial racialism; that is the work of petty officials, small traders, and colonials who have toiled much without great success. And it is well known that in South Africa the white labourers are quite as racialist as the employers and managers and very often a good deal more so. Again, we must remember that it is not a question of *magic* being in conflict with *science*, but of a superstitious peasant sizing up the scientific pretensions of an often ill-educated and not particularly clever colonial, and drawing his own conclusions. Even when we educate native intellectuals and assimilate them com-pletely so that they become our equals—a feat which is not impossible and has indeed often been accomplished—we find in the end that we are no further on in the work of interpretation and understanding which we believe should bring the two 'mentalities' closer together. We shall see why not later on.   For the moment all I will say is that if such an intellectual becomes wholly assimilated to our culture, he is lost to his own people and can no longer get on with them, while if his assimilation is not quite complete, he will suffer painful psychological conflicts and will become subject to feelings of hostility which, paradoxically but understandably enough, will be vented upon the Europeans.

The undeniable fact that the psychological attitude of the native has long been in our favour has blinded us to its character as a re-action. To-day that character is only too apparent and cannot be overlooked.

The psychological phenomena which occur when two peoples at different stages of civilization meet and mingle can probably best be explained and understood if we see them as the reactions to each other of two differently-constructed types of personality. Indeed, to talk of the interaction of groups or of the interaction of personalities which may be considered typical of each group is to discuss the same problem with two different vocabularies from two different points of view, for the personality is simply the sum total of beliefs, habits, and propensities, organized and linked one to another, which go to make up the individual *as* a member of his group. The true thinking subject whom social psychology should study is the individual, Gaston Bouthoul says in his *Traité de Sociologie* (p. 398). But elsewhere in the same work (p. 375) he rejects the idea of a distinction between the personality and the individual: 'Certain sociologists have tried to draw a distinction between individuality and personality. Durkheim believes that the difference resides in the fact that the personality is the individual socialised. But this is a false distinction, for the simple reason that there is no man who is not a social being. To think otherwise is to indulge in unreal and misleading abstractions.'

This simple argument, however, is not conclusive. Clearly we do not expect to find a real individual in the pure state as the 'savage of Aveyron ' [1] may perhaps have been, but the abstraction is still valid. The individual consists of what is inherited in the chromosomes, the genetic stock with which a man enters upon life. As an individual he represents the species to which he belongs and, within that species, the line from which he has sprung. The personality, too, is inherited up to a point, but the inheritance is a social one and is preserved only if the human environment is relatively stable. The personality represents, not the species and line, but the social group and the family—the latter as human environment and not as genetic source. The fact that these two elements are always combined in a single human being in no way justifies our regarding them as one and the same thing. A new-born child is an individual but has not yet acquired a personality. His hunger, his tears, his play are attributes of his individuality and of the biological species. Later, his enduring attachment to his mother, his respect for his father, his love of justice and his fear of abandonment will form the basis of his nascent personality. There is no denying that an individual becomes a personality as he learns to be a member of society, and this is the more apparent the less individualist the social ideal. But even in a very

[1] Early in the nineteenth century some sportsmen discovered and caught a boy aged about fifteen, who was living 'in a state of nature' in the forest of Aveyron. He was brought up, rather unsuccessfully, by the Abbot de l'Epée. Since then 'wolf children' have been found in the same way in India. Anthropologists have occasionally speculated as to what light such cases throw on 'natural man', thus taking up the question more or less at the point at which it was left by Psammetichus the King of Phrygia (Herodotus II).

advanced society, where the ideal personality was highly individual-ist, it would still be possible to point out a fundamental difference between that type of individualist personality—whose individualist traits originate in the social background—and the individual pure and simple, whose psychological (and physiological) characteristics derive solely from the biological species. Individualism might even be considered as a further development of the personality. To clarify the point we might recall Comte's classification of psychology into the biological and the social. But Comte's idea was too simple; between the individual organism and the social being there is precisely a person, with his own unique experience and his own unique history. He is distinct from his history as his memory records it. He cannot be explained in terms of the laws of habit or conditioned reflexes. But his personality has grown out of these habits and reflexes in the course of this history through his reactions to his environment, and especially his social environment, and that means first and foremost the family, the environment of the small child.

Thus we can pass from the structure of the group to the structure of the family, from that of the family to that of the personality: three aspects of the same human reality. And it may be that the best way to approach certain problems of collective psychology is, instead of studying the social group from the outside, to seek its inner reflection in the structure of personalities typical of the group.

Just as there may be some divergence between the characteristics of the species and those of a given member of it, so a given personality may not entirely coincide with what is thought of as the group mentality. But there are *types* which represent accurately enough in the one case the species and in the other the social group. Of course the more homogeneous the society, the easier it is to find members typical of it. If, then, we study the effects which two different types of personality have on each other, we shall discover socio-psycho-logical facts of the highest importance, and learn to understand certain sorts of xenophilia and xenophobia, racialism, nationalism, and clannishness and in a general way the reasons why there is friendship or conflict between different human groups.

Now, if there is one place where these things can be observed more easily than anywhere else, it is in the colonies. In a colonial situation the difference between the two types of personality brought face to face is greater, probably, than in any other, assuming—though it is not strictly true in every instance—that the colonizing peoples are among the most advanced in the world, while those which undergo colonization are among the most backward. The other characteristic features of a colonial situation—domination of a mass by a minority, economic exploitation, paternalism, racialism, &c.—are either the direct outcome of the relationship between the two peoples, as, for instance, paternalism, or they are distinctly 'colonial' as a result of that relationship. Colonial exploitation is not the same as other forms of exploitation, colonial racialism is different from other kinds of racialism. . . .

A policy of segregation, it may be noted, is powerless to prevent an interaction between the two types of personality once they have been brought together. Indeed, such a policy is itself a consequence of this interaction; the barriers it sets up in the outer world have their counterparts within the individual. From the purely psychological point of view it can be said that segregation is harmful both to those who impose it and to those who submit to it. Fortunately there is very little likelihood of its ever being introduced in the French colonies; the French, on the contrary, long held truly Utopian beliefs about the possibilities of assimilation. But such beliefs were possible only so long as colonial relations remained at the level of crude charity and blind pedantry. Assimilation can succeed if the personality of the native is first destroyed through uprooting, enslavement, and the collapse of the social structure, and this is in fact what happened—with debatable success, however—in the 'older' colonies.[1] But we can hardly recommend the introduction of slavery on the grounds that it will reduce the colonial peoples to a molten state and so enable us to pour them into a new mould; assimilation is only practicable where an individual has been isolated from his group, wrenched from his environment and transplanted elsewhere. It is absurd, therefore, to suggest that what is possible for individuals must also be possible for whole groups; too much hope has been founded on the success of isolated cases. When they have reached a certain number, of course (it is difficult to say how many; the figure has perhaps already been passed), they are bound to have an effect on the situation as a whole, though what effect it is impossible to forecast: certainly something very different from what may be expected by those who still cling to their faith in the virtue of a policy of assimilation.

[1] The French term *vieilles colonies* refers to colonies which remained after the eighteenth century and had been based on slavery—such as the Antilles and Réunion.

In the past people have in this way failed to distinguish clearly between the question of the assimilation of the single individual and the question of the mutual adaptation of two groups with different mentalities.   Some regarded the isolated cases as exceptions which proved nothing; others, on the other hand, saw them as conclusive proof of assimilability and felt that they should serve as a model for the masses.   It was generally believed that an individual consisted of what he had inherited (from the race) and what he had learnt, while education was naïvely thought of in purely academic terms.   The problem of assimilation then amounted to finding out whether the cultural graft would take and bear in the hereditary stock: in other words, it was felt to be a question of *natural aptitudes*.   I shall only say a few words about this, in order to show why it is of no interest to us.

To the question whether such and such a 'colonial' group is as intelligent as the average European group there is, I think, no acceptable answer.   If we were to judge solely by everyday experience we should find ourselves confronted with a series of impressions, each contradicting the one before.   For example, a typical Malagasy would be able to pick his way intelligently through a maze of subtleties which would quite bewilder us, and then he would fall down on some simple common-sense question in which we should see no difficulty at all.   But we should not be justified in drawing any conclusions from these impressions, for we should not know how much to attribute to his acquired mental habits and how much to his innate capacities.

We might perhaps try to overcome this difficulty by making use of intelligence tests.   We should then get a figure which would represent the intelligence of the average Malagasy child as compared with the intelligence of the average European child of the same age.   This would be a real indication of intelligence (always allowing for the accuracy of the index), but in fact we should not be very much further forward, for intelligence develops more or less as the social environment permits.   The tests measure intelligence by discounting *scholastic* acquisitions, but they do not discount *social* acquisitions, and so they are really valid only in the measurement of the natural aptitudes of persons of the same social environment.   The European grows up in a social environment which is more intelligent, in the sense in which I am using the word, than that of the Malagasy—for there is undoubtedly a social intelligence which is neither the average intelligence nor a function of the natural aptitudes of each individual in the group. And then there is always the chance that if the Malagasies were to devise their own intelligence tests—which is not beyond the bounds of possibility—the results would turn out to be in their favour!

In any case, the measurement of natural intelligence is not very useful in itself, for experience tends to show that the difficulty is not lack of intelligence but the fact that there are psychological obstacles, deriving from the social environment, which hinder the development of the intelligence. Once they are removed, the intelligence usually proves to be adequate.

Apart from obvious cases of mental deficiency, the idea of inborn intellectual aptitudes, which has never any very clear meaning, proves to have none at all in group psychology, for we have no means of gauging latent capacities except through observing manifest abilities, and these depend, at least for their development, on the social environment.

I have been referring in the main to intellectual capacities because it is these which in the past have attracted most attention. But the same is no doubt true of all natural aptitudes. When an author states that observation has shown that such and such a race lacks an aptitude for, say, attention, reasoning, &c., he is using faulty language. Let him say if he likes that a native of a certain race lacks attention, that a certain type of education, though successful with Europeans, has failed to make him attentive. He will then be stating the results of his observation correctly—if he has observed accurately. But in using the word aptitude he is suggesting to the reader that it is a matter of a fundamental incapacity, and we do not yet know enough to be able to pronounce on such matters.

One fact which appears to me to be very significant is that the crumbling of the old social structures in certain parts of Africa has resulted in an unexpected burgeoning of intelligence among the negroes. Consequently, an entirely different estimate of their alleged aptitudes is given to-day from that given fifty years ago. This should be enough to put us on our guard against the danger of estimating latent aptitudes from manifest abilities, which are all that we can observe. These estimates are arrived at by comparing a native with a European of the same age and at the same scholastic level, on the—erroneous—assumption that we know all about the natural aptitudes of the European! Aptitude-testing is, of course, still of some use if it is undertaken with a definite end in view, as, for instance, for the purpose of choosing from a group of native children those who, at the time of the test, are most likely to derive benefit from a specific type of schooling.

In order to prevent any misunderstanding, I shall say a few words about those isolated individuals who become assimilated into an environment different from the one into which they were born. Do they raise the problem of the unity of the personality?

A logic more verbal than real would lead us to suppose that someone who has grown up in two very different environments runs the risk of acquiring a dual personality. In actual fact, of course, that cannot happen. It might be said, in the manner of a Kantian axiom, that when the same individual participates in them, two different environments are but the parts of one and the same environment. People adapt themselves to a double environment rather as they do to bilingualism; it is simply a matter of a change of attitude, which does not affect the essential unity of the personality beneath. Naturally, the personality is to some extent modified by this apparent duality, but it continues nevertheless to follow the general law of development of the personality. According to this law, all elements which are in any way capable of coexisting are integrated into a single whole, while those which are incompatible with the rest are repressed. Thus every personality is unified, but the unification is never complete, because there is always something repressed. Those who pass from one environment to another and preserve their unity through a process of integration and repression are particular instances of this general law. When referring to them I shall use the expressions 'their European personality', and 'their native personality', but they are of course simply two aspects of the same individual—two *personæ*, we might say, two parts played by the same actor. But that is perhaps not entirely accurate, for there is reason to believe that in a non-civilized individual it is not easy to distinguish the *persona* from the inner personality. Only civilization makes it possible to distinguish between them, and it is not yet clear how a personality originally constructed on the 'non-civilized' model can later produce a second, 'civilized' personality. These, however, are mysteries which are best left till later.

All the material used in this book is drawn from Madagascar. My *indirect* knowledge of other colonial peoples leads me to believe that some of my conclusions are of general applicability. My personal experience of Malagasy customs and their psychological significance has frequently made me feel that I understood what other observers have reported about other peoples. But it is for them to judge, for there is no substitute for personal experience: I have too often seen how fatally easy it is to fall into error the moment one embarks on ethnography by hearsay. Most of the general theories which have now been discarded as purely hypothetical—to say no more—were formulated by armchair ethnographers from the evidence of travellers who, more often than not, had not set out as impartial witnesses. At the risk of offending, I must remind the reader that in spite of all their love and devotion the doctors, missionaries, and so on can hardly be called disinterested observers, if only because they came with the idea of changing, converting, civilizing. In order to understand their testimony we need to bear this purpose in mind; we need, that is to say, to take into consideration the situation I have been calling *colonial*. It is not absolutely essential to have experienced such a situation in order to be able to comprehend it; on the contrary, nothing is easier to imagine, as I shall show. But at the same time these products of the imagination are the source of all illusions, and the task of analysis consists primarily in sifting out the real from the imaginary.

This statement must not be taken too literally, however. There is no hope of our arriving at an objective truth through describing a fellow human as a distinct and separate being, for we can only bring him to life through the stuff of our own consciousness, and to be objective in these circumstances is to arrange as best we can, and to some extent to organize our own feelings and fancies in the presence of the other person. This is not an extension of scientific objectivity but rather a kind of social relationship; hence the value of direct, personal experience. We may resist the relationship in an attempt to attain 'greater objectivity', but in so doing we may well be eliminating something essential.

This book sets out to describe colonial situations as primarily the results of misunderstanding, of mutual incomprehension. It may be objected that this is the case with all human situations, and that is of course true: we could in fact approach the problem from this angle. It may be that this element is simply more pronounced and easier to detect in a colonial situation than elsewhere. European colonizers have battled successfully against hunger, sickness, slavery, ignorance —for all these evils have recoiled somewhat before their attack—but in spite of their good works they have failed to achieve friendly relations with the 'colonized' and we are now inclined to think that theirs was the wrong way to go about it.

The colonizers of the heroic age—the era of colonial expansion —were fully convinced of the superiority of the civilization they represented. Their strength came from their knowledge that, though they represented this civilization, they did not embody it. They did not set themselves up as models; they offered to others their own ideals, something greater than they.[1] But the fact that they possessed superior power persuaded the natives of the overriding need to imitate and, like schoolchildren, to obey. Psychologically the result was at first beneficial. At that stage it was impossible even dimly to perceive the reciprocal misunderstanding on which the situation was based, nor could it have been foreseen what successes and failures the effort at imitation was to meet. It would be pointless to pass judgement now on what happened then, especially as there was undoubtedly much goodwill on both sides at the outset, but we may be sure that those early events were the cause of the present situation. We should not, however, delude ourselves, as is commonly done, by thinking that if only the colonizers could have been more generous, more charitable, less selfish, less greedy for wealth, then everything would have been very much better than it is now—for in that case they would not have been colonizers. We must not, of course, underestimate the importance of economic relations, which is paramount; indeed, it is very likely that economic conditions will determine the whole future of the colonial peoples. And it cannot be denied that there have been and still are shocking abuses in this direction which have outraged public opinion. But they are not to be explained solely in terms of economic interest and exploitation. North American negroes may be less well-treated than white workers, but it is not because it is more profitable to treat them in this way, for that is not the case: in fact they are ill-treated because they are treated *as negroes*, that is to say in a way which escapes definition in economic terms. The 'colonial' is not looking for profit only; he is also greedy for certain other—psychological—satisfactions, and that is much more dangerous. Accurate observation of the facts would no doubt show us that he very often sacrifices profit for the sake of these satisfactions.

[1] This is what gives the missionaries their strength to-day.

It would not be difficult for a 'shrewd businessman' to make a good deal of money, as in Europe, by more or less honest means, without acquiring the characteristics of the colonial. But you will rarely come across such a man in the colonies. Why? Because there is no need for him to leave Europe. In other words, in a colonial situation economics are colonial and it is the adjective, not the noun, which interests us.

The colonial peoples have long been aware of the meaning of this adjective. They draw a clear distinction between the European proper and the colonial European; after all, they have had plenty of opportunity of watching the one turn into the other. Malagasies living in France get along with the French very well on the whole, but they carefully avoid anyone who has spent any length of time in Madagascar. So it appears that a Europeanized native can live in a European environment without any 'situation' necessarily arising, but of course we cannot forecast what might happen if Malagasies came to Europe in greater numbers.

It is difficult—and the difficulty is part of the situation—not to pass moral judgements on the feelings which the encounter breeds on either side. Besides, these judgements can to some extent legitimately be passed precisely in the name of morality. But that is a standpoint which all too easily blurs the vision, and I shall avoid it so far as possible, for I do not wish either to excuse or to condemn; suffice it if I explain how the seeds of the psychological situation which is only now bearing its bitter fruit were sown right at the very beginning. Even if it had been my purpose to try to suggest ways of remedying the defects in 'colonial policy' I could not have done better to begin with than to offer such an explanation.

The main object of this book is not to show how such problems can in theory be dealt with. An assortment of ideas, borrowed from various schools of psychology, has been applied quite unsystematically, so that any reader who is well versed in the theory of analytical psychology may find himself puzzled.

If one had to reduce the psychological theory to one system, I believe one could do it by applying the ideas of Karl Abraham, and especially of Melanie Klein. For example, the cult of the dead, such as is found among the Malagasies, would come near to being an institutionalized form of Melanie Klein's internalized 'good object' theory, according to which the individual preserves a 'good object' to which tribute must be paid. This cult, in contrast to the sort of mourning for stated periods we know in Europe, is continuous and acts as a protection against melancholia and as a cure for it, without having the same effect against what Klein calls 'persecutory anxieties'. I think one could use this phrase as a starting-point for a precise description of the 'primitive' personality. The 'wholly phantastic' world which Melanie Klein has found in infants,[1] and has attributed to persecution, is also to be found in 'primitive' people and continues with them in a quite special way.

But as a matter of fact the psychological analysis had a quite different point for me at the time I was writing this book. I was more interested in my own psychological make-up than in the psychology of the subjects under observation, who presented a less complex problem. For instance, I had often been astonished by the penetration and exactness of thinking shown by some old colonials when they analysed for my benefit the hidden reasons for certain native behaviour; but if I revealed my astonishment to them, they would at once reply that the natives were beyond comprehension and would always remain so. I was forced to realize that the colonials were reluctant to admit that they understood the native as well as they in fact did, and I saw that the problem for human beings, however much they differed from one another, was to acquire, not the ability but the *will* to understand each other. It is as difficult to see something of one's self in all men as it is to accept oneself completely as one is. For this reason I became preoccupied with my search for an understanding of my own self, as being an essential preliminary for all research in the sphere of colonial affairs.

That was how my study of social relationships coincided with research into my own personal problems. Moreover, this study also happened to coincide with a certain moment in history, a crisis in the evolution of politics, when many things that had been hidden were brought into the light of day; but it was only a moment, and time will soon have passed it by. I often had my doubts as I asked myself what was lasting and what was transitory in the observations I made; and I consoled myself with the thought that I would have successors who would correct my mistakes.

In the following pages the reader will find, first, a description of the general characteristics most typical of the Malagasy personality

[1] *Contributions to Psychoanalysis*, p. 238.

in relation to the structure of the family and the cult of the ancestors (Part I).

Then (in Part II) there is an analysis of the attitude of the European colonial to the image of the native.

The remaining chapters are devoted to an examination of the different aspects of the interhuman relationship which arises in a colonial situation.

Part I

DEPENDENCE

CHAPTER I

DEPENDENCE AND INFERIORITY

Dependence

THE celebrated inferiority complex of the coloured peoples, which is so often invoked to explain certain traits of their behaviour, is no different from the inferiority complex pure and simple as described by Adler. It springs from a physical difference taken to be a drawback—namely, the colour of the skin. But a difference of this kind gives rise to a complex only if it can in fact be accounted a disadvantage; at any rate it must be perceptible as a difference. In practice, therefore, an inferiority complex connected with the colour of the skin is found only among those who form a minority within a group of another colour. In a fairly homogeneous community like that of the Malagasies, where the social framework is still fairly strong, an inferiority complex occurs only in very exceptional cases. Its rarity probably alters its effects, for a person suffering from it will not find all around him those examples of compensation or sublimation which are usually of such comfort to an 'inferior' individual. But this difference is only superficial, and the fundamental nature of the Adlerian inferiority complex remains the same.

Furthermore, these exceptional cases of inferiority occurring in a homogeneous community obviously have nothing to do with skin colour, but are due to individual feelings of inferiority of various kinds. As with Europeans, any difference can cause a feeling of inferiority, once certain psychological and sociological conditions are fulfilled. The extreme rarity of the complex among typical Malagasies (it is practically never found except in a Malagasy who is already thoroughly Europeanized) therefore seemed to me to require explanation.

In seeking it I have been led to attach considerable importance to a group of psychological and social conditions which together I shall call 'dependence'. It is these conditions, as I shall endeavour to show, which explain why the development of the inferiority complex is slowed down, and indeed stifled, in a community like that of the Malagasies. Dependence and inferiority form an alternative; the one excludes the other. Thus, over against the inferiority complex, and more or less symmetrically opposed to it, I shall set the dependence complex. And these two different psychological climates serve to characterize two different types of personality, two different mentalities, two different civilizations.

The fact that when an *adult* Malagasy is isolated in a different environment he can become susceptible to the classical type of inferiority complex proves almost beyond doubt that the germ of the complex was latent in him from childhood. If we were to proceed farther in this direction we should very probably—as, indeed, we shall see later in connexion with dreams—encounter the Freudian castration complex. All I need say at present, however, is that the germ remains inactive in normal conditions—that is, while the individual feels himself securely held by the traditional bonds of dependence. It could also be maintained, as I shall show, that there is a potential dependence complex in the 'inferior' European. It is repressed, however, and this makes it difficult for us to perceive and appreciate it in others. A European who is more or less the victim of an inferiority complex tends to *feel*—and not simply to *consider*— an objective position of dependence as a sign of inferiority. He may rebel against it or react by displaying 'symptoms'. The Malagasy, on the other hand—and in this there is reason to believe that he does not differ radically from other non-civilized peoples—feels inferior only when the bonds of dependence are in some way threatened. This difference is probably the key to the psychology of the 'backward peoples'. It explains the long stagnation of their civilizations. It accounts for their belief in magic, and elucidates what seems to us at first sight incomprehensible in their psychological reactions—that mentality which we have long considered incapable of 'assimilation' to our own.

At a later stage I shall be describing the whole corpus of phenomena which are connected with psychological dependence, but I should like to make a few preliminary observations now.

It would be far from true to say that the Malagasies conform to a single type. There are many different ethnic groups among them, and although in the present state of our knowledge it is difficult to give an exact figure with any confidence, nevertheless it is possible to distinguish about twenty different groups at varying stages of development. The most backward are 'primitive' in the very vague sense in which the word is used at the present time. Others have to a greater or less extent undergone European influence, and it is of course these who interest us most. To be precise, then, we shall be studying *the dependence complex among Malagasies in course of colonization, and more particularly among the Merina.*

However, our knowledge of individual psychology among the Malagasies will necessarily be less complete than it would be of Europeans. I have been able to obtain some descriptions of dreams, and these I have analysed. I have also given my interpretation of the sustained relations I have had with certain Malagasies. But there is no hope of obtaining psychoanalyses of typical Malagasies; there never have been any, and it is extremely doubtful if there could be any. Apart from the difficulty presented by a language which, though broadly comprehensible, is capable of formidable subtleties and equivocations, it would still be necessary for the Malagasy to grant the European a degree of confidence he would not accord even his best friend. Finally, we do not find in him that disharmony, amounting almost to conflict, between the social being and the inner personality which is so frequently met with among the civilized and offers the analyst a means of access to the psyche. The oriental 'face' is different from the Jungian *persona* in being more firmly welded to the whole being.

All this would seem to suggest that the ego is wanting in strength, and that is borne out by the fact that hallucinatory disturbances and panic appear the moment the feeling of security is threatened. The individual is held together by his collective shell, his social mask, much more than by his 'moral skeleton'. And this, with but slight modifications, must be true of many other 'primitive' societies. It can be proved from the way these societies treat the sick, the possessed, the bewitched—all those who in Europe would be classified as neurotics. They are usually dealt with by means of initiation dances, ceremonies, or sacrifices, all of which are intended in one way or another to bring the sufferer back into the fold, with or without his evil spirit. Curative ceremonies of this kind have been known to exist in Madagascar, although to-day there are only distorted and barely recognizable traces of them left. (See for instance what the Reverend Father Cotte has to say about them in his *Regardons Vivre une Tribu Malgache*, Paris, 1947, pp. 225-32.)

Dependent behaviour

The 'dependent' behaviour of the Malagasies—and also, as we shall see, of other 'primitive' peoples—has almost always been misunderstood, but Europeans have never failed to notice it and to be astonished by it. Usually they first encounter it on the occasion of an exchange of services, and the sequence of events is generally something like this. A Malagasy receives from a European some favour which he badly needs, but would never have dreamed of asking for. Afterwards he comes of his own accord and asks for favours he could very well do without; he appears to feel he has some sort of claim upon the European who did him a kindness. Furthermore, he shows no gratitude—in our sense of the word—for the favours he has received. It is absolutely essential to interpret this behaviour correctly if we are to comprehend a type of mentality so different from our own.

Here, by way of illustration, is an example of this type of behaviour.

The young Merina who acted as my tennis coach went down with fever. I visited him and as he obviously had malaria I ordered a small supply of quinine to be sent to him. He would never himself have asked me for the medicine, even though he was in great need of it, and he had not been in the habit of seeking favours from me. I used to pay him after every lesson, so that we were quite square each time. Off the courts he would bid me a rather shy good-day whenever we met in the street, but there our relationship ended.

After I had given him the quinine, a change came about. One day, at the end of a lesson, he shyly pointed out to me that his rubber shoes were worn out and that mine, although rather shabby for me, would suit him very well. I handed them over to him readily enough, but two or three days later he came to look for me outside my coaching time and told me, without any trace of embarrassment, that he was in need of cigarette papers. Now at the time cigarette papers could be bought only on the black market, but they were neither scarce nor very dear, and the young Merina earned enough at each lesson to buy several packets of them. There was therefore something incongruous in his request which required looking into. What exactly did it mean?

It meant this: that when I sent him the quinine, my 'debtor' did not see the action simply as a helpful gesture which I had extended towards a sick man. He failed to appreciate its objective and impersonal nature. In fact he did not see it as it really was, but strictly subjectively; he was aware only of the relationship of dependence which was thereby set up between himself and me—not between a tennis-player and his coach, not between a healthy man and an invalid, but between our two selves. It must not be supposed that there was any question of interested motives or of a desire to create such a relationship simply in order to exploit it: his psychology was not that far developed, or degraded.   On the contrary: the relationship itself was enough for him—it was itself reassuring. It was the relationship, ultimately, which took away his fever: he was cured, not so much because quinine is an excellent remedy for malaria, as because a Malagasy who has a protector he can count on need fear no danger; what means his protector may employ to safeguard him is of little interest to him.

In fact the gifts which the Malagasy first accepts, then asks for, and finally, in certain rare cases, even demands, are simply the outward and visible signs of this reassuring relationship of dependence. They are essential to what might be called the life of the relationship. Therefore, the more he values it, the more he is driven to multiplying the visible signs of it. In the case of my tennis-coach, I could not help smiling as I gave him the packet of cigarette papers he had asked for. After that smile he asked for nothing more; he was sensitive enough to a hint to give up a relationship in which I was not wholeheartedly engaged. He knew well enough that he could easily have obtained other favours from me, but that was not his main interest. For my part, I could have fostered and encouraged the relationship which a casual gesture of mine had launched. I could not, however, have broken it off later except at the risk of making him feel abandoned, perhaps betrayed, and of rousing his enmity or even hatred—at any rate some negative emotion which would have been directed either against me or against himself.

Only when it is thoroughly degraded does such a need for dependence change radically in nature and become mendicity. It may be noted that the latter is found virtually only in certain tribes, or even families: a detailed study would no doubt reveal that it originated in certain family customs. Furthermore, most Malagasy beggars invariably appeal to the same persons—the same 'patrons', one might say. In other words, the bonds of dependence are not wholly depersonalized, even in these cases. In its uncontaminated state, however, the relationship is strictly personal. The Malagasy does not seek dependence on any conditions, at any price, on just anyone.

Lack of gratitude

As I have said, feelings of hostility, conscious or otherwise, are liable to arise when the bonds of dependence have snapped—when, that is, the Malagasy feels he has been abandoned. This fact is at the bottom of the belief widely held by Europeans in Madagascar that the Malagasies have no sense of gratitude.

This phrase, when used in the context of European psychology and morality, is wholly misleading, for by his failure to express gratitude the Malagasy proves in his way his nicety of feeling and his discernment. His reaction is archaic; among the various layers which go to make up what we consider the normal personality the feeling he experiences would be found fairly low down, for in us it is infantile, repressed. Our repression of it is perhaps the main reason why we are unable to appreciate it in him. There are other reasons, however, as we shall see.

We must also bear in mind certain moral prejudices of ours which prevent us seeing things as they really are and but for which we should realize that dependence excludes gratitude. That this is so is shown by the fact that we have to *teach* European children to be grateful, and even then there is an element of hypocrisy in it, for the child cannot really learn gratitude until he has attained a certain independence.[1]

That is one of the reasons why we tend to repress as 'bad' the infantile feelings which were associated with dependence, while the Malagasy does not. There is no need, I think, for me to point out the grave and sometimes tragic misunderstandings to which this situation is liable to give rise between Europeans and colonial inhabitants.

The reader will find almost the whole gamut of these misunderstandings in the writings of travellers who have been struck by the natives' lack of gratitude, not specially in Madagascar but in all the countries which used to be called 'primitive'. Lévy-Bruhl quotes

---

[1] The word for 'thank you' (*mishoatra*) is spoken by the donor as well as by the recipient in Madagascar; the same is true among European children.

from them freely in Chapter XIII of his book, *Primitive Mentality*, pp. 410 f. Although there are differences which I am unable to explain for lack of the necessary personal knowledge, it is clear that the kinds of behaviour described are examples of dependent behaviour in the sense in which I have used the expression. But the authors he quotes failed, one and all, to understand the significance of the behaviour they described, and it might be worth our while to consider why. Lévy-Bruhl himself, in spite of his customary penetration, was somewhat misled by the mistakes made by the travellers, and in particular, as I shall show, he was unable to rid himself of the idea of *payment*, which falsifies the interpretation.

This chapter of *Primitive Mentality* is divided into three parts. The first part contains quotations from doctors. Bentley interprets the reactions of his Congolese patients as a demand for compensation and considers it a shocking reversal of the 'normal' situation: the patient asking for fees from his doctor! Mackenzie's interpretation is hardly better, but his description is patently more accurate than that of Bentley. The cured man says to the doctor: 'Your herbs cured me. *You are now my white man.* Please to give me a knife,' and he adds, '*I shall always come to beg of you.*' But, like Bentley, Mackenzie sees it as 'a most wonderful transposition of relationship', and after relating a discussion in which he tried in vain to make the man see that he should be grateful, he says, 'I gave the man up as a very wonderful specimen of jumbled ideas.' Mr Williams, who worked among the Fiji Islanders, describes how a sick man who was receiving treatment asked for food: 'The reception of food he considered as giving him a claim on me for covering; and, that being secured, he deemed himself at liberty to beg anything he wanted, and abuse me if I refused his unreasonable request.' Here we find resentment (i.e. abandonment) also reported. Again, an injured man was treated, but when he was refused something he had asked for he 'showed his sense of obligation by burning down one of the captain's drying-houses, containing fish of the value of three hundred dollars'. We may be perfectly sure that the behaviour here described, though less delicate in form, is exactly comparable with the type of behaviour I have been describing among the Malagasies.

In the second part of the chapter Lévy-Bruhl offers an explanation based on the assumption that the native does not understand the treatment given him. But the man who says, '*Your herbs cured me,*' and who goes on to say, 'You are now my white man,' seems to have understood it well enough. However, there is no need to embark on a discussion of this point, for in the third part of the chapter Lévy-Bruhl is compelled to admit that these 'inexplicable' reactions occur even in situations where there is no question of medical treatment at all: a white man has only to perform some service for the native to elicit this behaviour from him, even if there is nothing which he could have any difficulty in understanding. For instance, a Congolese native whose canoe had capsized asked the missionary who rescued him to 'dress' him. When he refused, the man became 'abusive' and had to be locked up in the store and fined two goats by way of a 'lesson' to make him more grateful in the future.

The explanation Lévy-Bruhl offers is that the native thinks he has a right to compensation because he has suffered some loss in the mystical sphere. The native, he believes, argues thus: 'Henceforward you (white man) are my refuge and my support, and I have the right to reckon on you to compensate me for what your intervention has cost me with the mystic powers upon whom my social group depends, and upon whom I myself have depended till now.' But how could it cost anything, mystically, to be saved from drowning? Why did not the man who said, 'Your herbs cured me', make any reference to loss?

Psychoanalysis helps us to discover what has happened: the travellers who report these incidents project upon the native their own desire for reward, and it is this projection which prevents them understanding the psychology of dependent behaviour, and makes them see it as a reversal of the proper order of things. Lévy-Bruhl's analytical method did not reveal this projection, and he himself was misled by it. He realized well enough, however, that the native is in reality 'neither "ungrateful" nor "unreasonable"', as he is bound to appear in the eyes of anyone who has cared for and saved him, *and who is conscious of having rendered him signal service, often from purely disinterested and humane motives*. It is to be hoped that this humanity may not confine itself to dressing his ulcers, but that it may strive towards sympathetic penetration of the obscure recesses of a consciousness *which cannot express itself*' (the italics are mine). But in the light of analysis we can say that if these attentions had been given with complete disinterest—that is, *without any expectation, conscious or unconscious, of gratitude*—the observers would have run less risk of error and they would not have hoped to find among the manifestations of dependence a consciousness of gratitude, the very idea of which is entirely lacking, at least among typical, un-degraded cases. Furthermore, the misunderstanding is not the result of the native's *inability to express himself*. He expresses himself extraordinarily well when for instance he says, 'You are now my white man. I shall always come to beg of you.' In what way is this formula less clear than any of the phrases we normally use to express gratitude, acknowledgement, or thanks? Why should it be odder to ask than to promise? It is just a matter of a different attitude, an attitude which is unfamiliar to us, or rather which we have repressed in ourselves. All these phenomena, then, are to be explained by the persistence of dependence as an essential part of the native's personality, which is constructed along different lines from our own. It is this difference in structure which accounts for the absence of a sense of gratitude.

Clearly, therefore, the existence of a feeling of gratitude presupposes a loosening of the bonds of dependence. What, then, are we to conclude about the structure of our own personalities? The common idea that gratitude is primarily a matter of an exchange of services against expressions of thanks is unacceptable, for it would soon lead to a feeling that there was no indebtedness where no real gratitude was felt. True gratitude seems to be an attempt to preserve a balance between two feelings which at first sight seem contradictory: on the one hand the feeling that one is very much indebted, and on the other the feeling that one is not indebted at all. It implies a rejection of dependence and yet at the same time the preservation of an *image* of dependence based on free will. It is perhaps the prototype of the obligations assumed by the independent individual outside the framework of group behaviour.[1] That is why gratitude cannot be demanded, even though in a way it is obligatory, and why, in spite of appearances, it can exist only where persons are equal. Dependence proper, at least in the form in which it is found in Madagascar, is incompatible with equality.

Before going on to look for the cause of this 'dependence complex' I should like to make clear the meaning of the term 'infantile' which we are inclined to apply to it. There is a certain amount of justification for our using the word, because such behaviour would be infantile in us. But if we allow ourselves to think that it is also

---

[1] This kind of bond, independent of group tradition, plays a part in the development of the personality and of civilization. It is a break-away from traditional bonds, and prepares the way for the Christian idea of 'love thy neighbour . . .' But first it is necessary for a God, a Jupiter, to protect the unknown guest, or for the Eternal Father to make all men brothers, before such a transition is possible.

infantile in the Malagasies, we are risking imitating the colonials whose paternalist attitude stems from the belief that 'negroes are just big children'. In fact, of course, these traits of behaviour in the Malagasy *are* infantile, for everything in the adult goes back to his childhood. This is borne out by the fact that the Malagasy regards the inferiority behaviour of the typical European, with his tendency to boast of superiorities which are in part imaginary, as an infantile trait of character, for he sees this kind of behaviour in his own group only among children, before inferiority and dependence become differentiated, as it were.

CHAPTER II

THE CULT OF THE DEAD
AND THE FAMILY

Ny olombelona hoatra ny ladimboatavo, ka raha fotorana, iray ihany.
The living are like the branchings of a pumpkin stem; at the base there
is but one stalk.—Proverb.

WHEN faced with a serious difficulty, the typical European tends to
rely on his self-confidence or his technical skill. His main concern is not to prove *inferior* either to his own idea of himself or to the
situation. But the main concern of the Malagasy, when his security
is threatened, is not to feel *abandoned*. He has practically no confidence in himself and very little in technique, but relies on certain
protective powers without which he would feel utterly lost. The
origin of this attitude is to be found in the way in which the need for
security (the psychological need, of course) is satisfied during the
Malagasy's earliest experiences, and these experiences are determined
by the pattern of Malagasy family life.

The most important factor in Malagasy family life is a body of
customs or beliefs, coherent, firm, and deep-rooted, generally known
by the name of ancestor-worship, or the cult of the dead. A study of
these beliefs or customs—the two words are synonymous here—will
reveal both the basic pattern of Malagasy social life and the fundamental structure of the typical Malagasy personality.

Ethnographers suggest that there once existed a whole 'civilization'
based on the cult of the dead and closely connected with the cultiva-
tion of rice in irrigated paddy-fields. This civilization, they say,
stretched from the Indian Ocean to Melanesia. At that time, it
appears, the maternal uncle played an important part in family
customs. In Madagascar to-day there are only faint traces of these
ancient ways, for instance in the part still played by the maternal
uncle at the time of circumcision, and in some old proverbs. But
however interesting it might be to try to reconstruct the past hypo-
thetically from these relics, it must be realized that they are mere

survivals and no longer functional. I shall ignore them and shall confine myself to a consideration of the cult of the dead as it exists to-day.

The cult is met with in varying forms throughout Madagascar. There is no need for me to describe the variations in detail because the differences are purely superficial. The essential belief is the same everywhere: it is that the dead are the sole and inexhaustible source of all good things: life, happiness, peace, and, above all, fertility.[1] The Malagasies say and believe that the dead are the invisible root of their race and that the living are only its temporary offshoots. They are the originators of all the customs, and as everything is custom to the Malagasy, from the instincts of animals to the forms of plants and even the laws of the physical world, that is tantamount to saying that they rule all things. They are at one and the same time God of the universe, Nature, and the guardian spirit of the family. But we must beware of conceiving these beliefs in European form, as dogmas. They are so firm that they can safely be left vague. No one ever feels a need to clarify them. They are not systematic, and if a European inquirer should try to find out details about them by asking questions, all he will get in reply is a bewildering host of fanciful suggestions. Supposing, for instance, that he should ask who originated the customs (the instincts) of the animals: the answer is obviously, the ancestors. But if he should go on to ask which ones, some will tell him the men of past ages and others the ancestors of the animals themselves. The detail is of no importance to them: any answer will do. Their attitude is the same as that of people all over the world towards the firmness of the earth beneath their feet; if someone should ask them what makes it so firm, they will invent all sorts of fantastic explanations, simply because they have never found it necessary to ask the question. In trying to find out what the 'cult of the dead' really is, we shall discover what a belief is and how it differs from an opinion. A belief of this kind is unassailable, and inaccessible both to reason and to experiment. The great tenacity of belief and unconcern for opinions which the Malagasies show in this matter is the more remarkable in that they are perfectly capable of splitting hairs or of following the most tortuous discussion on other matters. The ancient game of *mifampiady karajia*, which consisted of a comic play on the meanings of words, bears witness to their

---

[1] This belief is found elsewhere; the Melanesians whom Maurice Leenhardt describes (*Do Kamo*, p. 77) call their ancestors *bemu*, life-givers.

nimbleness of wit, as also do their present skill in legal proceedings and their shrewdness in business dealings.

The strength of this belief in the dead, which becomes apparent once all the trivial opinions overlying it have been stripped away, explains why no missionary, either Catholic or Protestant, has ever dared to attack it.

In the book to which I have already referred, the Reverend Father Vincent Cotte describes this belief as he found it among the Betsimisaraka, a fairly backward tribe, in the following way (pp. 71–72):

'The ancestor continues to form part of the family of the living. The dead man or woman, however recently he or she may have died, and regardless of his or her status in the family, immediately takes precedence over the living. Have you not noticed how, before they drink, the natives will let a few drops of the liquid fall on the matting? It is not to get rid of some impurity but an offering made to the ancestors who are always presumed to be present. . . . One often hears it said of the ancestors that they are *Zanahary ambonin'ny tany*, gods on earth. The natives will themselves explain that this means that they are the trunk of the bamboo-tree from which the branches—men—emerge.'

But the Reverend Father permits himself to conclude (p. 73) that ancestor-worship and Christianity can be syncretized into 'a new Christian mentality which, without losing what it is entitled to retain from the cult of the ancestors, may nevertheless be enriched by new and more humane ideas whose dynamic force is constantly renewed by hope'.

There, in those embarrassed phrases, is the missionaries' admission that they found this kind of belief too firmly lodged in the foundations of the personality for their arguments to reach it. They forgot that St Augustine identified ancestor-worship with paganism. St Augustine knew from his own experience that conversion is not a matter of a change of opinion or a profession of faith, but a modification of the whole personality. Thus although there is practically no Malagasy who is not a member of some Christian church, there are very few for whom Christianity is anything more than a social mask. The mask is adopted readily enough, but beneath it there subsists an archaic type of personality founded, not upon a belief in a remote eternal Father, but upon the nearer and much more powerful image of earthly fathers who have died.

Here we have the key to a phenomenon which is the direct result of the bringing together of two different types of personality: beliefs may be held at two different levels, and do not conflict with each other. Observers have accused the Malagasies of contradicting themselves, of disregarding the principle of the excluded middle, and combining incompatible ideas, as if they had hit upon some defect of logic or intellectual incapacity. In point of fact there is no reason at all why the Malagasies should not adopt our opinions while remaining exactly what they have always been, what, deep down, they feel themselves to be—that is, the visible sign of the invisible force of the dead. There is nothing to prevent them topping their tombs with a Christian cross or having their dead blessed in a church. They are even ready to say that their dead, too, have been converted and accompany them invisibily to church to sing hymns. Indeed, it suits them very well to adopt this attitude. But there is very little chance of persuading a Malagasy seriously to consider whether the dead could cease inhabiting the earth and to some extent taking part in the daily life of the living. He could do that only after passing through a grave crisis in the course of which the whole structure of his personality would be changed. This, in fact, is what happens to those rare individuals who are genuinely and in the full sense of the word converted.

The personality of the occidental was long ago transformed by a breaking with the ancestral customs and the removal to heaven of a universalized paternal authority. That, roughly speaking, was how Europe was converted from paganism to Christianity. In the Malagasies, however, the essence of the pagan mentality still persists; we are scarcely able to recognize it because it is practically unknown in our ancient history except in the guise of a polytheistic mythology. Had the Malagasy been a polytheist the missionaries would have raged and fumed against him, for that was an adversary they were prepared for. But when they found themselves faced with a cult of the dead which lacked most of the characteristics we normally associate with religion—because its roots lay deeper than religious convictions—they did not think they were failing in their mission by leaving it alone.

We are not concerned here with the oft-debated question whether or not Christian missionaries should adapt religion to the customs they find in existence; the reader will find that question dealt with in, for instance, Chapter IX of Westermann's *The African To-day and To-morrow*. Nor are we concerned with the question whether the *lolo*,[1] the phantom which walks by night and appears in dreams, can be identified with the substantial soul. It is not theology we are interested in, but psychology, and psychology teaches us that conversion is a reshaping of the personality. In our own case, conversion opened up a new era in our history; except in very rare instances conversion has never meant this to the Malagasies.

To revert for a moment to the ethnographic aspect of the cult of the dead, one example will suffice to show that its basic beliefs may be expressed in forms so varied as to seem hardly comparable. Until quite recently it was the habit of the Sakalava of the Morondava region to adorn their tombs with wood carvings of incredible obscenity—the more incredible as all Malagasies are extremely modest. The purpose of these sculptures, however, was to recall and make visible (and perhaps accessible) the fertility of the dead: they were, so to speak, dream-images clothing the sculptor's profoundest convictions about death. On the High Plateaux, on the other hand, the tombs of Imerina are unadorned. However, when a disinterment takes place, the sterile women of a village will squabble with ludicrous ferocity over a mat on which the corpse has been set down for a moment. In other words, whereas at Morondava fertility is believed to reside in more or less indecent carvings, in Imerina it is thought to be present in a quite ordinary mat, just bought at the market, on which a *faty* (the sanctified body of a dead man) has been put down for a minute or two.

It is in this light, incidentally, that we must see the outbursts of sexuality which sometimes occur at funeral ceremonies; we should not regard them as what in Europe we mean by *orgies*. To sum up, beneath all the variations which we might well call superstitious, there is a single deep-rooted belief: that though the dead may turn to dust they will none the less continue to be the true fathers and alone possess fertility and authority. This fertility and this authority are simply delegated to the living fathers by the dead, whose deputies they are.

There is nothing of the sacred or the mystical in the customs connected with the dead, for these omnipotent dead are no other than the

---

[1] The word *lolo*, by a curious coincidence, has the same double meaning as the Greek word ψυχή, 'soul' and 'butterfly'. The transition from one meaning to the other in Greek is usually explained by reference to the idea of humidity—cf. ψῦχος. There is little doubt that in Malagasy the dual meaning is due to the fact that the chrysalis resembles a shrouded corpse and that the butterfly emerges from it like the soul from the body of the dead or sleeping man.

silk-swathed corpses sleeping in their stone cots in the depths of the family vault. The vault is opened periodically to admit new shrouds and to enable first one corpse, then another, to be given an airing for a while. It is all done very prosaically and in the spirit of a country jaunt, of a picnic almost. If a European asks if he may enter a vault, he is told: why, of course; the family will consider it an honour. May he take a flashlight photograph? Why not?—the family will keep some prints. There are no rites, no compulsory gestures; such customs and prohibitions as exist are those of everyday life. A European burial is like a nightmare, and seems expressly designed to impress upon the soul an awareness of the importance and awful grandeur of death. The fact is that Europeans believe in *death*, which is for them a subject of grave doubts and questionings, while the Malagasies believe in *the dead* and, having the corpse under their very eyes, they feel no need for ceremony and stage-effects.

In order to understand the position of the Malagasy child in a family the most important part of which is formed by the ancestors, we must imagine a European family in which all the money and all authority are in the hands of a paralysed and bedridden grandfather. Then let us suppose that there is a child in the family, who learns from what he hears that this paralytic, who is seen, if at all, only on ceremonial occasions, is held in immense respect and awe. He knows that on feast-days people try to amuse him a little and pretend that he has eaten and drunk with gusto, while the old man, for his part, through a succession of grimaces which are rather hard to interpret, somehow or other conveys his wishes, which are promptly carried out as if his displeasure could bring ruin to the family. Then, if the child were to be convinced that this situation would never alter, and if he were to discover that the same held good for all other families, he would be in the same position as the Malagasy child. The reader will no doubt agree that in such circumstances the child is unlikely to wish, and will certainly not be able, to rival such authority; indeed, he will never even conceive the idea of having, one day, a will of his own residing in himself alone.

There is no need for me to explain in detail how the 'will' of the dead is expressed in dreams, portents, and prophecies. It is strictly obeyed, even by an 'evolved' Malagasy, that is to say one who is sufficiently Europeanized to behave in every other respect like a European. Europeans are often indignant at the capriciousness and 'bad faith' of the Malagasies, at their changes of front and failure to keep their word. But they can hardly do otherwise if they are to obey the dictates of their dreams and forebodings. By way of excuse they offer the reasons which they consider to be the most polite and plausible. The European is shocked at these continual 'senseless' lies, but the Malagasy cannot tell him the real reason for his actions because he knows he will come up against an incredulity that nothing he could say would ever overcome. His failure to make any attempt to convince shows how firm are his own convictions. We can persuade a European child to stop believing in ghosts by drawing upon common-sense arguments, and in so doing we are helping him to build up his personality on the model of our own. But with a Malagasy who believes in the dead it is quite another matter. It would be as difficult to make him give up his belief as to persuade a European genuinely to doubt the existence of the outside world. Rather than adopt an attitude which appears to him sheer madness, a man will seek any and every means of defence. Here we are touching upon a problem of a more general nature, for very often the insane are precisely those whose personalities have in some way been upset, and we know from experience that it is impossible to influence them by common-sense arguments. They, too, very quickly give up trying to convince us. In the Malagasies, however, the personality is in no way deformed; it is not *abnormal* but simply *different*. Their deepest convictions and ours cannot be compared with each other, for they exist at different levels.   They are mutually comprehensible as opinions, inasmuch as they can be discussed, but as beliefs they form part of the very foundations of the personality, and if they were uprooted the whole personality would have to be rebuilt.

In these conditions ancestor-worship cannot be dismissed as a mere ethnographic curiosity. We may say, with the broadmindedness we believe to be a product of civilization, that 'every country has its customs', and the Malagasy will echo us in one of his proverbs. But to us customs are simply prejudices towards which we may be tolerant or indulgent, whereas to the Malagasy they are literally life-giving; they are the basis of his whole existence and not mere eccentricities for which he must be pardoned. To say that the cult of the dead is part of the customs is not to say that its observance is a mere habit or routine, as our customs have become in the course of our progress towards self-sufficiency. It would be no exaggeration to say that the dead and their images form the highest moral authority in the mind of the 'dependent' Malagasy, and that for him they play the part filled for the European by the moral conscience, reason, God, King, or party. . . .

In ourselves, however, more important than this moral pantheon, this mythology of authorities, is the continuous, barely conscious debate in which the Ego negotiates with the Super-ego and the Ideal its chances of existence. It begins with a guilty desire or an agonizing longing to escape from autonomous authority by seeking refuge in some higher authority, and this flight has given our civilization its distinctly evolutionary character. The theme is familiar enough in *mythical form*, and the story of little Tom Thumb can be found even in Malaya. But only the West has the courage to live out its myths. The story of Tom Thumb has been lived out to the letter, for instance, by Descartes, who deliberately courted abandonment, invented a device for not losing himself in the forest of doubt, triumphed over the terrors of malevolent authority (his particular ogre is called the Evil Genius), and found in God the higher authority who delegated to him his freedom and independence—just as Tom Thumb became a grown-up through the protection of a king, with whose assistance he was able to forget his father the woodcutter. We all know how difficult this road is: it is paved with anguish; it leads man not only to liberty but also to misery—Western man, that is, of whom Dr André Berge said in a striking phrase which sums up the whole situation, that he tries clumsily to behave like a grown-up without always being ready for the orphaned state.

The non-civilized man, however, if his personality is constructed like that of the Malagasies, is obviously totally unfitted for the orphaned state and he absolutely never, clumsily or in any other way, tries to 'grow up' as we do. It may be that he can lead his life in this way because of his belief in the dead. Or it may be that he is compelled to believe in the dead because he cannot lead his life in any other way. Nothing in our present state of knowledge helps us decide which of these possibilities is correct.

In the Malagasy family the father is the natural interpreter of the will of the dead. He does not perform any rites, however. The imported religion has thus had this further effect, of relegating the religious spirit of the Malagasies to the tombs and of drawing their social life into the orbit of the Church, with the result that there is a strange vacuum in family life.[1]

---

[1] The Reverend Father Vincent Cotte noted this situation in connexion with the Betsimisaraka, but offered no explanation (*Regardons vivre une tribu Malgache*, pp.

Among the *Hova*, who are the *Merina* bourgeoisie, the father keeps tight hold of the purse-strings and controls economic life down to the smallest detail. The mother obeys his instructions and acts as intermediary, transmitting the father's orders to the children and the children's requests to the father. Outside school and religious duties the children have nothing to do except mend their clothes, look after the chickens and the kitchen garden, and similar small jobs. In between they laze about. They are not given any money, for fear they should get into trouble. They read only what the priest or occasionally the teacher recommends. If they do anything naughty they do it secretly and in silence; they are never boisterous or openly disobedient. If they are not behaving well enough, the mother has only to threaten to tell the father and they become quiet again; sometimes she warns them that the *vazaha*—the European—will be angry. The *vazaha* is primarily a substitute for the father-image, but in the unfortunate rôle of bogey-man he is undoubtedly the object of morbid fears, although I have found no trace of him in the unconscious in my analysis of dreams. However, dreams are much too important to a Malagasy for him to impart any and all of them to a European, especially those in which a European figures.

The Malagasy mother enjoys considerable real influence in the family but possesses no actual authority; the position seems to suit her psychologically, and all observers have remarked on the difference between the *ramatoa* (the women) and the *rangahy* (the men), to the advantage of the former. Perhaps it is because the woman does in fact leave her father and mother, whereas the man can never break free from his father even when the latter can only watch and guide him from afar, from the depths of his tomb. This would be a profitable subject of study; all I can do here is to point it out and hope that others will take it up; it would, of course, require the examination of individual cases.

In the Malagasy home, the child's main attachment is to his mother, whose job it is to protect him both from outside dangers and from the father's wrath, and so to satisfy his more or less conscious need for security. He is hardly ever parted from the mother; she carries him everywhere with her on her back, wrapped up in his *lamba*, head and all. The habit adults have of sleeping completely enveloped is

173 to 175). For a detailed description of Malagasy family life, see an article by P. Boiteau in the 1945 special number of *Revue de Madagascar*, entitled 'La structure sociale'.

probably due to their memory of this position and its comfort; their breath keeps them warm, and the *lamba* stretched from head to foot also acts as a mosquito-net. The dead are shrouded in exactly the same way. Childhood, sleep, and death are thus, as we might have expected, symbolically linked.

The child, then, permanently attached as he is to the mother, is not a subject of conflict. He can only be threatened, as my analysis of dreams will show, *through* the mother. It is always a surprise to find how good the Malagasy child is; he is never rowdy, like the European child, whose bad behaviour is the result of his intermediate position between father and mother.

There are families in Europe which at first sight seem very like the Malagasy family as I have described it; the father's absolute authority over the child is exercised through the agency of the mother. But the children are noisy, violent, and aggressive, though the father has only to exert his authority for them to become quiet and shame-faced. It might seem that all this turbulence is necessary for the child to create and store up the quantity of independence he will need later on when he, in turn, is 'head of the family'. But that is not so; his boisterousness is primarily a protest, an unconscious assertion that the father is but a man like other men and that he, the child, is a man just like his father. The assertion is not made, however, without some dim awareness of the dangers inherent in it; hence the unruliness. The Malagasy child, it is obvious, is in quite a different position.

According to Freud, circumcision (which is practised among the Malagasies) strengthens the authority of the father, symbolizing acceptance of that authority. But the rite appears to be less emotionally charged among the Malagasies than it is among the Jews, and it engenders no suspicion or hatred of the uncircumcised. The difference in its meaning for the two groups again offers an interesting subject of study which I can do no more than note in passing.

When circumcision takes place in Madagascar, the foreskin is sometimes placed 'under the sign' of a forked tree—a sort of totem pole probably representing the *Omby maranitra*, the bull with the sharp horns. In the traditional address the tree is said to represent the ancestors—but it stands erect in the village, symbol of the virility of the circumcised. Another symbol is, or used to be, a branch selected from a strong forest tree.

It is interesting to compare these customs with the tree-worship of the Melanesians (see *Do Kamo*, by Maurice Leenhardt, for instance),[1] but they are best understood in terms of the dream-symbolism I shall be explaining later on. In any case, whatever the influence of circumcision on the minds of the Malagasies, paternal authority, for all its force, is still a derived authority and at all points it extends beyond the person of the father. The European child knows he will take his father's place and inherit all authority; the Malagasy child knows that this can never happen. The source of paternal power is, for him, lost in the night of time, without, however, diminishing in strength in the process: rather the contrary.[2]

When the rebels, armed only with pointed sticks, went in to attack troops armed with rifles, they advanced in step in serried ranks shouting 'Rano, rano', which means 'Water, water'. This cry was very soon explained by prisoners; it was, they said, a magical formula intended to turn the bullets into water as they left the rifles. The sorcerers had invented it. It rapidly spread all over the island wherever there were disturbances. I remember Malagasy doctors and lawyers who had received a European education seriously wondering 'whether it was true'. The symbol, it seemed, was a very potent one, and I sought to find the reason. Even some of the European soldiers began to have doubts and to panic when their fire proved ineffective through faulty aiming or the use of old cartridges. They laughed in talking about it afterwards, but it is very likely that in the moment of danger the symbolism of the rebels' cry roused in them that terror of impotence which is often dramatically represented in nightmares as the misfiring of weapons.

The psychological sequence in the Malagasy rebels was probably this. The father-image was projected on to the vaʒaha they were attacking. The rifle symbolizes the male sex organ. In the child nothing but 'water' comes out of it. See, the child is felt to say, I am not competing with my father; my penis is good only for urination. That is his defence against the fear of mutilation, a defence against anguish. In order to be able to attack the father, in the person of the vaʒaha, the Malagasy rebel had to persuade himself that the father, too, was only a harmless child. This unconscious process is very revealing: in a similar situation a European would try to use magic to

---

[1] Cf. Ch. Renel, 'Les amulettes Malgaches', Chap. III, in *Bulletin de l'Académie malgache*, 1915, p. 63.

[2] It happens on rare occasions that the death of the father provokes a grave crisis in the son, who then repudiates his mother. This fact has been noted by Cailliet in his *Essai sur la psychologie du Hova*, p. 110. I regret that I have never personally encountered an instance of this interesting phenomenon.

raise his arms to the strength of those of the opponent upon whom the image was projected, and would thus assert his own virility. The Malagasy, however, deprives the father of virility and tries to reduce him to the level of childhood impotence. Thus, instead of protesting, like the European, that he is a man like his father, the Malagasy appears to claim that all men are children. He projects his own dependence on everyone else. The word for 'child' appears frequently in the names of Malagasy tribes, and ultimately it is only the dead who are to the Malagasy what adults are to European children.

CHAPTER III

THE THREAT
OF ABANDONMENT

Freedom and independence

THE universality of the dependence 'complex' can be deduced from the frequency of the dreams in which security is first threatened and then to a greater or less extent restored. The parental couple, *Ray aman'dReny*, appear in them, but the father usually assumes a threatening role. The child is placed between the dread authority of the father and the beloved protection of the mother; the two opposite aspects of the same feeling (fear and security) are thus clearly divided. It may be noticed that in three of the dreams (epilogue to this chapter) the mother's protection proved inadequate, and of those three dreams two were told by girls, while the third was reported by an inquisitive and so-to-speak experimentally minded boy, who had wanted to see—what he saw in fact was how the mother yielded to the father. But the material is too slight for me to pursue the analysis of the Œdipus complex among the Malagasies; for a thorough analysis I should need far more data.

Dependence, as I have said, is not the same thing as inferiority, for even when the Malagasy knows or feels that he is inferior he does not compensate in the way a European does by claiming equality or superiority. On the contrary, he tries to rectify the situation by establishing a dependence relationship on the pattern of that of the child with his parents. The words *Ray aman'dReny*, which literally mean 'the father and also the mother', the parental couple, are those the Malagasy uses to address personages he deems worthy of respect —the administrator or the governor, for instance—and with whom he would be happy to establish a strong bond of dependence. When he has succeeded in forming such relations with his superiors, his inferiority no longer troubles him: everything is all right. When he fails to establish them, when his feeling of insecurity is not assuaged in this way, he suffers a crisis. This may, as I have shown, revive old memories of abandonment and lead to an outburst of hostility.

I have tried to verify this point by reference to observations concerning other colonial peoples. This is what D. Westermann says in *The African To-day and To-morrow* (p. 70) about the behaviour of the African: 'He knows no crawling humility, no slavish flattery, and he is not easily embarrassed. Within his own circle he is never in a position where he does not know how to behave or what to do. . . . In public meetings he deports himself with dignity and has no difficulty in expressing his opinions in well-turned phrases.' Farther on, the author offers his interpretation of the facts—an interpretation which, as I shall show, is scarcely accurate: 'He does not suffer from social disabilities, for *there is hardly any economic dependence*, nor is there a distinction between servant and master, rich and poor. *Hence nobody suffers from an inferiority complex*' (the italics are mine). This explanation is unacceptable: social inequality is not the necessary cause of an inferiority complex. But as the author gives us a full description of the facts, we can find the real explanation a few lines farther on: 'This consciousness that one is surrounded by friends and can always rely on their support helps to give everyone both in his attitude to life and in his manner that self-reliant assurance which strikes everyone as so pleasing in the "uncivilized" African.'

So we see that the position of the African, though different in certain particulars, is manifestly comparable with that of the Malagasy: he has no inferiority complex because he knows whom he can count on, but they are his equals, and not his superiors. This explains his open and agreeable manner. The division of society into tribes and age-groups is no doubt largely responsible for his feeling of security, for it ensures close union between all those at the same level. It is for this reason, too, no doubt, that the ancestors are mere memories. The Malagasy, in contrast, counts on his superiors; he is directly dependent on the ancestral stock. His whole attitude, in fact, is different. But there is no need, I think, to bring racial differences into the matter and to contrast the oriental temperament with the African.

The Malagasy's dependence 'complex' pervades his whole personality and colours his adaptive actions and reactions in all fields. But dependence, either on the family or on society, which is the soil in which the complex grows, is not peculiar to the Malagasy: it is shared by all children, whatever their environment. Likewise they all experience inferiority. It is a fact, however, that whereas most Europeans resolve their dependence complex by repressing it or sublimating it, most Malagasies avoid the consequences of inferiority by accepting dependence. This fundamental difference is clearly the result of differences in the family situation; the Malagasy child, as I have shown, does not feel that he is in competition with his parents.

Inferiority and dependence, as I have said, form an alternative, and if for some reason or other dependence fails (or is rebuffed), then inferiority may make its appearance. It is a remarkable fact that a psychologist, Fritz Künkel, detected the operation of this law—in a slightly different form, of course—among Europeans in Europe. The conclusions he draws, however, are not acceptable as such, and it might be worth our while to consider his arguments. I did not know Künkel's work when I was discovering dependence among the Malagasies and its connexion with inferiority; in fact his work remained virtually unknown in France until Oliver Brachfeld gave a summary of it in his *Sentiments d'infériorité*. It was through this summary that I came to know of him. I would refer the reader to it for the details, and shall mention only the main points here.

Künkel's conception of the sentiment of inferiority was similar to Adler's, but he attributed it to a different cause. Whereas Adler saw it as the consequence of a physical defect, or at any rate of a physical difference taken to be a defect, Künkel thought that it was the result of the betrayal of the child by those nearest him, or what I have called abandonment. The use of the word betrayal dramatizes the objective situation and indicates the subjective context in which the analyst should examine it.

It is true of the Malagasies, psychologically, that so long as they do not feel abandoned—or betrayed—and so long as the satisfying relation of dependence is preserved, they are not subject to the inferiority complex. One question which it is difficult to answer with absolute certainty is whether the difference between the dependent child and the 'betrayed' child is an objective difference—as Künkel seems to think [1]—or whether, as I believe, betrayal is not rather the

---

[1] Naturally, Künkel's theory is much more complex than it appears from a summary. In a passage in his *Einführung in die Karakterkunde*, for instance, he says: 'It was not absolutely proved whether the inhumanity of the parents (of the *betrayed* child, whose case he is analysing) was such as it appeared in the eyes of the desperate child. But the purpose of the investigation was not to establish what had taken place, objectively, in this family, but what had come to pass, subjectively, in the soul of the child. The rift between the child and his parents was only too real. . . .'
It may be noted that whenever the analyst comes upon an event which has had a

imaginary consequence of a ('guilty') desire for independence, born of a will to power. If Künkel had been right, the Malagasies and un-contaminated 'primitives' generally—to whom, indeed, he expressly refers [1]—would still have been living in a sort of psycho-sociological paradise from which Künkel and other Europeans would have been chased at the time of the original betrayal.   In that case, in trying to deliver the Malagasy from his dependence—as we must do if he is to attain to freedom and acquire a complete personality—we should be leading him along the rocky road to inferiority. Nor should we have the excuse that it is a necessary evil, that inferiority, however un-comfortable, is the only way we know of promoting the progress of the individual, for according to Künkel it would be an absolute and incurable evil, the only possible remedy for which would be a return to lost dependence. And that, in his view, would be a return to a sort of feudalism.[2] His theory no doubt applies rather less than he thinks to Europeans who have resolved their dependence complex. It does apply, however, to anyone who through an affective re-gression has come to regret his lost dependence, and we must find out whether it would also apply to the 'primitives'—as logically it ought—the moment we 'relieved' them of their dependence. Though it is true that dependence is a hindrance to them on the path of progress, it is at the same time a wonderful protection against a troubled conscience, which is the heavy price we pay for our progress.

Certainly the failure of dependence, or more probably in the case of the European its rebuff, is one of the causes of the growth or the coming to light of the inferiority complex.   It may be remembered that an adult Malagasy cut off from his normal environment is liable to show signs of inferiority, which is almost irrefutable proof that the complex was already present in him in latent form, but masked by dependence.   Reverting to dependence, however, is only one of the possible solutions, and is a real regression.   Künkel's preference for it

traumatic effect, not because of what it was but because of how it appeared to the child, he cannot stop there, but must go on to look for the reason *why* it so appeared.

[1] In his book, *Let's be normal!* Künkel says, 'The lives of all of us begin in full harmony with our environment. As subjects we are at first not to be differentiated from the subjects around us. We live simply in the general subjectivity of mankind as if every human being being lived as we did. The infant is, to a certain extent, in the state of primaeval mankind. It could only remain in this condition if such a primaeval people existed. It may be said, therefore, that the behaviour of an infant is based upon an illusion. His behaviour is not actually justified by his environment. . . . The child suffers from the disparity between its own behaviour and the behaviour of the environment. The en-vironment construes the child's unhappiness as an unjustifiable demand or even as an egoistic claim, whereas the child feels that he has been betrayed by the adults.'

[2] At least according to Brachfeld in *Sentiments d'infériorité*, p. 100.

is suspect. Surely the best way of resolving the complex would be to attain a complete and independent personality—to become an apprentice to freedom. Man has invented many means of sublimation, ranging from God to mathematical truths by way of love of one's neighbour and professional and social obligations—in fact all the duties which will enable him to purify the bonds of dependence, so that he may progress towards his ultimate object, which is to attain a freedom founded neither upon dependence nor upon independence, but upon responsibilities freely assumed. A feeling of responsibility is essential to the attainment of an independent personality. If the collapse of dependence merely breaks the bonds without putting anything in their place, then clearly the man who finds himself suddenly independent in this way will no longer be able to tolerate guidance, but will yet be unable to guide himself. He will then fall prey to Pascalian despair, existentialist anguish, dereliction. The paths to freedom are more tortuous than this vertical drop into independence or Künkel's straight path back to dependence.

We must not, however, underestimate what is of value—even if we have good reason to suspect a regression—in the course Künkel advocates, namely, a return to a feudal world where the bonds restored between men would deliver them from themselves and from their torments. If left to themselves, the majority of Malagasies would, it is certain, spontaneously and even unthinkingly strive to recreate a feudal type of society. They would call it a republic or a democracy, but their need for dependence would drive them almost inevitably to organize a society composed of clientèles grouped about patrons in the way they like best.[1] They would lack the courage to face the terrors of a genuine liberation of the individual.

Even with the help of Europeans, the road to freedom would not be easy for them. It seems likely, at least according to Westermann's observations, that the African negro, however dependent he may be on his group, would attain freedom more easily, for even in his dependent state he is accustomed to equality among members of the group and brotherhood among members of the tribe. The Malagasies lack this advantage, or perhaps lost it some centuries ago—those of them, at any rate, who have not remained sufficiently 'primitive' to be still organized in tribes. It would, indeed, be interesting to find out whether, paradoxically, the tribal and therefore most backward parts of the Malagasy population were not yet the

[1] See Part III, Ch. V, on the *fokon'olona*.

easiest to 'liberate' because of their less hierarchical, more homo-geneous grouping—because they have not yet acquired the taste for feudal subordination.

If we were to ask the colonialists for their opinion, they would say: 'The Malagasies do not need freedom; they do not know what it is: if you force it on them they become unhappy, and that makes them vicious.' This verdict is unacceptable as such because it springs from a biased view. The colonialists' impressions of Malagasy psychology are vitiated by their own psychological defects, which I shall describe later on. They know of the need for dependence, for they exploit it; they live by it. They do not want it to be removed; rather would they maintain it. They do in fact foster it by instinc-tively adopting a paternalist attitude, with too much affection and too much punishment. The experiment has worked out well for them and therefore, pragmatically speaking, there must be some-thing to be said for it. What that amounts to is this, that living in an untroubled state of dependence would—and does, wherever these conditions occur—give the Malagasies a certain psychological comfort. Even Europeans who are not colonialists, but are susceptible nevertheless to a somewhat old-fashioned style of wisdom, might consider this comfort a good in itself and might hesitate to take it away from people who have up to now undoubtedly enjoyed peace and happiness of a kind, on the pretext that progress was essential—an attitude which might well embarrass us if we were to discuss it at the moral level. There are people of conservative taste, those who favour the *fomba taloha*—the old-time customs—among Europeans as among Malagasies. Among the latter they are usually old people who until recently had the political support of the French authorities. They are disappearing now and giving place to younger and more active generations. The European conservatives no longer have a voice either: it is too late. Thus there is no need for us to consider this possibility, which we might find it difficult to oppose on philo-sophical grounds, for it is no longer possible to return to this state of comfort based on dependence of all kinds. We may regret it, but our regrets would be vain.

It seems, then, that there is no alternative to the painful apprentice-ship to freedom; that alone will solve all the problems amid which both Malagasies and Europeans are floundering—it is a medicine which will cure them both. If it appears sweet to the one and bitter to the other, it is an illusion in both cases. The way will be much harder for the Malagasies than they imagine, while the Europeans have no idea of the extent to which a genuine and successful liberation of their subject peoples—if it could be brought about without conflict, which unfortunately they make unlikely—would liberate them too, without harming their 'interests' to anything like the extent they fear. Needless to say, an essential precondition for the liberation of the individual is the sincere application of a policy of democracy and racial equality. But that is not enough by itself. The colonials who are anti-democratic are not all colonialists. Some, though not many, have adopted a conservative attitude, not out of self-interest or a feeling of racial superiority, but because they are dimly aware of the inadequacy of political reforms to solve psychological problems. They blame the democratic ideal itself for the accidents which are apt to occur when an attempt is made to put it into practice. They believe, not without reason, that a people so thoroughly fixed psychologically in the attitudes I have called dependent, could not pass from this archaic state to a modern one without undergoing some crisis of adolescence. But this conservative attitude—and its adherents are not all Europeans—appears to have had a harmful effect, for it has succeeded in delaying and hindering reforms without preventing them altogether. The conservatives' opposition, which will avail nothing in the end, has merely aggravated the situation, and the deterioration in relations gives an appearance of proving them right. But as the reader must know in situations of this kind failures can be made to prove anyone right. Obviously if the conservatives had managed to prevent any change at all, there would have been no crisis! But it is equally true that the crisis would have been less serious and more manageable if the reforms proposed had met with less stubborn opposition.

The dependent personality and repression

Although the concept of dependence seems to be the one which will best explain the psychology of the Malagasy who has been 'colonized' and is now in course of evolution, it is doubtful whether it would be equally valid with respect to more 'primitive' communities, those which have hardly been touched by our civilization, if in fact there are any remaining. . . .

In them we should very probably find some form of dependence, but it is unlikely that it would be dependence on the parental couple alone or that it would be transferred to the same substitutes, the most important of which, for the Malagasy, are the family ancestors. Mythical ancestors, kings living or dead, the group as a whole, the tribe, substituted idols, perhaps, like the *solo* [1] of the ancient Merina— all these would no doubt be found in the rôle of guardians of peace and security and protectors both against external dangers and against feelings of guilt, for the two are always closely linked in the unconscious. A study of these forms of group dependence would be very interesting in itself but would not, I think, help us forward in our investigation of psychological dependence, for in communities of such a kind the individual can hardly be distinguished from the collective, since all the separate conscious minds resemble and reflect each other. Dependence, in such cases, is something solid, universal, and undifferentiated. The bond between mother and child will of course remain and will retain its affective force, but it will necessarily play a less prominent part in a society where all the children of the same age are bound together into a homogeneous group. The village square is as friendly and familiar a place for such children as their own homes, at least during the daytime. The child clings less fiercely to vertical family ties when he feels supported by a whole network of horizontal ties, even if he knows he must wait till he has attained a certain age and pass through a series of initiation ceremonies before they are confirmed. Relations between individuals are consequently very different, and if people of this kind are cut off from their normal environment they will tend to look for a group to which they can belong rather than a person upon whom they can depend. They will also find it easier to make firm friendships with equals.

We do not know how Malagasy society developed, for we have no means of placing the different types of social organization in chronological order without resorting to hypotheses which are at the best merely plausible. It is a simple matter of fact that among the Merina, who are considered, rightly or wrongly, the more highly developed of the Malagasies, attachments are primarily vertical, and horizontal ties are negligible. We may wonder whether horizontal attachments would spontaneously form—or, it may be, reform— the moment the vertical dependences became dangerously weakened. Observation of Malagasies who have been called up for military service suggests that they would. A far-sighted administration ought,

---

[1] *Solo*, in Malagasy, means substitute.

in any case, while respecting the vertical relationships, at the same time to try to encourage and strengthen horizontal ties, especially among children, through school friendships, sports societies, scouting, and so on, always guarding, however, as far as possible against their turning into vertical relationships through the appointment of leaders or masters psychologically prepared to accept the projection of parental images.[1] By this means it might be possible to ward off certain difficulties likely to arise in the future, or to moderate their psychological effects by sparing individuals the anxiety resulting from a feeling of abandonment.

It may be objected that the vertical ties are strong and not yet ready to be broken. We cannot be certain about that. Of course there is no question of the parent generations 'betraying' their children (in Künkel's sense), but, as we have already seen, a child can experience as betrayal his projection of his own desire for independence, about which he unconsciously feels guilty. For, objectively, anything is enough to make the child feel betrayed, even the lightest and most well-earned punishment, if the subjective conditions are ripe.[2] So, then, in the present period of unrest the psychological need for dependence and its unconscious acceptance may be seriously disturbed without there being any change, outwardly at least, in the general sociological structure of the family and the cult of the dead. There is some conflict between the older, conservative

---

[1] This verticalization of ties, with the projection of the father-image on a 'patron', has often had a harmful influence and frustrated measures which might otherwise have served a useful purpose, but the reason for their failure has not been understood. Here is an example. There has been a considerable development of trade unionism of recent years in Madagascar, and this should have led to progress in psychological growth through the development of a sense of responsibility and social and occupational unity. Unfortunately the Malagasies have always chosen to lead their unions, not the men best able to protect their interests, but the 'notables' most likely to exercise paternalist authority, and prone to make use of trade union activity for their own gain—which fails to shock the majority of union members. The need for dependence has almost always hindered (and even halted) the development of a real trade union spirit, and has thus deprived the Malagasies of almost all the psychological and moral benefits they might have derived from this activity. And, as usual, this experience doubles the tasks for the future; what might have been achieved without great difficulty by starting from nought and taking account of the psychological situation, can now be achieved only after a painful effort of correction has first been made.

[2] A. Hesnard, in *Freud dans la Société d'après-guerre* (p. 78) says: 'There is an astonishing disproportion between the childhood events which appear from the affective history of the individual to have been pathogenic, and these same events as they were in reality, that is to say on the scale and in the proportion in which they were seen by the adults who participated in or witnessed them. . . . The poisoning of entire lives by a terrible social inferiority complex . . . is thus often due to some stupid and vulgar admonition by a parent who, when questioned about the traumatic event, no longer even remembered it, so childishly unimportant did it seem.'
This, no doubt, is what Künkel means by 'betrayal'.

generations, and the more progressive-minded youth. The nature of the conflict is, however, rather obscure because the young are both more conservative and more revolutionary than the old.

Meanwhile, dependence continues to give the average Malagasy a greater feeling of security while relieving him of the need to show initiative or assume responsibility. It is easy to see why the Malagasies are lovers of routine. As with some Europeans, it is because it makes them feel safer. To depart from routine is to wander in pathless woods; there you will meet the bull who will send you running helter-skelter home again. No doubt there was a time when routine, adhered to in every detail of life, was a great guarantee of security. But—and we shall see later why—the very existence of the *fady* (taboos) is due to the way in which the feeling of insecurity is assuaged. The Malagasy's routine—which is not the result of conservatism, for he is perfectly ready to adopt a new routine—has something in common with the rituals of the obsessed; it protects him against his unconscious fear of insecurity. There is more than just this, though, in the Malagasy's kind of routine. A Malagasy will take pleasure in performing some complicated administrative task, observing with pedantic correctness every rule and regulation, and not skipping a single formality, even if it serves no purpose at all. In this he is not very different from some non-Malagasy officials, and the resemblance warrants our saying that in both cases there are probably certain psychological obstacles and that they are of the same kind, whatever form they may have taken at an earlier stage of the individual's development in each case. However, it is not difficult to discover that a respect for red tape in the European civil servant is very often a weapon he uses to defend himself against the public and a means of inflating his own importance—to the extent of being aggressive and malicious at times—in compensation for his feeling of inferiority. The Malagasy, on the other hand, adopts the formalities in order to enter a large family which will afford him a secure place: for him, a scrupulous observance of the rules of the game is his guarantee of the strength of the ties securing that place in the whole structure, and therefore removes the risk of any unforeseen—and consequently dangerous—occurrence.[1] We must guard against over-

---

[1] There is a description of the behaviour of the 'inferior' European in Adler's *The Neurotic Constitution*. The inferior person develops a cult of means by which to attain the end he desires. He endeavours to be different from others in order to feel superior. He feels he is a martyr to his own demands. The Malagasy respects forms, desires no superiority, and does not make himself a martyr.

simplifying the matter and believing that the Malagasy official is scrupulous because he is afraid of 'trouble' or of losing his position. There is no deliberate intention; it is his general attitude which compels him to multiply the strong hierarchical bonds of dependence, for he loves to feel anchored by such bonds.

If a situation arises which requires him to show initiative, to settle a question without reference to any rule or precedent, he at once loses his head and appears quite unintelligent. Even at school, pupils may be brilliant at making subtle logical or grammatical analyses but will be unable to deal with questions which are fundamentally quite simple. And in everyday life, opinions on important matters are given only in the form of ready-made formulas, the 'proverbs' which enshrine the wisdom of the ancients. Though illogical and extraordinarily elastic, these formulas are always felt to be convincing in arguments or disputes.

The Malagasies may at times appear to be entirely lacking in common sense, but they reveal a remarkable intelligence once it is allowed free exercise within the framework of rules and formulas. Old Malagasy lawyers are formidable practitioners of legal procedure. Every Malagasy can compose poetry by regrouping ready-made phrases in a great variety of ways, and can improvise word-puzzles—like the Hain-Teny—with great subtlety and finesse. Another aspect of this capacity is what the Malagasies call suppleness, a quality which (in their eyes) consists in reaching one's objective without check, without a conflict with anyone, and without violating any of the known rules. To Europeans, of course, this suppleness looks very much like hypocrisy and it shocks those who do not understand its real nature. The Malagasies, for their part, are often shocked and demoralized by the way the Europeans, who brought such detailed and formal regulations into the country, mock and ridicule them and occasionally even violate them.

The words in which D. Westermann, in his *Noirs et Blancs en Afrique*, pp. 45–46, describes the dependence of the African, could very well be applied unchanged to the Malagasy: 'The springs of his actions are predominantly social and not individual, and he is profoundly affected by public opinion. His conscience is rooted in the approval of the community; it depends upon the daily security provided by the group and not upon any individual action. Personal responsibility is avoided to the greatest extent possible.' It appears, however, that the African group, the tribe, is a more solid unity than

Malagasy society, which has a looser general structure, but is rigidly linked to the ancestors.

In spite of his docility, the Malagasy has no real professional conscience, but that is not for the reasons which would account for its absence in Europeans. He lacks it because he personalizes his relationships where he does not formalize them, and where there is neither formality nor person, there is nothing. Do your best to please the chief and obey the rules; there his ethics ends, and naturally that is not enough to make him conscientious.[1] Even respect for the truth is replaced by consideration for the person to whom he is speaking; he does not say what is true but what he feels it appropriate to say. This is apparent in certain linguistic peculiarities; the word for 'yes', for instance, means 'I agree with you'; the word for 'no' means 'I am not in agreement'; to the question, 'Has it not rained?' the reply 'No' means that it has rained. This mode of conversation reveals a desire to make one's position clear with regard to persons rather than to things.[2]

For the sake of completeness I should perhaps mention in connexion with the dependence complex the fact that semi-evolved Malagasies (and no doubt also, many of those whom we consider 'civilized') place absolute faith in divinations. The commonest form of divination practised at present is that of the *sikidy*. (Seeds are used; the diviner picks up handfuls at random, and according as the handful contains an odd or an even number he lays down one or two, building up groups somewhat like Braille characters. Once the first row is laid down, a second is deduced from it in accordance with certain rather complicated rules. The result is read rather in the way a fortune-teller reads a pack of cards.)[3] The injunctions of the *sikidy* are always strictly obeyed, and this explains the often incomprehensible behaviour of Malagasies when they change their plans without apparent reason, give up a profitable enterprise for a less profitable one, and so on. They will never admit that they are following the *sikidy*; to Europeans they invent excuses which are very often

---

[1] What he lacks is a certain development of the super-ego. His conscience remains attached to the persons in whom authority resides, to their edicts, and the social customs. He has not what the philosophers would call an 'autonomous' moral authority: dependence excludes autonomy. E. Cailliet, in his *Essai sur la psychologie du Hova*, noted these psychological traits (pp. 26–31), but without analysing them.

[2] See G. Berthier, *Note sur les coutumes du peuple malgache*, p. 26 (concern for politeness in replies).

[3] For further details, see Berthier, ibid., p. 89. The fortune revealed by divination is somehow identified with the will of the ancestors.

absurd and simply irritate him. They also obey the dictates of their dreams.

Sorcerers are very different from the diviners who perform the *sikidy*. They are withdrawn and very difficult to approach. They do as they like and cause horror by disregarding the customs, as for instance by dancing on the tombs at night. By way of reprisal the sorcerer himself is buried, not in a tomb, but at the roadside, where he may be trampled on. He is a sort of voluntary victim, a scapegoat personifying evil, but one who accepts his role. It is easy to see that in order to play this part the sorcerer must have cast off all the bonds of dependence. How does he manage to break free? Does he perhaps transfer his dependence to imaginary beings, in the way we do? His 'professional' life is so carefully hidden that it is impossible to find out how a man *becomes* a sorcerer. It would appear, from the energetic way the diviners deny it, that it is possible to pass from 'honest' magic to sorcery, and this is probably a temptation the diviners have to guard against. In any case the characteristic feature of the sorcerer is not that he practises magic, but that he is 'charged' with evil, in both senses of the word. He is accused of selling poisons more often than of casting spells—although these two branches of activity are not so clearly differentiated by the Malagasies as by ourselves. The most plausible theory that can be put forward to explain the existence of the Malagasy sorcerer is that man spontaneously forms an image of evil and that this image fascinates him; the sorcerer is the man who identifies himself with the image, and there are social paths (ceremonies, initiations, beliefs of various kinds) whereby this identification can be transformed into a 'situation' in the community. That is sheer hypothesis, of course, and though it would explain the characteristics of the Malagasy sorcerer, it would not explain those of magicians and witch-doctors.

To return to my main theme—when the Malagasy, with his dependent personality, is confronted with someone whose personality is free and independent, like that of the adult European, he cannot easily adapt himself to it.

The first attempt at adaptation takes place on the mythical level by means of a process of rationalization which I must mention because it is still 'true' in the eyes of the Malagasies. They think that the European has no soul. This is a living belief which they do not attempt to reduce to a formula, and it is firmly held because it is linked with the belief in the dead. To them it seems self-evident—a fact which gives us some insight into their concept of the soul. Ironically enough, of course, the very people the Malagasies accuse of having no soul are precisely those who thought to bring them the doctrine of the immortality of the spiritual substance.

The fact is that to the Malagasies the soul is virtually identical with dependence: it is that which requires the observance of the customs and respect for the *fady*; it is that which unites the family and the tribe; it is that which reappears, after death, in the dreams of the living, and so on. Proof of the Europeans' lack of soul is the fact that they have no cult of the dead and no white ghosts. To say that the white man has no conscience, that he does what he likes, that he has no soul, or that he has no ancestors is, for the Malagasy, to say the same thing in four different ways. I have never obtained from a Malagasy an account of a dream in which a white man figured— although this is not conclusive, for a Malagasy would never relate such a dream to a European.

The Malagasy in his way is unhappily aware of the white man's inferiority complex, just as the white man dimly—though to his advantage—comprehends the Malagasy's dependence complex. The Malagasy realizes that there is in the white man some force which drives him to seek constant change, to try out novelties, to make incessant demands, and to accomplish extraordinary things just to 'show off'. He understands it the more easily since the inferiority complex, though masked in him by his acceptance of dependence, is not entirely absent and in some circumstances becomes clearly apparent. On such occasions his Malagasy comrades say he is 'trying to play the *vazaha*', and make fun of him. Playing the *vazaha* and swanking are virtually synonymous, and the Malagasy who begins to act in this way will not get very far or derive any great satisfaction from it unless he has been uprooted from his environment at an early age—for assuredly there is nothing to prevent a Malagasy acquiring a personality of the European type if he has been brought up from infancy in a European environment. But such a Malagasy will be a European and will have the complexes of a European. There may be some traits of character linked with the physical temperament, the manner of expressing emotion, for instance, which persist by way of racial characteristics—but even that is doubtful.

The situation is quite different in those cases, and they are not a few, where a Malagasy has during his youth—and not, be it noted, in infancy—acquired a European personality which is superimposed upon the Malagasy personality he already possessed. If he represses his Malagasy personality he is to all outward appearances a European, but his original personality has not been destroyed and will continue to manifest itself in disguise. If he returns to his own people his repressed personality will be awakened again by the environment. He is then rather in the position of a repressed homosexual among overt homosexuals, a situation which, as is well known, is liable to give rise to hatred, either conscious or otherwise. This explains why 'assimilated' natives have so very little influence, why the policy of bringing back to Madagascar Malagasies who have been thoroughly Europeanized in Europe, in the hope of fostering Franco-Malagasy friendship, does not pay off as well as might, *a priori*, be expected. The complexes of the 'assimilated' drive them to seek the company of Europeans, but they are never received by them as equals. They are ill at ease in all societies, and the failure they embody heightens rather than diminishes consciousness of racial differences.[1]

If the Europeanized Malagasy is not to repress his Malagasy personality he must integrate his European elements into it—a difficult task for which his own goodwill and skilfulness are not enough; it is necessary in addition that the European and Malagasy environments should not place insurmountable obstacles in his way. If he fails in his task, his European personality will probably be just a slender *persona* and our 'civilized' man will have but a thin European veneer. The unenlightened would see this veneer as the cause of the familiar displays of vanity and manifestations of degradation; their observation of the facts would be correct but their explanation of

---

[1] This failure is a good example of those false verifications by experience which are so frequently met with in the study of inter-racial relations.

To all appearances, in fact, these Europeanized Malagasies differ from Europeans proper only by the racial characteristics determined by their genetic stock, the most obvious of these being the colour of the skin. Thus it appears that the conditions are present for a verification by the 'method of difference' as conceived by inductive logic. The difference in skin-colour is enough, in fact, for the European colonial society to refuse to receive these evolved natives into its midst (though it finds room for them in the administration). The Malagasy reacts to these difficulties with symptoms of inferiority, a need for compensation, feelings of abandonment, and so on. But his reaction is taken by the European for a racial characteristic, and racialism, which was at first spontaneous, becomes deliberate, and claims to be based on impartial observation. Typical Malagasies, for their part, noticing what happens to Europeanized Malagasies, draw their conclusions too. Thus, paradoxically, the more 'civilized' the colonial inhabitants become, the greater is the awareness on both sides of irremovable racial differences. These differences acquire exactly the importance attributed to them. Seen in this light, our old claim that we wanted to assimilate the Malagasies seems somewhat hypocritical, since in fact we denied them social assimilation. We may conclude that but for this hypocrisy assimilation would have been perfectly possible. But there is no doubt to-day that as a result of new unconscious convictions, this possibility has quite disappeared.

them wrong: vanity is the price that is paid for failure and is a compensation for inferiority. The Malagasy is better off if he is deliberately hypocritical—and this, too, happens at times. Usually, however, things are less simple, for the original personality does not remain intact under its mask: in place of an almost megalomaniac vanity, resentment and hostility appear. These traits—vanity, hypocrisy, resentment—have sometimes been attributed to the Malagasies as a whole, but this is a mistake, for they are the consequence of unsuccessful Europeanization.   Unfortunately, as things are at present—at any rate in Madagascar—Europeanization fails more often than it succeeds. It is more successful in Europe, for European society offers fewer obstacles, and there in any case the Malagasy personality is eventually repressed.

The Malagasy who can be most useful to us in forwarding Franco-Malagasy collaboration is the one who has preserved his Malagasy personality intact, adapting it, but not concealing it. A real understanding of this fact would lead to a total revision of our teaching methods, for all we do at present is to instruct the masses without adapting them to our civilization, and to cultivate the *élite* while suppressing their personalities, neither of which methods really improves the situation.

It is worthy of note that disturbances broke out at the very time when a number of Europeanized Malagasies were returning to Madagascar. Some of them—those who had been truly assimilated—broke with their compatriots, and thereafter had no influence on them. Others, whose assimilation had been incomplete, fomented and led the revolts, for they are the people most likely to develop a real hatred of Europeans. Caliban's dictum:

> You taught me language; and my profit on't
> Is, I know how to curse . . . ,

though   over-simplifies the situation, is true in essence. It is not that Caliban has savage and uneducable instincts or that he is such poor so   that even good seed would bring forth bad plants, as Prospero believes. The real reason is given by Caliban himself:

> . . . When thou camest first,
> Thou strok'dst me, and mad'st much of me . . .
> . . . and then I lov'd thee

—and then you abandoned me before I had time to become your equal. . . . In other words: you taught me to be dependent, and I was happy; then you betrayed me and plunged me into inferiority. It is indeed in some such situation as this that we must look for the origin of the fierce hatred sometimes shown by 'evolved' natives; in them the process of civilization has come to a halt and been left incomplete.

In contrast, the Malagasy whose personality has been neither repressed nor masked, who has preserved his original dependence complex in all its purity, is not generally a prey to hostility towards the European. During the recent rebellion there was a number of cases where Malagasies who came to assassinate isolated Europeans explained that they did so with regret in obedience to their chiefs, to whom they had sworn oaths of allegiance, and not out of any hatred.

From the very beginning of the revolt these assassinations were represented as atrocities; although at the time we had very little information about what was going on we were always given very detailed accounts of any episode that was likely to arouse unconscious sadistic tendencies. . . . Such investigations as it has been possible to make since suggest that in almost every case there were distortions and exaggerations which were not even conscious or deliberate. Even where officials of the police department were responsible for circulating these rumours they were impelled rather by their own unconscious sadism than by an official policy. In fact it was not the accounts of Malagasy atrocities only which were exaggerated. Reports of the acts of violence committed by Europeans were exaggerated too, in the same proportions *and by the same people.* The lawyers defending the Malagasies who were brought to trial took care to mention the ill-treatment inflicted on the prisoners (to make them 'confess') only when they could produce positive evidence in the form, say, of medical records or bodily scars. But, surprisingly enough, the Europeans who took a more or less direct part in the ill-treatment boasted about it and, without a thought to the harm they did themselves in the process, represented it as torture of a far more lurid kind than in actual fact it was. (Which is not to say, of course, that it was not adequate to achieve its object, that of making the prisoners sign statements obviously prepared in advance.) A particularly bloody and highly-coloured description of the Fianarantsoa 'chamber of horrors' was so shocking as to provoke an official inquiry: the inquiry revealed nothing more than the abuses— odious, but more prosaic—of police 'routine'. The description had in fact emanated from certain rather neurotic individuals who had taken part, in a semi-official capacity, in the police interrogations. They had posed as veritable torturers in order to satisfy—relatively cheaply and in imagination only—tendencies to which they had in reality yielded only in a very mild degree. Considerable allowance must therefore be made for a kind of imaginary sadism, and that being so the amount of torture and the number of rapes and cruelties attributed to the rebels will not be so surprising. There was the description, for instance, of the horrible death of a young civil service clerk upon whom a 'live autopsy' was said to have been carried out by his own native doctor: he cut him up, it was alleged, exactly according to the rules, tying the arteries as he went along and keeping the man alive right up to the end by injecting him with camphorated oil! (I shall spare the reader the details.) In spite of the absurd improbability of a story of this kind, people were so ready to believe such tales that it was unwise for a European who had retained a modicum of judgement to appear sceptical. In this case, too, an investigation took place some six months later. It revealed that the native doctor had displayed the utmost devotion to his master, who was ill, and had done all in his power to help him escape from the rebels. The Government has since rewarded him for his efforts. There were relatively few cases as extreme as this, but many of a milder kind could be found.

Given this reservation, however, to put us on our guard against all unverified atrocity stories, it must be admitted that the rebellion and its suppression occasioned a great deal of violence in which some streaks of real cruelty can be seen. But the Malagasies' cruelty bears no resemblance to the picture of it which the European spontaneously —and almost inevitably—forms in his imagination. Their ferocity towards their victims was rather that of the 'inexperienced' killer, crazed with feelings of guilt, than the skilled refinements of a sadistic torturer. It is obviously difficult, during a period of unrest, to perceive the psychological factor operating in the horrified witnesses, or in those who later peddle these stories for the sake of the unconscious satisfaction they gain from them. Moreover, a murder is in itself cruelty enough, without the addition of torture, to cause a profound disturbance. . . .

We shall be better able to judge exactly what degree of cruelty to attribute to the Malagasies if we consider how they sacrifice their oxen in the course of funeral ceremonies—a practice which, though distasteful to us, is not sadistic. They are fond of the beast they intend to kill. They begin by playing with him; then the game becomes a struggle in earnest, and as the ox defends himself they become indignant and angry, and in the end they kill the 'wicked' creature with distressing fury, saying that he 'jolly well deserved it'. The Spanish toreador's bull is considered noble: whence does it derive its nobility if not from that of the Spanish soul? The Malagasies' sacrificial ox, on the other hand, just before its death, is considered to be intractable, viciously naughty, stupidly disobedient, and all without a hope of success. These characteristics indicate, in projection and by opposites, as it were, the dependence complex. Exactly the same psychological features are to be found in the game children play of sacrificing an ox. A child takes the place of the ox, and he is pretty roughly handled by his comrades. Cailliet notes these facts very accurately in his *Essai sur la psychologie du Hova*, p. 20.

The numerous stories which circulated among the European population, depicting the Malagasies as perpetrators of revolting atrocities (I shall refer later to their sexual ingredients), were not all officially denied or else they were denied too late. Their originators were probably not deliberately seeking to create a lasting misunderstanding between Europeans and Malagasies, but that is what they may well have done. In very truth, however, they *created* nothing; their unconscious feelings of hatred merely *emerged* in the stories and roused in their hearers similar feelings which had up to then been repressed.

The image of the European plays much too big a part in the Malagasy's thoughts for him not to give him a great deal of attention. In normal times the presence of the European is very comforting; he assumes responsibility for so many offences against the customs and looks so strong and easily capable of shouldering the burden of guilt. In him the Malagasy sees at once the absolute master, the protector, and the scapegoat—images which in Europe would never be so completely fused. But in spite of these reassuring factors the European is always a source of ill-defined anxiety for the Malagasy: he can do what he likes and is unpredictable; he has no standards, and his attitudes are extraordinary—he is disappointed if the fruit is not ripe, even if it is the wrong season! He is liable to want the impossible and to demand it. He thereby sets a bad example which may weaken the precepts handed down from the ancestors. Fortunately he is strong; if he were weak, 'what on earth would happen to us?' people ask.

Thus everything connected with the European—the way he washes, the way he eats, his habits of life in general—all become the subject of a somewhat legendary learning, as the habits of beavers or ants are to us. This knowledge is to some extent prized among the Malagasies, in the same way as we in Europe prize a knowledge of the habits of the animal societies I have just mentioned. The European, however, who has always something of an inferiority complex, interprets the value set on knowledge of his ways as a valuing of himself; he takes it as a tribute to his immense superiority. But the really typical Malagasy takes an interest in the white man, and even unconsciously identifies himself with him, without actually making any comparison between himself and the other, or feeling inferior, while at the same time adopting a dependent attitude. In these circumstances it is easy to see why 'first contacts' are so easy to make; it is easy, too, to see why the observers whom Lévy-Bruhl quotes found the natives first so dependent, then so abusive as if they did not know their 'place'—the place, that is, that the observers had assigned to them, as the result of a barely conscious process of valuation to which they alone assented.

If we look at the external facts alone, we cannot help realizing that the dependence relationship is reciprocal in nature: if the master has a servant, the servant likewise has a master, and though he does not compare himself with him, he nevertheless takes pleasure in the value of the thing he possesses. The man Mackenzie cured said distinctly, 'You are now *my* white man.' The same is probably true in Europe of the psychology of the staff of luxury establishments; they are naïvely devoted to their rich and elegant patrons because they identify themselves with them and no longer suffer from their subservient positions. It is the poor patron who humiliates them. This is an important element in the psychology of dependence. The reader will find many examples of it in Robert Drury's *Journal*, published in 1729. At the time when Robert Drury was living in Madagascar after being shipwrecked, the petty kings of the Malagasies were all very anxious to get possession of a white man. They attached great value to such a possession, but this value had nothing to do with esteem for the white man himself.

These relationships are difficult to understand properly because we are always too prone to think that they are explained by motives of self-interest. (For instance, people assume that the servant likes the rich patron for his tips, but in fact it is very often the poor man who gives the larger tip out of sheer nervousness, and he is all the more despised for it!) In the case of the petty kings, it has been thought that they considered white men useful possessions because they were knowledgeable about most things. We need only read Drury's *Journal*—which is very interesting in itself—to realize what a mistake that is. Those who offer this explanation over-estimate the importance the Malagasies attached to European technique; in fact they saw it as a mere curiosity. No doubt they very much appreciated the manufactured goods the Europeans brought with them, but they had practically no desire to know how to make them. Drury, like a good European, learned much more from the Malagasies than they bothered to learn from him. However, he was perfectly prepared, still like a good European, to teach them all he knew.[1]

The reciprocity in the dependence relationship, whereby the Malagasy, as it were, takes possession of the person upon whom he is dependent, and in that way values him, has certain more obscure psychological foundations. Without trying to elucidate them in their entirety I should like to give some indication of their nature. There is a satisfaction to be gained, as I have said, from knowing about other animal species and their customs, and this, too, might be seen as a kind of appropriation. We are now touching upon the psychological ground in which totemistic beliefs are rooted. Behind the totem lurks the image of the ancestors and, further behind still, the image of the parents as the small child conceives them. Psychoanalysis suggests that this image of the parents, the first of all human images to confront the infant child, is very probably adult man's only means of escaping solipsism—or narcissism—and of apprehending others as real live beings. The strange beliefs collectively known as totemism [2] might then be explained by the need to apprehend even

[1] Malagasies to-day are very anxious to learn from us.

[2] There are only traces—recognizable ones, however—of totemism in Madagascar. It would be arbitrary to consider them as survivals of an earlier system; we do not know. Here are some examples: among the Merina, certain families pass on *fady* (taboos) connected with various animal species. There are personal *fady* like those of the King Andrianampoinimerina connected with the dog. The dog then acquired a new name—*alika* instead of *amboa*. The ox appears to have been *fady* at one time; it is said that a king, half-legendary, removed this *fady* some centuries ago. The Tandroy, who are rather backward inhabitants of the south of Madagascar, commit suicide when they lose an ox they are fond of. Other tribes take for their ancestors lemurs or crocodiles. The commonest word for lemurs is *babakoto*, which means something like ancestor-child.

This assimilation of the image of the child with that of the ancestor can also be found in the unconscious of the European, where, indeed, it was first discovered by psychoanalysis. See Ernest Jones, *Papers on Psycho-Analysis* (3rd ed., 1923), Chaps. XXXVIII and XXXIX.

other living species, at least at first, through this human *imago*. In children's dreams or drawings there is a constant recurrence of animal forms representing the mother, so much so as to put the likelihood of assimilation beyond doubt. Totemism thus becomes comprehensible and we find that we are not so far removed from it as we should like to think.

Totemism is the opposite of the mechanistic theory, a theory which was propounded by a philosopher who had been wrestling with the problem of the existence of other people; he was in the habit of seeing them as no more than 'hats and coats' and never quite succeeded, in spite of the Princess Elizabeth's questioning, in giving them any more life than that of mechanical toys driven by will and reason, both almost entirely depersonalized—for almost anything can be willed, and reason is identical for all men. The interesting point, however, is that children, instead of treating animals as machines, treat machines as living things, the more highly prized because they are easier to appropriate. Children's appropriation is a virtual identification and they play at being machines (steam-engines, motor cars, aeroplanes) just as 'primitive' peoples play at being the totem. The psychological state in the two cases is probably very similar. The totemic attitude would then be that which occurs when another being is apprehended as living and existing, through the naïve projection of the original *imago*. The failure of this projection would lead to narcissism in one of its various forms or to solipsism.

It is against this psychological background, which is barely accessible to the conscious mind, that we must endeavour to sketch in the picture of the white man as the Malagasy may at first see him. We shall then discover—as I shall show later on, and as Emile Cailliet indicated was possible in his *Essai sur la psychologie du Hova*, from which I shall quote [1]—how it may interfere with his image of the ancestors.

[1] Since this book was written, Mr H. F. Hanneman has published an interesting article in the *Monde non chrétien* (and also in the *International Review of Missions*), called 'Le culte du cargo en Nouvelle-Guinée'. It shows how the image of the white man, in the eyes of the Papuans, coincides with that of the *Tibud*—the ancestor-gods.

In his introduction to this article Maurice Leenhardt says: '. . . The Oceanians often place the paradise which is inhabited by their dead on an island they name and which they say is beyond the horizon. That of the people of Buka was called Sune. When, once a month, a ship from Sydney brought goods for trading, the natives went on board, bought freely, and delighted in all the possibilities of wealth laid out before them. One day a captain forbade them to come on board. This caused discontent among them, protests, and finally a revolt, which the administration feared it might have to quell by force of arms. Everything became clear when it was discovered that the natives, who had confused the names Sune, their paradise, and Sydney, believed that the monthly steamer and its cargo were a miraculous gift from the ancestors and that the ancestors themselves had come in the form of white men. They went on board

At all events it is clear that the dependence relationship contains no element of comparison or self-appraisal, no effort to 'situate' oneself otherwise than within that special order of things which is the system of dependence. This is true, of course, only so long as the relationship remains pure—so long, that is, as the feeling of security guaranteed by it remains intact. This is what distinguishes it radically from the attitudes which go to make up the inferiority complex.

When a European child stops 'being' an aeroplane he becomes, in imagination, an airman. He looks at real airmen but does not compare himself with them, and so escapes the feeling of inferiority; on the contrary, he is exalted by his identification of himself with the airman. Moreover, he can later convert his dream into reality and himself become an airman—though this possibility is quite un-

---

because they felt at home there. But they could no longer see the white man as god-ancestor when he suddenly became unkind.'

There is no doubt, as we shall see from Part III, Ch. V, that in a certain way white men are the ancestors. There are two observations I should like to make in connexion with the above text.

1. Confusion of the names Sune and Sydney is not the real explanation of what happened, for it would apply only to the people of Buka, whereas the same attitude towards the whites and their cargoes is found in places where no such confusion of names is possible. That explanation is purely coincidental, therefore. The true explanation would show that the people of Buka were *prepared* to make this confusion by their general behaviour as Melanesians.

2. My second and more serious comment is that the mythical explanation is probably accidental also. The myth, like the confusion of Sune with Sydney, is a story offered by the Papuans to justify an attitude they adopt spontaneously and unconsciously, following upon the transference to the white man of deep feelings they had earlier transferred to their dead. This is easy to prove because the transference and this attitude are much more widespread than the myth. It is recognizably the attitude described by the observers quoted by Lévy-Bruhl; it is the attitude of typical Malagasies, though they would indignantly deny it or burst out laughing if anyone suggested to them that the white men were ancestors!

Mythologists think that myths are beliefs, but real beliefs are situated at a greater depth; they are the fundamental and vital attitudes of which myths are merely the reflection in the imagination: they indicate the beliefs in the way a dream might indicate psychological structure.

A mythologist reading this might think it a pity that we had not been able to find an ancient myth to explain Malagasies' present behaviour. But it would be a waste of time to look for one, and even if one were to be found, it would explain nothing, but would, on the contrary, itself require explanation in terms of the deeper psychological attitudes indicated by this behaviour, which psychoanalysis is able to elucidate. Otherwise we should be obliged to admit, what is absurd, that the incarnation of the ancestors by white men is an unconscious myth of the Malagasies! To the psychologist these transference reactions are elementary phenomena; the myths with which they may be embellished are purely accidental. Analysis reveals the fundamental beliefs.

It would be interesting to know how the people of Buka reacted when they were told that Sydney was not Sune, and what happened to the transference thereafter.

There is a third point which I shall refrain from commenting on because it will be cleared up later in this book; it is the difficulty of explaining why the natives should have revolted against the ancestors, in the form of white men, when they ceased being kindly—as if the dead could not prove fearsome without provoking immediate rebellion!

necessary to the original game. The Malagasy, however, may suddenly find himself, the instant the bonds of dependence snap, on the brink of an abyss of inferiority, and in danger of falling in. In that case an earlier identification may result in distressingly negative phenomena. In other words, the Malagasy can bear not being a white man; what hurts him cruelly is to have discovered first (by identification) that he is a man and *later* that men are divided into blacks and whites. If the 'abandoned' or 'betrayed' Malagasy continues his identification he becomes clamorous; he begins to demand *equality* in a way he had never before found necessary. The equality he seeks would have been beneficial before he started asking for it, but afterwards it proves inadequate to remedy his ills—for every increase in equality makes the remaining differences seem the more intolerable, for they suddenly appear agonizingly irremovable. This is the road along which the Malagasy passes from psychological dependence to psychological inferiority.

The idea that the 'benefits' of the Malagasy can be increased by our giving him what he lacks, in the way a sum of money can be increased by the addition of other sums, is valid only if it is a matter of material objects such as food and tools. Applied to political, moral, or psychological 'advantages' it appears just a trifle silly. . . . If we try to alter only some aspects of a personality which is constructed differently from our own, we ought not to be surprised if the whole personality undergoes a change. Thus, it is just when the Malagasy is beginning to resemble us a little that he turns roughly from us. Our mistake lies in assuming that the personality as a whole can be treated in the way we treat the schoolboy's mind—as an empty vessel waiting to be filled. Those schoolmasters who thought that there was nothing in the mind which had not entered through the doors of the senses—and by that they meant that there was nothing in the memory except what had entered through the ears listening to the teacher or the eyes fastened upon the school-book—were ready to believe that there was nothing good in the personality but what had been put there deliberately, like plants in a garden, and that whatever happened to be growing there could be dug up like weeds. This schoolmaster's philosophy has ruled Europe with a rod of iron and is ultimately responsible for the present character of the European, with all its good and bad qualities. But if it is applied to personalities of a very different type, what is 'added' either remains an alien element or else in the long run brings about a modification of the whole personality, some elements being integrated and others repressed.

Thus, an education confined to providing the colonial inhabitant with new tools could be very useful if it left the personality as a whole untouched and had no direct cultural import, but a culturally-biased education can disrupt the personality far more than one would expect, unless—and this is probably what most often happens—it is accepted simply at the level of the *persona*, as knowledge for the sake of knowledge, and a source of vanity—purely academic and bookish and not integrated into the whole being. We have yet to find an educational method which is somewhere between these two extremes. For the moment we must be content not to influence the personality or unwittingly undermine it. With all this in mind we can better understand what Christianity could have done for the peoples with dependent personalities—and what it signally failed to do.

Dependence threatened

People say that we do not realize we possess a particular organ until something goes wrong with it. Similarly it may be that the dependence relationship has only now sprung to our notice because it has already been partly undermined. The individuals who have come into contact with representatives of the other civilization—and it applies to both sides—have been more profoundly affected by the encounter than might at first be supposed.[1]

To my mind there is no doubting the fact that colonization has always required the existence of the need for dependence. Not all peoples can be colonized: only those who experience this need. Neither are all peoples equally likely to become colonizers, for, as I shall show later, certain other equally definite predispositions are required for that role. There are other ways of being conquered than that of becoming a subject colony, and other forms of domination than the colonial—assimilation, association, economic exploitation; there is extermination at one end of the scale, and absorption of the victor by the vanquished at the other.

[1] It must also be remembered that the elements which come into contact with each other first are in one way or another the most 'eccentric'. They would have had less chance of meeting had they been more firmly held within their respective social structures. This fact no doubt explains the exaggerated character of the acts of dependent behaviour noted by the observers whom Lévy-Bruhl quotes and which I referred to earlier. The exaggeration seems to be due to a state of dissatisfaction which aggravates the hunger for dependence.

Wherever Europeans have founded colonies of the type we are considering, it can safely be said that their coming was unconsciously expected—even desired—by the future subject peoples. Everywhere there existed legends foretelling the arrival of strangers from the sea, bearing wondrous gifts with them.[1] From the early seventeenth century onwards any shipwrecked sailor was welcomed with open arms, and the chiefs quarrelled over possession of them. True, these Europeans were on occasions massacred. But we cannot tell to what extent they may have frightened the natives by their strange behaviour and their incomprehensible demands. Certain it is that at the start there was nothing indicative of racial hatred; whatever there was rather favoured the white man than otherwise, at least in Madagascar.

When the colonizer first appears, it is not as an enemy but as a stranger, as a guest. In Madagascar he is called *vazaha*, an expression which means as nearly as possible, 'honourable stranger'.[2] He seizes authority only when at length through his persistent demands —the native finds him insatiable [3]—he has provoked part of the population to display defence reactions. It is in this sense that we can say that the colonies were conquered. But in most cases, in its ordinary meaning, it is a distortion of the facts to make them fit a preconceived pattern, for the armed forces employed would have been inadequate for the task had we not been helped by our un-conscious accomplices in the souls of the natives themselves. In 1947, after fifty years of colonial rule, tribes allegedly unwarlike, armed only with pointed sticks—which the communiqués described as assegais—attacked positions defended with Lewis guns and hand-grenades. Yet at the time when Madagascar was first conquered the Malagasies had been drawn up in armed formations—and had fled at the first shots fired. It cannot have been force alone, therefore, which vanquished Madagascar; force would not have conquered and kept the island had not the Malagasy people, long before our arrival, been ready for our coming.

---

[1] One of many examples of these beliefs may be found in *Notes, Reconnaissances et Explorations*, Antananarivo, 1897, 2nd vol., p. 196.

[2] *Vazaha* has recently acquired a pejorative sense. After the revolt, the *boto* at the hotel where I used to dine in Antananarivo took to calling me *Rangahy*, which is the word used to address a Malagasy as 'sir'. Surprised by this new form of address, I looked for an explanation; it was a way of telling me that they were not confusing me with the colonialists.

[3] That is the impression invariably produced on a personality psychologically dependent by a personality psychologically inferior.

Moreover, the Europeans themselves only made a show of believing in military force; they knew instinctively, and barely consciously, where their strength lay—in a certain 'weakness' of personality on the part of the Malagasies. They were not to know that their position of dominance was due to the fact that in the network of dependences they occupied roughly the same position as the dead ancestors. . . . But they were aware that the psychological situation favoured them, and knew that force alone would be powerless once that situation changed. Proof of this is the alarm and anger with which they greeted any attempt by the natives to gain emancipation. This was not the reasonable reaction of men sure of their own strength preparing to meet a danger with energetic measures. Those few Europeans who, because they were unaffected by the contagion, were able to observe the colonials' reactions dispassionately will confirm that it looked very much like panic and that there was a tendency to take violent, spectacular, rather pointless or downright harmful actions. In the following chapter the reader will find an account of the psychological causes of this attitude.

From the very beginning of the revolt, in March 1947, the Europeans in Madagascar began to behave in a paradoxical and consequently very revealing fashion. Those who were in the area of the revolt displayed great self-possession and courage, and after the initial surprise which caused some loss of life, there were virtually no more casualties. The story is told, for instance, of the colonial who held out single-handed against three hundred assailants, with only a shotgun and twenty rounds, for ten days before being rescued.

In places far from the actual disturbances, however, a mixture of fear, excitement, and anger gained possession of the Europeans. In the capital they took defensive precautions out of all proportion to the real danger, to the extent of depriving other parts of the country which were more closely threatened of the help they badly needed.[1] The emotion generated was evidently unrelated to the degree of real

[1] For instance, one of the Antananarivo hotels, two steps from police headquarters and with a self-propelled gun almost on its doorstep, obtained for its defence two machine-guns which were entrusted to the residents. (They were sorely needed on the east coast where the colonials were beleaguered.) Armed Senegalese soldiers mounted guard outside the rooms of the officers' wives. Hotel residents, armed, patrolled the town. These patrols served no purpose, for there was no sign of real danger, nor did any ever arise in the town. The danger, at that moment, was over a hundred miles away. But the significant point is that two months later, when the rebellion had spread as a result of repressive measures which roused uncertain terror everywhere, danger in fact drew near to Antananarivo. Then, the European inhabitants of the town recovered their calm completely and behaved with normal good sense. What better proof could there be of the purely emotional character—to say no more—of the earlier reactions?

danger. There were many little tell-tale signs: verbal slips, for instance—when the rebellion seemed to be dying down a man, refusing to be reassured, said: 'I am not unhopeful of further outbreaks', as if he wanted rather than feared them. The revolt appeared to have some sort of fascination, and the Europeans' actions, which they took to be purely defensive, were, unknown to them, acts of defiance and provocation. They behaved, in fact, rather like an angry schoolmaster whose orders have been disobeyed and who, to gain some psychological satisfaction, resorts to violence, but violence of a peculiar kind, a theatrical sort of violence: he makes a scene, strikes a pose, creates a spectacle for himself and his friends, in accordance with a mode of thinking more superstitious than practical, and derives some inner solace from it. This was the meaning of the noisy sorties of armed men in the evenings; they returned home satisfied and slept soundly for the rest of the night. They justified their behaviour by saying that it was necessary to frighten the Malagasies, although what the immense majority of the Malagasies needed far more was to feel that they were not being abandoned. The Europeans knew well enough that their behaviour was likely to rouse peaceful Malagasies and drive them into the arms of the rebels. But, irrationally, they derived a certain satisfaction from running this risk.

It could be maintained from the purely psychological point of view, and leaving aside all moral considerations, that the use of force *can* solve problems; we all know that in war the soldier finally makes peace with himself while making peace with the enemy. But he must first have recognized himself in the enemy, have shared his perils, his misfortunes, and his courage: in other words, he must have been a combatant and have seen the combatant in the enemy. This is hardly possible in a colonial war. Anger, threats, defiance, provocation do not bring with them absolution. This was understood somewhat belatedly, and ceremonies of surrender were organized to try to make the pacification of the revolt look like an agreement between opposing forces. Unfortunately nobody believed in it. Even war has its laws which we cannot afford to disobey.

In conclusion, it may be said that the conduct of the Europeans cannot be explained solely in terms of their carefully calculated interests, nor by their fear in the face of danger. On the contrary, it can only be explained by the nature of the complex-determined feelings roused by a colonial situation. In the next part of this book I shall try to indicate the origin of these feelings.

EPILOGUE TO PART I – DREAMS

Mᴀʟᴀɢᴀsɪᴇs' dreams faithfully reflect their overriding need for security and protection. All the dreams quoted below were, it is true, recorded at a time of public disturbance, but their authors had seen nothing of the disorders and knew about them only from hearsay. The following nightmare, described by a twenty-three-year-old Merina cook, is—so far as can be judged from the samples I have been able to collect—typical of the dreams of thousands of Malagasies.

The cook's dream. 'I was being chased by an angry black bull. Terrified, I climbed up into a tree and stayed there till the danger was past. I came down again, trembling all over.'

The bull stands for a Senegalese soldier. It was not possible to push the analysis any farther in this instance, but other dreams, set forth below, leave no doubt as to the correct interpretation.

The tree stands for the mother, as in European symbolism, and the symbol is easily explained: when danger threatens, the child rushes to its mother; she picks it up off the ground, and it can then put its tongue out at the enemy from a safe distance. Or again, the child can hide 'in the shade' of the mother, among her skirts, as among the foliage of a tree.

Lastly, behind the figure of the Senegalese (the bull), who represents external danger, there undoubtedly lurks the psychologically deeper image of the father, as will be shown by other dreams of the same type.[1]

---

[1] There is a little-known Merina *Key to Dreams*, which is a mixture of symbolical interpretations and superstitions. Dreams about bulls have a prominent place in it. Being attacked by a bull is supposed to warn the dreamer that he is threatened by sorcery, the bull representing the sorcerer. If the dreamer is caught on the bull's horns it means that the spell will be effective and he must seek protective magic. The colour of the coat must be noted because it indicates the colouring of the originator of the sorcery.

From the point of view of psychoanalysis, of course, this 'interpretation' is simply

Dream of a thirteen-year-old boy, Rahevi. 'While going for a walk in the woods, I met two black men. "Oh," I thought, "I am done for!" I tried to run away but couldn't. They barred my way and began jabbering in a strange tongue. I thought they were saying, "We'll show you what death is." I shivered with fright and begged, "Please, Sirs, let me go, I'm so frightened." One of them understood French but in spite of that they said, "We are going to take you to our chief." As we set off they made me go in front and they showed me their rifles. I was more frightened than ever, but before reaching their camp we had to cross a river. I dived deep into the water and thanks to my presence of mind found a rocky cave where I hid. When the two men had gone I ran back to my parents' house.'

Psychoanalysis might perhaps have revealed why there were two men, but apart from this point the dream is essentially the same as the preceding one: the rifles replace the bull's horns.

Josette's dream. The dreamer, a young girl, got lost and sat down on a fallen tree-trunk. A woman in a white dress told her that she was in the midst of a band of robbers. The account goes on: '"I am a schoolgirl", I said, trembling, "and I lost my way here when I was going home from school," and she replied: "Follow this path, child, and you children will find your way home."'

Here it appears that the mother's protective powers are inadequate; in fact the mother seems to be dead: she is lying stretched out on the ground. Josette relies for protection on the fact that she is a schoolgirl and on some woman in a white dress—evidently a teacher or nurse. A point to note is the passage from the singular to the plural in the woman's reply, for solitude *is* danger (I am alone and lost) and safety lies in numbers (we are all together). The passage from danger to safety in the dream led to this revealing lapse in the telling of it.

Dream of a fourteen-year-old boy, Raẓafi. He is being chased by (Senegalese) soldiers who 'make a noise like galloping horses as they run', and 'show their rifles in front of them'. The dreamer escapes by becoming invisible; he climbs a stairway and finds the door of his home.

---

another document on this type of dream. We learn from it that fear of the bull is associated with the image of the sorcerer. Thus there is a link between the image of the sorcerer and that of the father, just as with us there is a connexion between the image of the mother and that of the witch.

Among the Malagasies the image of the mother (so far as I know) is never anything but protective, although in dreams there often arises a dramatic situation in which the protective power of the mother appears inadequate. Indeed, these are the typical anxiety-dreams.

The sexual significance of the rifles is obvious. The sound of galloping horses and the desire to be invisible are probably to be explained by the fact that the child has witnessed the sexual act: he has both *heard* and *seen*. It becomes clear—and it will become clearer later on—that it is in so far as he is felt to be an aggressor threatening the mother that the father is identified with all dangers. The child, moreover, somehow identifies himself with the mother who is 'in danger'.

Proof of the existence of a mutilation complex is found in the dream of a young girl, Elphine (thirteen or fourteen years old). The complex exists in girls as well as boys. Among the Malagasies when a baby boy is circumcised it is the custom for the maternal uncle to eat the foreskin.[1] In this little girl's fantasies her penis is eaten by her father (probably as a punishment for other fantasies). The feeling of danger thus symbolized by the father was called forth by the dangers besetting the Malagasies during the disturbances of the time.

Elphine's dream. 'I dreamed that a fierce black ox was chasing me. He was big and strong. On his head, which was almost mottled (*sic*) with white he had two long horns with sharp points. "Oh how dreadful," I thought. The path was getting narrower. What should I do? I perched myself in a mango-tree, but the ox rent its trunk. Alas, I fell among the bushes. Then he pressed his horns into me; my stomach fell out and he devoured it.'

Most of the remaining dreams would add little to what has already been brought out. More than half the dreams selected at random are of the same type; a few, however, show individual variations.[2]

Raẓa's dream. In his dream the boy heard someone say at school that the Senegalese were coming. 'I went out of the school yard to see.' The Senegalese were indeed coming. He ran home. 'But our house had been dispersed by them too.' 'Dispersed' is a mistake, owing to association with the idea of 'piercing' (compare above, the horns with which the ox rent the trunk of the mango-tree).

The dream reveals the desire to see for oneself, and this desire is an offence for which the child is punished. It may be assumed in this

---

[1] This is a survival from an old form of family organization.
[2] The dreams from which those given here are drawn come from various sources, but in the main they have been collected in schools in the form of French homework. Those which appeared to be inventions have been eliminated, not because such fantasies are without interest but because their interpretation is more difficult. By contrast with the real dreams they were all very 'optimistic'.

case, as in that of Razafi, that what the child has seen is the mother's weakness before the father, who 'pierces' her. The distress the child experiences as a result of this discovery is renewed in the face of danger. Of course discoveries of this kind are bound to be much more frequent among the Malagasies than they are among Europeans, for a Malagasy family usually lives all together in one room and its members sleep on plain mats.[1]

The protective power of the mother is somewhat uncertain; in two of the dreams cited above it proved ineffective. It may therefore be asked whether the father never plays the part of protector. The answer is: yes, but in different circumstances.

Dream of a fourteen-year-old boy, Si. 'I was walking in the garden and felt something like a shadow behind me. All around me the leaves were rustling and falling off, as if a robber was in hiding among them, waiting to catch me. Wherever I walked, up and down the alleys, the shadow still followed me. Suddenly I got frightened and started running, but the shadow took great strides and stretched out his huge hand to take hold of my clothes. I felt my shirt tearing, and screamed. My father jumped out of bed when he heard me scream and came over to look at me, but the big shadow had disappeared and I was no longer afraid.'

In this dream a first interpretation would suggest that the father was protecting the child against a ghost, a *lolo*, representing the power of the ancestors. Anything connected with the ancestors points to the father. Vague childhood fears attach themselves to the ghostly images of the ancestors as soon as the child has learned of their 'existence'.

But the father, it will be noted, affords no protection during the dream, only afterwards, when the child wakes (the account is not clear, the dreaming and waking states being mingled in it). It could be maintained that the dangerous being represented by the *lolo* is once again the father. In other words, the real father is protecting the child against the dream father. Rustling and falling leaves as a symbol of fright are found in the folklore of many countries. They may possibly be a symbol for the mother, in which case in spite of apparent differences the dream would fall into the same category as the others.

The conclusions which may be reached from a consideration of the dreams as a whole are, first: that the children feel they are in danger because their parents are afraid. Then, the cause of fear is the

[1] Cf. *Notes, Reconnaissances et Explorations,* 1897, vol. 2, p. 542.

Senegalese soldier (a fear which at the time was objectively justified). He is disguised in the form of various classic symbols (the bull, for instance), but behind these symbols lies the image of the father, merged with that of external dangers. In the last dream there appears to be an effort to deny that the father is dangerous (we might even say—though there is no evidence for it—*to deny that the father is afraid*, for that would be well within the logic of this kind of thinking: the father's fear *is* the danger). Finally, protection is usually maternal; it is never in doubt, but it is sometimes ineffective, and it is in that form that we find distress most commonly expressed.

Part II
INFERIORITY

CHAPTER I

CRUSOE AND PROSPERO

THE dependence relationship requires at least two members, and where a colonial situation exists, if one of them is the native of the colony, the other is likely to be the colonizer, or rather the colonial, for he it is who offers us the more interesting subject of study. The real colonizer is almost of necessity a man of strong character, a creator rather than an accepter of relationships, at least at the outset. It is only later that he becomes a colonial. The typical colonial, on the other hand, finds the relationship ready made; he takes it up, adapts himself to it, and very often exploits it. And in any case, whether he accepts it passively or seizes upon it greedily, the relationship changes him more than he it. It is precisely this transformation which sets a stamp on him, which makes him a colonial. And it is this which we must now study if we are to find out the exact psychological nature of the relations which form between the European colonial and the dependent native—if we are to understand how and why these relations change with time and what effect they have on the two members.

The reader will see that in trying to discover how it is that a European, to all appearances indistinguishable from other Europeans, can become, sometimes in a very short space of time, a typical colonial and very different from his former self, I have reached a conclusion which is at first sight paradoxical—namely, that the personality of the colonial is made up, not of characteristics acquired during and through experience of the colonies, but of traits, very often in the nature of a complex, already in existence in a latent and repressed form in the European's psyche, traits which the colonial experience has simply brought to the surface and made manifest. Social life in Europe exerts a certain pressure on the individual, and that pressure keeps the personality in a given shape; once it is removed, however, the outlines of the personality change and swell, thus revealing the existence of internal pressures which had up to then passed unnoticed.

Of course that is simply a metaphor; what I want to bring out is that what happens to a European when he becomes a colonial is the result of unconscious complexes, and these I propose to analyse. The shape assumed by a deep-sea fish when it is brought up to the surface is due to differences in pressure, certainly, but it is also due to its own internal anatomical structure. Logically, what my theory amounts to is this, that a person free from complexes—if such a person can be imagined—would not undergo change as a result of experience of the colonies. He would not in the first place feel the urge to go to the colonies, but even should he find himself there by chance, he would not taste those emotional satisfactions which, whether consciously or unconsciously, so powerfully attract the predestined colonial.

These complexes are formed, necessarily, in infancy; their later history varies according to whether they are resolved, repressed, or satisfied in the course of a closer and closer contact with reality as the age of adulthood is reached. The best description of them is to be found in the works of some of the great writers who projected them on to imaginary characters placed in situations which, though imaginary, are typically colonial. The material they drew directly from their own unconscious desires. This is proof enough that the complexes exist even before the colonial situation is experienced.

It is easy, for instance, to establish that Defoe had no other model for Robinson Crusoe but himself. Of the 'real Robinsons' known at the time none had been able to withstand the solitude. Selkirk, the best known, had entirely lost the power of speech. The man who was taken off Mauritius was mad, and John Segar died on seeing white men again. It is just because it is a fable that the story of Crusoe, which came straight from the author's unconscious, makes such an appeal to our own. Defoe himself, in a letter to Bishop Hoadley in 1725, said that the tale of Robinson was an allegory of his own life. He only realized it (as Flaubert did his identification with Madame Bovary) later on. We know that he wrote the novel in two parts. The second part (travels on the Continent) he wrote to order for his publisher, and he wrote it laboriously and with difficulty. But the first part—the one which interests us—he wrote straight off by force of inspiration, at the dictate of his own unconscious. I shall show how all this is confirmed by a passage in the *Serious Reflections* which I shall quote later on.

The story of the friendship of Robinson and Friday no doubt

accounts for many colonial callings. However, it is not this unsurprising aspect of the novel to which I want to draw attention, but the fact that it reveals the colonial vocation *in esse*, as it exists in the unconscious before there is any question of influence or emulation—and as it must necessarily have existed in the unconscious of Defoe. He was not to respond to the call; nevertheless in 1702 he was responsible for a strange proposal for an expedition against Spain's American colonies, and he officially offered to lead it. It was only in his later years, when he was nearly sixty, that he satisfied a long-felt desire—we shall see which—by writing his novel about Crusoe.

Shakespeare's *The Tempest*—he, too, wrote it in his old age—presents a situation which is, psychoanalytically, almost identical with that of Crusoe. We can be sure that Shakespeare had no other model but himself for his creation of Prospero.

It is characteristic of this type of story—the remark applies equally, for instance, to the *Odyssey*, *Sinbad the Sailor* and *Gulliver's Travels*—that the hero has to face either the perils or the miseries of exile; they are either punishments or, as it were, scarecrows, the two ideas being easily linked in that of prohibition. The reason for them is usually a wrongdoing, deliberate or otherwise, and it constitutes disobedience of the gods, the customs, or more generally the father. Prospero had neglected the duties of his office and had been betrayed by his brother in complicity with a king—psychoanalytically a king is a father-image. Even the real travellers, Baudelaire, Trelawny and many others, obediently conform to the unconscious schema.[1] The story-book travellers encounter parental prohibitions in the form of monsters: Cyclops, the Roc bird, the cannibals. They are full of regrets—'Ah, how much better it would have been. . . !' and so on. When they get back they have nothing but misfortunes to relate: 'So we worked at the oar' says Robinson, 'and the wind driving us towards the shore, we hastened our destruction with our own hands. . . .' Nevertheless their adventures rouse envy in their stay-at-home readers, especially if they are young.

Prospero is the least evolved of all these literary figures, according to the criteria of psychoanalysis, for he is endowed with magical power, and so is not required to display those virile and adult qualities to which Ulysses and Crusoe owe their salvation. Crusoe

[1] A particularly interesting traveller to study is R. L. Stevenson. In his story Ariel and Caliban are called Jekyll and Hyde. In the remote Pacific he found courage to grapple with the image which had driven him that far, and began writing the *Weir of Hermiston*. He died before victory was won, leaving his chef-d'oeuvre incomplete.

is psychologically the least archaic, as is shown by his faith in technical skill—he is a veritable Jack-of-all-trades. He is in line with the current of ideas flowing from Locke to the Encyclopaedists; Prospero, on the other hand, is reminiscent rather of Bacon, who thought in terms of experiment but dreamed of magic; nor is he the only character in the play to repudiate technique, for there is Gonzalo, too, the Utopist. Between them, therefore, these characters appear to cover the whole of the subject we are studying. Chronology is of no importance, and so we shall begin with an analysis of Crusoe and see what we can learn from it.

First, it is very significant that he is much less unhappy when he is absolutely alone than when he is afraid he may not be. I must dwell on this paradox, for our familiarity with it dulls our surprise at it; man is afraid because he is alone and his fear is the fear of other men. Fear of solitude is fear of intrusion upon that solitude. (It is the same in *The Tempest*: Prospero's solitude is finally broken in upon.) Contemporary critics even pointed out this 'contradiction' in Robinson Crusoe. But perhaps it was not a contradiction, after all.

At all events, every sign of another living thing, a goat, a footprint, anything put fear into the heart of Crusoe—even his parrot, which was nonetheless a first configuration of the companion he both dreaded and desired in an ambivalent complex of feelings. (It will be easier to understand the role of this parrot, which learns to talk, after reading the passage from the *Serious Reflections*, which I shall quote later on.) In fact, Daniel Defoe's story recounts *the long and difficult cure of a misanthropic neurosis.* His hero, who is at first at odds with his environment, gradually recovers psychological health in solitude. He comes to accept the presence of creatures upon whom he tries to project the image—at once terrifying and reassuring—of *another*. Then he has a friend, 'dumb' at first, like his parrot. Later he has the courage to fight against the 'others' in the form of hostile cannibals. Finally he has to deal with a terribly bad lot who are, however, more akin to himself, and he manages to subdue them by his authority. He even assumes the title of governor of the island. His cure is assured; he is even reconciled with the father-image, and, by the same token, with God (God is also mentioned in the *Serious Reflections*). So, then, Crusoe can return, like Ulysses, '*plein d'usage et raison*'— and money, too, gained chiefly through slave-trading.

Let us leave Defoe's case for a moment to consider that of his reader and discover why he finds Defoe's book so interesting. His interest itself is enough to show that there is in the child some trait which is partly misanthropic, or at any rate anti-social, a trait which, for lack of a better term, I would call 'the lure of a world without men'. It may be repressed to a greater or less extent, but it will remain, nonetheless, in the unconscious.

It is the existence of this trait which makes the idea of the desert island so attractive, whereas in reality there is little to be said for it, as the real Robinsons discovered. The desert islands of the imagination are, it is true, peopled with imaginary beings, but that is after all their *raison d'être*. Some of the semi-human creatures the unconscious creates, such as Caliban or the Lilliputians, reveal their creator's desire to denigrate the whole of mankind. Others are a compound of the bad creatures on whom the child projects his own desire to be naughty and the parents who forbid him to be naughty—for the father who tells his child that the wicked bogey-man will get him if he does not behave, himself becomes a bogey-man in the eyes of the child. And all external dangers, such as the wolf and the policeman, are felt to be his allies, especially as they are specifically referred to by the parents. We have already seen how often this fusion occurs in the dreams of Malagasy children where the 'naughty' (i.e. guilty) child is pursued by the wicked Senegalese soldier who is at the same time his father, both being represented by the bull.

It is a fact, however, that in spite of prohibitions, or perhaps because of them, the child longs to escape. Some time after he is four years of age he makes surreptitious attempts to venture out alone. Sometimes he 'loses' himself or he makes a tour of a block of houses and returns to his starting-point, as if he wanted to verify some topographical intuition or prove that the world is round. Sometimes he longs to be invisible, and hides himself; when his mother calls him anxiously he does not reply. She calls these escapades silly, but perhaps they are something more than mere games. Or again the child may long to go and hide far away from everybody, and so he goes to the bottom of the garden to play at being Robinson; the fact that several children may take part in this game makes no difference—it is still a flight from mankind, and intrusion must be guarded against.

The real attraction of solitude, however, is that if the world is emptied of human beings as they really are, it can be filled with the creatures of our own imagination: Calypso, Ariel, Friday. But if we are to achieve a complete and adult personality it is essential that we should make the images of the unconscious tally, more or less, with real people; flight into solitude shows that we have failed to do so. In *The Tempest*, when Miranda cries:

> . . . O brave new world,
> That has such people in't

we realize, with an emotion which reveals the importance of the fact, that she has accomplished in one step that adjustment of the archetypes to reality which her neurotic father had so surely missed. His scornful reply, ' 'Tis new to thee', proves that he is not yet cured. Where there is a preference for Ariel or Friday to real persons, it is clear that there has been a failure in adaptation, resulting usually from a grave lack of sociability combined with a pathological urge to dominate. These characteristics, which are traceable in the unconscious of Prospero–Shakespeare and Crusoe–Defoe, are very probably present in all children too, but they may develop in one of many ways.

The figure of Friday is no more fully portrayed than that of Ariel, nor, on the whole, is he more fully sexed. This repression of sexuality brings us back again to the world of childhood fantasies. It would be considered outrageous if such a creature dared to disobey, and Defoe would feel 'legitimately' angry if the *socius* born of his unconscious were to prove insubordinate. By comparison with these, Proust's prisoner Albertine is a free and fully-rounded figure. If it were my intention to pursue my psychoanalysis of Defoe and not to revert after this long digression to a consideration of the typical colonial, I should turn next to the novelist's favourite daughter, Sophia, who was in some ways remarkably like Miranda. Let us, however, look at this extract from Chapter I of the *Serious Reflections*, the second version of Crusoe's adventures:

'I have heard of a man, that upon some extraordinary disgust which he took at the unsuitable conversation of some of his nearest relations, whose society he could not avoid, suddenly resolved never to speak any more. He kept his resolution most rigorously many years; not all the tears or entreaties of his friends—no, not of his wife and children—could prevail with him to break his silence. It seems it was their ill-behaviour to him, at first, that was the occasion of it; for they treated him with provoking language, which frequently put him into indecent passions and urged him to rash replies; and he took this severe way to punish himself for being provoked, and to punish them for provoking him. But the severity was unjustifiable; it ruined his family, and broke up his house. His wife could not bear it, and after endeavouring, by all the ways possible, to alter his rigid silence, went first away from him, and afterwards away from herself, turning melancholy and distracted. His children separated, some one way and some another way; and only one daughter, who loved her father above all the rest, kept with him, tended him, *talked to him by signs*, and lived almost dumb like her father *near twenty-nine years* with him; till being very sick, and in a high fever, delirious as we call it, or light-headed, he broke his silence, not knowing when he did it, and spoke, though wildly at first. He recovered of the illness afterwards and frequently talked with his daughter, but not much, and very seldom to anybody else.

'Yet this man did not live a silent life with respect to himself; he read continually, and wrote down many excellent things, which deserved to have appeared in the world, and was often heard to pray to God in his solitudes very audibly and with great fervency.' (The italics are mine.)

Crusoe remained on his island for twenty-eight years, two months, and nineteen days. The girl mentioned in the above extract behaves like Friday, talking by signs. What is the significance of this anecdote in Defoe's biography? It is hardly to be supposed that Defoe himself spent twenty-nine years in complete silence! Yet the story has the stamp of truth upon it and very much resembles certain known clinical cases. In any event, whatever its origin, it must certainly have made a great impression on Defoe, since he retold it symbolically in the story of Robinson Crusoe, and we may remember that elsewhere he says in effect: Robinson is myself.

The 'case' of Defoe, then, broadly, is one of misanthropy, melancholy, a pathological need for solitude, the projection of his faults on to others, a sense of guilt towards his father, repressed affection for a daughter whose sex he preferred to ignore. . . . Thence emerged the story of Robinson, in the way a dream might occur. When this dream was published, however, all Europe realized that it had been dreaming it. For more than a century afterwards the European concept of the savage came no nearer reality than Defoe's representation of him, and it was on that figure that the European, if he was more or less infantile in character or, like Rousseau, unable to adapt himself to reality, projected the inner image of which there was no counterpart in the solid and too familiar world of reality.

But such a concept of the savage can be found in literature even before Defoe's time, as early as 1572, for instance, in Jean de Léry's *Histoire du voyage au Brésil*. He, however—and this confirms my theory—drew a picture of the savage precisely in order to contrast it with that of Europeans of his time whose manners he felt compelled by some bitter anti-social urge to censure. It was not by chance that the eighteenth century, which sang the 'Noble Savage', also produced the Revolution and the Terror: they all sprang from the same source. And this century was to choose for its hero a sentimentalist who was at the same time a 'persecuted' misanthropist.

It was in this soil that the taste for exotic literature grew. Certainly the success of Robinson Crusoe was in part responsible, but there are signs that the seeds had been planted much earlier—in *Télémaque*, for instance, and *The Tempest*; indeed, it appears to correspond to some need deep in the human psyche.

But whatever its real nature, this tendency towards misanthropy, which may first be expressed in a flight from other people, may, it is clear, later lead to a serious rupture of the image of these others or to a failure in the process of synthesis whereby that image is formed. The image falls into two parts which recede farther and farther from one another instead of coalescing; on the one hand there are pictures of monstrous and terrifying creatures, and on the other visions of gracious beings bereft of will and purpose—Caliban and the cannibals at one extreme (Caliban is surely a deliberate anagram); Ariel and Friday at the other. But man is both Ariel and Caliban; we must recognize this if we are to grow up. For a period during childhood we refuse to believe it, and it is the traces of this phase which remain in the unconscious that led Defoe and Shakespeare to write the works to which I have referred. The same unconscious tendency has impelled thousands of Europeans to seek out oceanic islands inhabited only by Fridays or, alternatively, to go and entrench themselves in isolated outposts in hostile countries where they could repulse by force of arms those same terrifying creatures whose image was formed in their own unconscious.

It would, of course, be possible to put forward all sorts of historical reasons to explain the success of colonization, and there is no denying the importance of the phenomena of economic expansion. But these causes were brought to bear on minds psychologically prepared, and if my analysis is correct no one becomes a real colonial who is not impelled by infantile complexes which were not properly resolved in adolescence. The gap between the dependent personality of the native and the independent personality of the European affords these complexes an opportunity of becoming manifest; it invites the projection of unconscious images and encourages behaviour which is not warranted by the objective situation, but is ultimately explainable in terms of the most infantile subjectivity. Colonial countries are still the nearest approach possible to the archetype of the desert island, and the native still best represents the archetype of the *socius* and the enemy, Friday and the cannibals. So, then, colonial life is simply a substitute to those who are still obscurely drawn to a world without men—to those, that is, who have failed to make the effort necessary to adapt infantile images to adult reality.

This is the conclusion to which my analysis of Robinson Crusoe has led me: I shall now consider the case of Prospero, and the reader will find my interpretation confirmed and given more precision.

The colonial situation is even more clearly portrayed in *The Tempest* [1] than in *Robinson Crusoe*, which is the more remarkable in that Shakespeare certainly thought less about it than did Defoe. Shakespeare's theme is the drama of the renunciation of power and domination, which are symbolized by magic, a borrowed power which must be rendered up. Man must learn to accept himself as he is and to accept others as they are, even if they happen to be called Caliban. This is the only wise course, but the path towards wisdom is long and infinitely painful for Prospero.

There is no doubting the nature of Prospero's magical power, for at his side we find his obedient daughter—and magic is the child's image of paternal omnipotence. Whenever his absolute authority is threatened, and however slight the threat, Prospero—our aspirant to wisdom—always becomes impatient and almost neurotically touchy. The essence of the problem is revealed at the outset; Prospero lays down his magic garment and prepares to tell Miranda the story of his life. In other words, he tries to treat Miranda as an equal; but he fails. He begins with 'Obey and be attentive,' and the recital is punctuated with other orders of the same kind, all absurd and quite unwarranted; later in the play he even goes so far as to threaten Miranda with his hatred. It is the same with Ariel; Prospero has promised him his liberty, but fails to give it to him. He constantly reminds Ariel that he freed him from the knotty entrails of a cloven pine in which the terrible mother, Sycorax, had confined him. This again means that Prospero has the absolute authority of the father. Caliban is the unruly and incorrigible son who is disowned. Prospero says he was 'got by the devil himself'. At the same time he is the useful slave who

---

[1] On the analytical interpretation of the text of Shakespeare's play, see Abenheimer: 'Shakespeare's Tempest', in the *Psychoanalytic Review* of October 1946.

is ruthlessly exploited. But Caliban does not complain of being exploited; he complains rather of being betrayed, in Künkel's sense of the word: he says, explicitly,

> . . . When thou camest first,
> Thou strok'dst me, and mad'st much of me; wouldst give me
> Water with berries in't; and teach me how
> To name the bigger light, and how the less,
> That burn by day and night: and then I lov'd thee,

but now

> . . . you sty me
> In this hard rock, whiles you do keep from me
> The rest o' the island.

Caliban has fallen prey to the resentment which succeeds the breakdown of dependence. Prospero seeks to justify himself: did Caliban not attempt to violate the honour of his child? After such an offence, what hope is there? There is no logic in this argument. Prospero could have removed Caliban to a safe distance or he could have continued to civilize and correct him. But the argument: you tried to violate Miranda, *therefore* you shall chop wood, belongs to a nonrational mode of thinking. In spite of the various forms this attitude may take (it includes, for instance, working for the father-in-law, a common practice in patriarchal communities), it is primarily a justification of hatred on grounds of sexual guilt, and it is at the root of colonial racialism.

I was given a clue to the explanation of this racialism while questioning a European colonial, who expressed the belief that the black race had become inferior to the white through excessive masturbation! The man himself was troubled by parental prohibitions in this respect. The 'inferior being' always serves as scapegoat; our own evil intentions can be projected on to him. This applies especially to incestuous intentions; Miranda is the only woman on the island, and Prospero and Caliban the only men. It is easy to see why it is always his daughter or his sister or his neighbour's wife (never his own) whom a man imagines to have been violated by a negro; he wants to rid himself of guilt by putting the blame for his bad thoughts on someone else. Caliban, in this hopeless situation, begins plotting against Prospero—not to win his freedom, for he could not support freedom, but to have a new master whose 'foot-licker' he can become. He is delighted at the prospect. It would be hard to find a better example of the dependence complex in its pure state. In the play the complex must be a projection, for where else could it have come from? The dependence of colonial natives is a matter of plain fact. The ensuing encounter between the European's unconscious and a reality only too well prepared to receive its projections is in practice full of dangers. Colonials live in a less real social world, and this diminished reality is less able to wake the dreamer. . . .

Among the castaways in *The Tempest* there is one rather strangely-drawn character: Gonzalo. The list of *dramatis personae* describes him as an 'honest old counsellor'. He once rendered Prospero great service, and Prospero treats him with immense respect. He is, however, simply a variant of Polonius, a garrulous old dotard, but more of a caricature. *The Tempest* repeats, in order to resolve it, the Hamlet situation: brother ousted by brother, guilty father (here the King of Naples), hatred of the mother, brooding instead of action—the latter a regression due to loss of real power. And in both cases, alongside the father, there is the uncle or some other father-image: a doddering and impotent old man. Gonzalo, the Utopist, dreams of turning the island into a Land of Cockaigne: [1]

> All things in common nature should produce
> Without sweat or endeavour . . .

no toil, no government, no institutions. His attitude is in fact identical with Prospero's and shows the same infantile regression—but he lacks the omnipotence of the father, that is to say magic, the power which is the cause of all difficulties and must be rejected. How reluctantly Prospero gives up his daughter to Ferdinand! And he cannot restore Ariel to liberty without asking him to perform yet one more task. He forgives his enemies, but only after he has avenged himself on them and thoroughly humiliated them. In Milan, where he will be duke in name only, he says, 'Every third thought shall be my grave'. In the Epilogue Prospero declares

> Now my charms are all o'erthrown,
> And what strength I have's mine own;
> Which is most faint.

In this, his will, he gives back everything he acquired by magic—all, that is, that he lost by betrayal, including his birthright. Surely the

---

[1] We shall see in a later chapter (Part III, Ch. V) with regard to the *Fokon'olona*, how the image of the Land of Cockaigne emerges after the suppression of paternalist power, like a more distant memory of childhood.

man who wrote this play must have harboured in his unconscious a strange and potent desire to possess power over men, if only by prestige, and this desire must in its way have been as powerful and as difficult to overcome as that of Defoe.

In any case it was from the unconscious that the two islands of these tales emerged. The parallels between the two works assure us that we are in the presence of archetypes: Ariel, Friday, Caliban, the cannibals. And as in these works of art these archetypes governed the imagination, so in real life they govern behaviour. The typical colonial is compelled to live out Prospero's drama, for Prospero is in his unconscious as he was in Shakespeare's; only the former lacks the writer's capacity for sublimation. The colonial's personality is wholly unaffected by that of the native of the colony to which he goes; it does not adapt itself, but develops solely in accordance with its own inner structure. It is inevitable, therefore, that misunderstandings should arise, for there can be no harmony between monads.

It is always worth while considering the opinions of the colonialists, for they are necessarily very revealing, and in this case they confirm my views. What they say in effect is: there is no misunderstanding to clear up; it would not be worth the trouble, anyway; the Malagasy personality is whatever you like to make of it—for in fact it does not exist; ours alone counts. In other words, they do not acknowledge the Malagasy personality. Nothing outside themselves affects them. After all, what sorts of personalities have Miranda, Ariel, and Friday? None at all, so long as they remain submissive. Caliban, it is true, asserts himself by opposing, but he is mere bestiality.

What the colonial in common with Prospero lacks, is awareness of the world of Others, a world in which Others have to be respected. This is the world from which the colonial has fled because he cannot accept men as they are. Rejection of that world is combined with an urge to dominate, an urge which is infantile in origin and which social adaptation has failed to discipline. The reason the colonial himself gives for his flight—whether he says it was the desire to travel, or the desire to escape from the cradle or from the 'ancient parapets', or whether he says that he simply wanted a freer life—is of no consequence, for whatever the variant offered, the real reason is still what I have called very loosely the colonial vocation. It is always a question of compromising with the desire for a world without men. As for the man who chooses a colonial career by chance and without specific vocation, there is nevertheless every possibility that he too has a 'Prospero complex', more fully repressed, but still ready to emerge to view in favourable conditions.

In his *Traité de sociologie*, p. 394, Mr Gaston Bouthoul says:

'Of all the elements which go to make up a society, its mentality is the most difficult to destroy. A man may be uprooted from his surroundings and taken to the antipodes or shut up in a cell, but the society to which he belongs will continue to live in him, in his beliefs and in the entire content of his mental life and the knowledge he takes with him. If such a man has the strength, or if he meets some of his fellows, he may build in some distant spot a society almost identical with the one he left behind. This was the case with many of the colonies.'

It is true that an *adult* man carries with him wherever he goes all that he is, and experience is powerless to add or subtract anything of any importance. What a man is, however, is not all manifest; he contains latent possibilities. In other circumstances—at the Antipodes, for instance—there is an inevitable shifting of the boundary between the latent and the manifest personalities. Thus, although it is the same material a man takes with him into the new environment, it assumes a new shape there, partly as a result of the difference in social pressure but also, and more particularly, as a result of the inner pressures of the man's own personality.

THE COLONIAL SITUATION AND RACIALISM

FRANCE is unquestionably one of the least racialist-minded countries in the world; also colonial policy is officially anti-racialist. But the effects of the colonial situation inevitably make themselves felt, so that a marked racialist attitude appears side by side with the official attitude, and, indeed, in spite of it. Even the administration officials themselves, although they apply France's pro-native policy humanely and conscientiously, are nevertheless subject to the psycho-sociological laws, and unless they are men of exceptional calibre, come to adopt attitudes which are coloured with racialism. Those outside the administration, of course, have no appearances to keep up.

The 'Prospero complex', which draws from the inside, as it were, a picture of the paternalist colonial, with his pride, his neurotic impatience, and his desire to dominate, at the same time portrays the racialist whose daughter has suffered an attempted rape at the hands of an inferior being. In the play itself, of course, the attempt is imaginary, but as the sexual aspect of racialism plays a large part in the unconscious, I shall endeavour to explain it forthwith. These rapes allegedly perpetrated by members of one race on those of another are pure projections of the unconscious. The fact that Shakespeare found them in his artistic imagination and had no need to go to the outside world for examples should be argument enough. I could add many more. For instance, there was obviously no real ground for the belief, widely held in the eighteenth century even among enlightened people, that apes would carry women off to rape them. Is there any more solid foundation for the belief, so firmly rooted in the unconscious of many Americans of the southern States, that the negroes are simply waiting till they are off guard to pounce upon the white women? Reports of rapes were circulating in Madagascar at the beginning of the revolt. It was not possible to investigate all of them; in the circumstances of the time it is unfortunately possible that some were true, but the ones I checked were all false.

In his urge to identify the anthropoid apes, Caliban, the Negroes, even the Jews with the mythological figures of the satyrs, man reveals that there are sensitive spots in the human soul at a level where thought becomes confused and where sexual excitement is strangely linked with violence and aggressiveness. As I have already said, the explanation is mainly a matter of repressed tendencies towards sadism, rape, or incest, the image of the misdeed which both frightens and fascinates us being projected on to others. Stories of such doings are very often used by prostitutes to excite certain of their clients; their effect is presumably to remove obstacles in the unconscious, and those obstacles are probably feelings of guilt. All these factors, which analysis has not yet succeeded in explaining in their entirety—all this mass of emotion charged with a rather savage sexuality—is an important though invisible element in the composition of colour-prejudice, or racialism.[1]

Racial conflict is not, however, a primary or spontaneous phenomenon. Racialism develops gradually in the course of events. At their first encounter persons of different races usually evince curiosity, liking and very often sexual attraction towards each other. Children show their liking in all simplicity. Moreover, romantic literature has made use of the sexual appeal of racial differences as if they reinforced the purely sexual differences. The more remote people are, the more they seem to attract our projections—the easier it is for a 'crystallization', as Stendhal called it, to take place. Whatever one may think before analysis, it is himself a man is looking for when he goes far away; near at hand he is liable to come up against Others. Far-away princesses are psychologically important in this respect. Who else could Trelawny have loved but the captive Arab girl he rescued during a fight? Psychologically he is one with Pygmalion; he can only love his own creation, his *anima*. Even in works without any exotic flavour, such as *The Red and the Black* and *The Lily of the*

[1] An argument widely used by racialists against those who do not share their convictions is worthy of mention for its revealing character. 'What', they say, 'if you had a daughter, do you mean to say that you would marry her to a negro?' I have seen people who appeared to have no racialist bias lose all critical sense when confronted with this kind of question. The reason is that such an argument disturbs certain uneasy feelings in them (more exactly, *incestuous* feelings) and they turn to racialism as a defence reaction. The argument is obviously stupid in itself; it seems to imply that there is no middle way between racialism and wholesale promiscuity! But whoever advances it in good faith little suspects, in his naïvety, how much it reveals the repressed sentiments upon which his racial 'theories' are based.

Valley, two of the great nineteenth-century French novels, we find, in addition to the maternal image filling the major role, the *anima* sketched in in the background—for Lady Dudley is English and Mathilde belongs to another century. It might be appropriate here to note what might be called the modern tendency towards exogamy, which is a consequence of the Œdipus complex. Romantic young girls like Ophelia or Virginie must be allowed to die, unless they are so different and so remote as not to risk interfering with the *imago* of the mother.

It appears, therefore, that our natural inclinations tend in part to draw us towards the most 'foreign' types of people. That is no mere literary illusion; there was no question of literature, and the illusion was probably very slight when Galliéni's soldiers chose young *ramatoa* as their more or less temporary wives. In fact these first contacts presented no difficulties at all. This was in part due to the healthy sex life of the Malagasies, which was unmarred by complexes. But this only goes to show that racial conflicts develop gradually and do not arise spontaneously.

The relatively easy-going nature of the Malagasies' sex life is, once again, due to the dependence complex, or rather to the social environment in which that complex grows and flourishes. To consider for a moment the case of the European boy; when he marries he has to solve two difficult problems at the same time: first, he must accept his own independence and leave the shelter of the family, and secondly—and this is a problem of a rather different order—he must choose a wife who will not cause a conflict between his *anima* and his maternal *imago*, the emotional force of which is greatly increased by the fact that he has feelings of regret and guilt at leaving his family. The frequency of such conflicts is apparent from the relationship commonly existing between husbands and mothers-in-law—so much so that it has become a familiar subject of popular jokes. The Malagasy youth, on the other hand, has no such problems to face because he does not feel obliged to break the bonds of dependence on his family. Dependence remains, and so he escapes the shock of separation. Moreover, he never appears to be troubled by the maternal image: it is always unambiguously protective, and his sexuality impels him unequivocally towards a *socia* upon whom he can project his *anima*.[1] In Europe the girl's situation is, necessarily,

---

[1] Homosexuality (*manifest*, naturally) is rarely found among typical Malagasies, but there is the curious case of the *men-women* who are not so easily explained away as the

the equivalent of the boy's; in Madagascar it is not, for she must leave her family, but the new dependence, on her husband, replaces the old without difficulty.

The sexual customs of the Malagasies have changed somewhat with time, but their main features have remained unaltered. Young people court in secret, but without restraint. If their provisional union proves fruitful, they marry; if not, they separate. The purpose of marriage is to have children. The sterile woman is disgraced and devotes her life to pilgrimages and magical ceremonies. A certain moral latitude is not incompatible with considerable decorum. Married partners are free if they are at a distance from each other because one of them has gone on a journey. The woman is very restrained in her expression of feeling; she is very obedient and docile, but capable of imposing her will insensibly through the exercise of patience and perseverance. Liberty never becomes licence or debauchery. Adultery leads to bitter quarrels, but there are never any neurotic consequences. Divorce is there in the last resort. The *crime passionel* and the love-suicide are unknown among the Merina. Songs and poetry extol desire and fidelity, mourn desertion, condemn deception and pity the ill-assorted, as they do the world over, but without anguish and without despair. An *affaire* is always taken seriously but is not given undue importance; it is never a mere pastime and certainly never a neurotic protest against an oppressive moral system.

All this being so, the first Europeans in Madagascar found a certain emotional comfort in the company of Malagasy women; this was not without value, but it was not without danger either. Here we find another of the effects of the dependence complex, for a personality constructed on the European model is in the end demoralized by a docile and inferior sexual partner. Ultimately he retains his liberty only if his partner is free and more or less his equal, and this is in fact usually the case in successful unions. When a European takes a Malagasy woman as wife or mistress, his subsequent transformation becomes so obvious, even to the most obtuse observer, that there has grown up a legend that the Malagasy woman uses philtres and poisons to retain her hold upon the *vazaha*—the foreigner. The philtres and poisons, it is said, gradually sap the will and intelligence.

European might think. These men dress like women and do women's work, but it is *in order to live with women*, and they have, it is said, a normal sexuality. Such cases are rarer now than they were.

This debilitation, it is thought, would account for the frequency and duration of such unions, which are otherwise inexplicable. That is clearly not the real explanation. Neither love-potions nor even sensuality ensure the permanence of these unions. The fact is that the Malagasy woman corresponds fairly closely to an archetype of the collective unconscious, like Friday or Ariel. Civilization forces us to build about this archetype a whole complex organization—very often bisexual—consisting of a *persona*, one physical aspect that is aesthetic or social, another physical aspect that is erotic, a will that is both free and obedient, an intelligence—and a host of other elements. . . . But the personality of the Malagasy woman is so little externalized that it acts like a mirror and reflects back to the European his own projections on to it. So, then, we are brought back to the observation which is, I believe, essential to our understanding of colonial facts: if a man lives in the midst of his own projections without truly admitting the independent will and existence of other people, he loses his own will and his own independence, while the *ego* inflates as it becomes empty. Mixed unions, however, are becoming more and more rare, or at any rate are diminishing in importance, partly because Europeans have learnt from experience to mistrust those they consider to be 'degraded', but more particularly because there now exists in Madagascar a European female population whose presence has completely altered the basis of the problem.

In the early days there was no spontaneous occurrence among Malagasy males either of collective jealousy towards the European or of individual contempt for the girls who lent themselves to such unions. On the contrary, Malagasy families were for a long time rather proud of being allied, even by so slender a bond, to a *vaʒaha*. This must have been due to their lack of an inferiority complex. Here again, of course, it is true that experience gradually changed their outlook. The birth of half-caste children was at first treated as a welcome event by both sides. It was naïvely supposed that interbreeding would serve to bring the two 'races' closer together. Even Galliéni, apparently, encouraged this 'policy'. But it soon became necessary to play it down because—for reasons I shall explain later on—the half-castes proved in the end to be a great source of trouble. The European women, too, when their numbers increased, had something to say about the matter.

The colonial woman is, as it were, the feminine counterpart of Prospero, but—and it is an astonishing fact—in Madagascar the

European women are far more racialist than the men. Sometimes their racialism attains preposterous proportions. For instance, at a mass sung for the souls of some European victims of the rebellion, women from the good Christian community raised an indignant protest against the presence of Malagasy choirboys. No man, however much a racialist and however little a Christian, would have gone that far. Similar observations have been made in other countries where racialism exists.

It would be difficult to make any confident analysis of this feminine racialism without individual psychoanalyses, but it may be noted that sexual unions between European women and Malagasy men are extremely rare, as much because the European woman does not satisfy the Malagasy's psychological ideal of womanhood as because the white woman would find herself socially in an intolerable position. Such marriages as there are between Malagasy men and European women have usually been contracted in Europe. There are not many of them, but they are a cause of uneasiness both to Malagasies and to Europeans. Difficulties arise within the Malagasy family because the white woman does not fit into the network of dependences, and is therefore felt to be an intruder; she for her part feels cut off from the European community to which, consciously or unconsciously, she cannot help feeling she still belongs. A European man who marries a Malagasy woman need not enter so completely into family life and is free, if he wishes, to leave his coloured wife at home and go and join his own kind as in the past. In point of fact, he will give up doing this after a time, and will allow himself to be drawn into the Malagasy community. But it will be of his own free will, whereas the white wife is obliged to form part of the family and can scarcely ever leave it to rejoin the white community. It may be that one day we shall be fortunate enough to find one of these white wives endowed with sufficient intuition and psychological insight to impart her experience to us, and that would be of great interest and value.

Needless to say, the mixed Franco-Malagasy community which it was supposed could be created through these marriages—and which a policy based solely on theory sought to encourage—has not been realized. If it exists at all, it is in the form of official functions, but politically sponsored, voluntary, meetings of representatives of the two sides are painfully reminiscent of those awkward social gatherings at which the rich offer cakes and condescension to the poor. Those who feel most uncomfortable are probably the more advanced

Malagasies—though they are best at concealing it. There is less awkwardness at ceremonial meetings where everything, including dress, is governed by protocol and everyone has his appointed place, and this is no doubt why such meetings are very popular with the Malagasies. Unfortunately for the official efforts at bringing about a 'closer understanding', they are not popular with the Europeans, who regard them as mere chores.

To sum up, all attempts at *rapprochement*, both official and unofficial, including those of the missionaries, have failed to bridge the gap between the two communities. On the contrary, they have served rather to 'reconnoitre' it—to fix its position more firmly, and in fact the indications are that it is widening daily. Europeans used to try to learn the Malagasy language and some succeeded in mastering it completely, but to-day the administration has to issue an order making such study compulsory and there are protests against it from certain officials. Europeans used to feel that they were in the Malagasies' country. Nowadays they feel that the country belongs to them and they tend rather to resent the presence of the Malagasies and to think them a nuisance. The Malagasies are well aware of these feelings and draw the obvious conclusions. A great psychological change has in fact come about in the course of a single generation, which may in part be due to the racialist influence of the European women. That, at any rate, is the opinion of those Malagasies who have given the matter any thought, though one should treat such opinions with reserve, for there could be many reasons for a misunderstanding betwee Malagasy men and European women.

At least one element in this feminine racialism is over-compensation for an inferiority complex similar to that of *nouvelles-riches* in Europe, whose relations with their domestic servants and social inferiors bear the stamp of over-compensation. There is undoubtedly some sexual tinge to it too: the white woman is constantly trying to impress it on the white man's unconscious that there can be no possible comparison between herself and the Malagasy woman. As for her attitude to the Malagasy man, the power of issuing tyrannical orders to him no doubt satisfies her unconscious urge to dominate a male figure. As there is no serious obstacle—except perhaps the danger of losing her cook if she is too aggressive—her character is bound to suffer as a result.

All this, however, is no more than latent racialism; it becomes manifest only when the Malagasy shows signs of shaking off the bonds of his dependence. What is resented in Caliban is not really his physical appearance, his bestiality, his 'evil' instincts—for after all it is a matter of pride to keep half-tamed apes or other wild animals in one's household—but that he should claim to be a person in his own right and from time to time show that he has a will of his own. In other words, we are perfectly happy if we can project the fantasies of our own unconscious on to the outside world, but if we suddenly find that these creatures are not pure projections but real beings with claims to liberty, we consider it outrageous, however modest their claims. Further, it is not the claims themselves which makes us indignant, but the very desire for freedom. Racialism, properly speaking, is simply a rather poor rationalization of our feelings of indignation. Indignation comes first—and I think I have indicated how deep in the unconscious lie its causes, even if I have not fully explained them—and later the explanation: the theory, newly discovered or merely parroted, of racial inferiority. The theory itself is always left very bare and rudimentary, and those who believe it most firmly are precisely those who would be least capable of explaining it. That is of no importance to them, however, for, by an irrational process of great emotional force, it is the strength of a believer's indignation which serves him as proof, and there is no lack of that.

It is probably hardly necessary for me to point out that the fact of belonging to a certain race is significant only in so far as one is conscious of it. Such consciousness is not direct but acquired, and of course it is more quickly acquired the more often a man meets personalities constructed differently from his own. In the ensuing effort to classify these personalities the idea of race occurs spontaneously, accompanied, moreover, by a feeling of its persuasiveness, which merely goes to show what emotional force these psychological phenomena possess.

As might have been expected, European racialism has evoked a corresponding Malagasy racialism, although naturally it is different in kind because of the difference in the structure of the Malagasy personality. In the first place the Malagasy does not consider that the European belongs to an inferior race. He simply says that Europeans in Madagascar are not the equal of those in Europe, without offering any explanation. Of course there are many things he criticizes in the European: his smell, certain physical traits of his, his lack of soul, his impatience, his vanity, but he does not invoke these characteristics in order to denigrate him. For there is no question in his mind of a moral judgement. Under European influence he becomes conscious of his race and of his duties towards it, in a way he never was before colonization. But his racialism is much more like the isolationism of someone looking for a new form of security than it is like the European's over-compensation for an inferiority complex: that is still exceptional and untypical among Malagasies. Again, the Malagasy's rationalization of his desire for racial segregation is different in kind from the European's rationalization. Why? Because the psychic raw material from which he constructed that rationalization is also different. It consists mainly of what might be called a fear of the contamination of the group—of *mésalliance*, if you like—and it gives the Malagasy's attitude the sexual tinge from which racialism is never wholly free. Among the Andriana [1] and the Hova, the two principal classes of the Merina, there was already a hostility toward *mésalliance* between the castes; it had only to be re-directed. Those who oppose mixed marriages usually justify their views by an argument concerning the offspring of such marriages. Malagasies are now convinced that mixing the blood is wrong, for, they say, the children of European–Malagasy unions inherit in the main the defects of the two races. During the revolt of March 1947 they were as hostile towards the half-castes as they were towards the Europeans.

A cursory examination of the case of those of mixed blood would appear to prove the Malagasies right, but for reasons other than those they give. The social position of the half-castes is such that they cannot avoid acquiring an inferiority complex, and their psychology is therefore quite different from that of pure Malagasies. They are few in number and ill at ease in both communities, for in both they are made aware of that mixture of similarities and differences which is the begetter, *par excellence*, of an inferiority complex. Moreover, if they have a Malagasy mother and a European father, who has no ancestors, of course, their early upbringing is Malagasy, but they do

---

[1] The *Hova* are the middle-class Merina; the *Andriana* are a noble caste. Ethnologists will perhaps allow us to draw their attention to the following coincidence: Cook met a similar community in the Sandwich Islands; the noble caste there was called *Eree Taboo* or *Eree Moee*. The second of these names means that everyone is obliged to prostrate himself before them, or, in the strict meaning of the word 'moee', to *lie down to sleep* in their presence (Third Voyage of Cook, March 1779). Now, 'Andriana' comes from the word *mandry*, which also means to lie down to sleep. This would seem to remove all doubt about the etymology of the word *andriana*, over which there has been some controversy. The etymology of the word *hova* is not known. The root signifies *change*, but it is impossible to detect any semantic association. One can only surmise what might be the significance of this obligation to sleep in the presence of chiefs,

not adopt an attitude of dependence while yet not receiving a normal European training. Furthermore, the fate of the boys is very different from that of the girls. With a little coquetry the girls, who are very often both pretty and intelligent, can make a place for themselves in the European community, where they can easily secure amorous or romantic successes. Naturally, the place they make for themselves in this way is very often of an inferior moral order and cannot fully compensate for their feelings of inferiority. They may run after this compensation by multiplying their 'conquests', but they will never wholly attain it. Of course they do not all choose the same course; some turn to religion or even take the veil, which is another way of solving their difficulties. . . . The men are less fortunate, however, and tend nowadays to engage in the black market and other more or less parasitic economic activities. It is they who display the celebrated racial inferiority complex in its purest form, with its fantastic compensations in the form of vanity.

As one would expect, half-castes born of a Malagasy father, who has ancestors, and a European mother have a different personality again, because of the difference in the parental influences. Malagasies and Europeans ignorant of the facts blindly attribute all these differences to heredity. Their racialist beliefs are thereby strengthened, and these again bolster up the belief in heredity.

We must now give these racialist feelings closer attention in order to discover how it is that they have so baneful an effect on relations between the two groups.

It is generally said that racialism leads to hatred, injustice, and violence, but it could surely equally well be said that hatred and injustice are causes of racialism. Racialism, either the European or the Malagasy variety, is a pseudo-rational construct—a rationalization—to justify feelings the source of which are embedded deep in the unconscious. Even apart from the rationalization these feelings could of themselves lead to injustice, hatred, and violence, but the rationalization, once constructed, in turn reacts on the original feelings and gives them a new and more vicious cast, as I shall try to show.

First, although the general concept of race already existed and racialism did not create it, yet racialism has given the concept a powerful emotional content, and, as we have seen, for the ordinary uncritical mind that emotional content alone suffices as proof and evidence. The racialist apprehends racial differences emotionally;

he is conscious of belonging to a particular race, and in another person he sees the race before he sees the man. For him, the race over-shadows the individual; the meaning of race itself is left intellectually vague, which is why it can be adapted to suit all emotional needs; in the European it is made to satisfy the overriding need for com-pensation.

A group infected with racialism acquires a cheap superiority; the more mature personalities may scorn it, but we may be sure that the mediocre will make great play with it. Since, however, the mentality of the majority inevitably has a more or less coercive influence on the whole group, there occurs an inversion of normal values and in-fluences within the group, to the advantage of the mediocre, who are the most rabid racialists. It is not that they are unintelligent but that they have a greater need to believe in racialism than the others; they gain more from it because they are more hungry for compensation. Thus we see that even within a race-conscious group the racialist attitude may be pernicious in its effects. There is a general deteriora-tion of intellectual and moral standards, but it goes along with a tightening of certain collective bonds, and from this some advantage is derived in compensation for the not inconsiderable loss, humanly speaking, suffered in other directions.

It is psychologically dangerous to feel important simply because of belonging to a 'superior' race, though the attitude could serve a useful purpose if it went hand in hand with a sense of duty and responsibility. But that is rarely the case with colonial racialism, which usually produces a feeling of superiority and nothing more, and unfortunately the feeling is all the stronger in those who are, in an Adlerian sense, inferior.

Similar facts could no doubt be found among the Malagasies too, but there they would be less frequent and obvious simply because the inferiority complex is so much more rare. They are to be observed where logically one would not expect to find them but where psycho-logically they are quite in keeping—namely, among the half-castes. Persons of mixed blood can obviously choose between the two types of racialism and naturally they tend to choose the one which will be most profitable to them—the European, though the Europeans do not in fact welcome them into their ranks. They look down on the Malagasy race in spite of being half Malagasy themselves, and never really seriously consider their own position. If they were to adopt the Malagasy, anti-European racialism they would be subject to very violent feelings of hatred,[1] whereas anti-Malagasy racialism is more easily satisfied, with scorn and condescension. Of course not all half-castes are racialists, but very few escape the temptation.

Malagasy racialism is much more difficult to disentangle than European. It appears both less rationalized and less emotional. The Malagasy's idea of his own race, which includes the dead ancestors, is much less abstract than the European's; it contains a much keener sense of community with his fellows, and is much more concerned with the thoughts and cares of everyday life, family feelings, and neighbourly relations. Fundamentally, race to him means his family, his community, the beliefs and customs which make up his life, and not, as in the European, a blind, violent, impersonal, and biological will to survive focused on the generations to come. This is one reason why his racialism is so much less aggressive and more defensive; he looks to it for protection, for a defence against intrusion, and does not seek to challenge other races by vaunting his own.

Nothing is gained by creating great vague concepts like that of race. All conflicts between individuals, families, tribes, even peoples, can be settled by peaceful means, through arbitration; some sort of compromise or working arrangement can be arrived at. But once the idea of race is allowed in, once the dispute becomes a racial conflict between two race-conscious peoples, then there is no hope of solution, even if the one people is under the yoke of the other. The only hope lies in abandoning the too-vague notion of race altogether. Unfortunately, however, no one who seeks compensation for his personal inferiority in the idea of racial superiority is likely to be willing to give it up; it has become necessary to him because of the psychological satisfactions it brings. It is fairly easy, if one acts in time, to prevent someone becoming a racialist, but once he has become one there is very little one can do; the very most one can expect of him is that he will hide his racialist convictions. . . .

[1] In those cases, of course, where the father is European.

Part III

PSYCHOLOGICAL DEPENDENCE AND POLITICAL INDEPENDENCE

PSYCHOLOGICAL HEREDITY
AND THE PERSONALITY

———————

THERE is a kind of psychological heredity whereby certain traits of character are handed down from generation to generation. For instance, parents suffering from a complex of some sort will tend by their behaviour to engender the same complex in their children. This form of heredity must be particularly persistent if it is true, as is claimed, that the characters of the various European peoples as described in antiquity are still recognizable to-day, even after all the intermingling they have undergone in the course of time, so much so that it is virtually impossible to link this constancy to any physiological heredity. Psychological heredity, however, does not operate through the simple passing on of good and bad qualities; it does not necessarily lead to similarity between the generations, but may indeed operate by contraries. To take a very simple example: though it may happen in some cases that a son has great will-power because his father was strong-willed, it may equally well happen in other cases that the son has no will-power because his father had too much.

It is more than fifty years now since the colonization of Madagascar was completed. Consequently those who were of an age to understand this important event when it took place must now be nearly eighty years old, and those who now hold the reins of authority know of it only through the preceding generation. This time-factor must be taken into account if we are to understand the present situation. The men who, half a century ago, made peace in Madagascar and who are now dead or at any rate retired from active life, had not been influenced or deformed in character by the existence of a colonial situation; the first contacts were thus made between personalities constructed on the metropolitan French pattern on the one hand and on the uncontaminated Malagasy pattern on the other. Apart from the initial clash, these contacts appear to have been fairly successful, so far as can be judged this long afterwards. But the descendants of these pioneers, both Malagasy and European, after living together for a period during which any difficulties which arose were resolved by an arrangement which appeared to lead to a better understanding, suddenly awoke to find themselves seriously at odds with each other. The principal reason for this was that experience of colonial life had altered them both. Judging its results from the purely human and psychological points of view, the experiment was in fact rather disappointing. The fact that non-colonial Frenchmen and un-Gallicized Malagasies got on together far better than do French colonials and Malagasies whom the former have had every opportunity of moulding into what form they pleased, deserves serious consideration, since it refutes that optimistic theory, for long implicitly recognized in official policy, that the longer people live together the more they understand each other and the closer they draw together.

It would require a very detailed and difficult analysis to discover exactly what has taken place. In the meanwhile we may legitimately offer certain hypotheses which, though not necessarily accurate in every detail, may yet provoke reflection and research which may eventually lead to a better knowledge of the facts.

I think the reader will agree in principle that once a personality is fully developed, no matter what its basic structure, so long as it is sound it is very little affected by subsequent events. If it is thrown into disorder or seriously deteriorates under the impact of events, it must surely be because the seeds of that disorder or deterioration were implanted in it in childhood in the form of latent conflicts. It is difficult to test this theory, however, because we have no means of knowing what germs of infantile behaviour are lying dormant in a personality.

A distinction must be drawn between those Europeans who were born and brought up in a colony—they are still in the minority, at least among adults—and those who were born and bred in Europe. The latter are markedly different from the colonizers of fifty years ago. For that there are several reasons. First, people who go to a colony to take advantage of a well-established colonial situation are a far different human type from those who set out to conquer a new country. Then, the colonial life they experience is very different from the life their grandfathers knew. Again, it may well be that the European himself has changed to a considerable extent, even in Europe; we are justified in thinking this by the frequent complaints one hears nowadays about the deterioration of relations between the younger and older generations in Europe. There may even be some connexion between the colonial crisis and the crisis through which European youth is now passing, if, as seems likely, the latter is due to a decline in the authority of the European father.

Europeans born in a colony are unlike their parents. They do not as a rule suffer from an over-compensated inferiority complex, as do the parents. If the community were homogeneous, as in Europe, the parental complex would naturally tend to create in them a permanent psychological state of inferiority. But in a colonial environment the fact of belonging to the privileged race offers easy compensations for inferiority and certainly diminishes its effects, and the children usually possess very firm and un-neurotic racial convictions, which are as much a part of their *persona* as of their unconscious. Such convictions are obviously based on the childhood experience of seeing the father exercise absolute authority over all Malagasies—an authority which to the child is unquestioned and unquestionable.[1] Later these children begin to feel superior even to metropolitan Europeans because they are in a better position to resolve or conceal their fundamental inferiority, because they are absolutely convinced, without any neurotic complication, of their superiority to the natives, while the Europeans have not that complete assurance, and when they become racialist it is by an act of over-compensation which, like all such acts, has its drawbacks. This is an important factor on the basis of which we may predict with a fair degree of certainty that in the near future the Europeans born in Madagascar will be openly hostile towards metropolitan Europeans. Indeed, the probability is so great that it ought to be taken into account now in the formulation of political plans and projects. It may well be, from the purely psychological point of view, of course, that these Europeans get on better with the Malagasies than those who come out from Europe, because the Malagasies' dependence complex fits in with this feeling of absolute superiority [2] more easily than

[1] The over-compensated inferiority of the parents becomes the psychological climate to which the children become adapted, and so it loses its compensatory characteristics.

[2] This feeling of superiority is easily maintained by processes of projection, which liberate the European. In the eyes of those who have had to give up trying to make a place for themselves in Europe commensurate with their ambitions, the Malagasy worker is *incompetent*. To those who would like to live by deceiving him, he is lying and deceitful, while to those who relish the leisures of colonial life he is, above all, lazy. Naturally, too, his pretentions are ridiculous in the eyes of the upstart, and so on. . . .

But the most curious effect of these projections, and one which enables us to understand what is perhaps essential in these feelings of superiority, is the sexual liberation the

with the more unstable attitude of metropolitans compensating for an inferiority complex. Moreover, the Europeans born in Madagascar have a keener sense of the Malagasy psychology and know how to foster and exploit the need for dependence.

Naturally, the fact of escaping the inferiority complex so easily by taking advantage of the presence of a whole dependent people is in itself psychologically a loss. For though compensation for such a complex is fraught with dangers, the only hope of human progress lies in a vigorous and manly liquidation of inferiority. Inferiority, provided it is resolved in good time, is the main driving force of western man, and provides him with the energy which sets him apart from all other peoples in the world. It underlies almost all the life-stories of our great men. And I think it would not be over-bold to foresee in the distant future the development of a new kind of white or near-white humanity over almost the whole of the southern hemisphere of the ancient world, a type more different, psychologically, from that of the north than any of the northern peoples are from each other from east to west. If national psychologies remain as constant as appears to be the case, we can already forecast what the main characteristics of this new type will be: lack of originality and creativity, a distinct taste for feudal types of organization, and a lively desire to avoid infection from the complexes of the northern hemisphere. Long-term prophecies of this kind must, of course, be seen for what they are—namely, a way of defining our intuitions about the present situation rather than a precise forecast of an unknown future. In any case the new white or near-white (white enough at any rate not to feel inferior in the southern hemisphere) human beings I have envisaged would on the whole be far less worthy products than are Europeans, unless as a result of having to grapple with fresh difficulties they acquired some qualities other than mere pride in the race of their birth.

Let us turn now to the Malagasy and find out what effect this 'psychological heredity' has on him.

The Malagasies who made the first settlement with their European guests—they are all dead now or too old to have any influence—

Europeans experience even when they have no direct contact with the native population. This liberation is so marked that people have tried to explain it as an increase in sexual appetite due to the change of diet, to the climate, idleness, or even to hypothetical radiations from the earth. The truth is that the colonial Europeans are able to rid themselves of the unconscious obstacles bound up with inferiority and guilt, owing to the presence all around them of an inferior and 'therefore' lustful and debauched people. It has often been observed that a racialist attitude has a sexually exciting effect.

appear to have been fairly satisfied with the dependence relationship they established. They were accustomed to living within a system of bonds, and the new bonds were no more difficult to bear than the old —rather the contrary. They considered the presence of the European beneficial and felt that his arrival held out to them hopes of progress. Progress they conceived in terms of an increase of skills and knowledge of all kinds; they wanted to become educated, to develop their country, to add to what they had in every field without, however, changing the nature of their relationship with the Europeans. But succeeding generations have grown up in a different atmosphere, for the following reason: the feelings of dependence which the first Malagasies transferred to the Europeans were formed in traditional conditions, within the family and tribal organization; they were all of a piece, and their transfer to a fresh object did not alter their structure. But the children of these Malagasies were brought up under the influence of parents who had already effected this transfer. It is difficult to make an exact analysis of this new influence, but it is obvious that the whole upbringing must have been different. It was not so much the object of their feelings which was at issue as their composition. The hoped-for progress has indeed been made, but not within the original emotional framework; feelings have changed, new needs have arisen, and the achievements have consequently lost almost all their affective value.

We are no doubt perfectly right in thinking that education, hygiene, and material comforts are good in themselves and that what has been accomplished so far in that direction in Madagascar is only a stage in a process which must continue. But people who lack nothing in these respects may yet be very unhappy if their personalities are disrupted or contain contradictions which they are unable to resolve.[1] Of course it is true that these contradictions are the driving force behind all real progress and development, in Madagascar as elsewhere—not without crises, though, and sometimes very grave ones, for progress leads the Malagasy into difficulties which he is hard put to understand, and the means of resolving his doubts and perplexities are not always within his reach. Ought he to break with tradition? That would mean giving up all the bonds of dependence,

[1] From the economic and social points of view an overall increase in material prosperity is a good thing in itself, but from the psychological viewpoint it is only the differences which count, and the concept of them in the subject's mind. An overall increase is appreciated only in so far as it can be measured against some standard. Its indirect effects are beneficial, however.

hence almost the whole of his family and social organization. If he were to abandon the cult of the dead he would feel like a plant cut off from its roots. He would have to pass through the painful apprenticeship to individualism. And if all the bonds were broken the Malagasies would in truth be no longer a people, but a mob. Of course that is not the way things will happen: the transformation will be neither complete nor instantaneous, and there are some bonds which will never be broken. Individuals will drop from their social niches one after another . . . and already we have a good idea what will happen to them: they will swell the ranks of the agents and petty traders, political agitators, labour recruiters, and so on, who represent this new type of 'uprooted' Malagasy. He is much nearer to us, psychologically speaking, than the traditional Malagasy, for he has to a large extent cast off the bonds of dependence and like us he has discovered inferiority and guilt; he has known anguish and perturbation. He may not necessarily represent the typical Malagasy of the future, but he is certainly the catalytic element which will precipitate change and development. Paradoxically, he is unaware of the part he is playing; whereas in fact and almost in spite of himself he is helping to demolish what remains of the traditional structure, he is nevertheless reactionary in his desires and advocates a return to the old ways. It is probable that, having himself abandoned these old ways, he is suffering from unconscious feelings of guilt about it. Hence his desire for change, which makes him a disturbing element and likely to speed up the process of change among those who have up to now retained their traditional relationships. Hence also his nostalgia for the old days. So in fact he is undermining what is left standing of the edifice he longs to preserve. . . . I think these observations are probably true of the psychology of many reactionaries the world over. It must be realized that this contradictory and dangerous attitude draws strength from complexes deep in the Malagasy unconscious, sources of energy not available to the democratic convictions of the more evolved Malagasies. Their more rational attitude appears to be contained wholly within the conscious part of their thinking. Fortunately, however, this does not mean that their ideas will not triumph in the end, but it does mean that they must find something other than the psychological energy of the unconscious for their support.

The new type of Malagasy who has thrown tradition overboard has a certain fascination for the traditional Malagasy. It is touch-and-go, however, whether he will follow his example or recoil in horror and seek refuge in the comforting traditions of the past. Up to the last ten years the Malagasies modelled themselves on the older generation—those who had come to terms with the French, sought to be called 'citizen', and preserved the Malagasy personality while adapting it to French influence. But they have all disappeared now or else are no longer in the public eye. The pattern of behaviour is set to-day by men whose personalities are already in course of change. The whole future rests with them, a future as yet impenetrable.

The crisis implicit in this future would be less a cause for anxiety if we could be sure that some sort of working arrangement could be reached, even temporarily, between the European personality and the evolving Malagasy personality. We are no longer justified in believing that things will sort themselves out in some providential way, and the Malagasies are now sceptical of the security offered them by the protective power of the dead and respect for the *fomba*. Things will be arranged only as we arrange them; responsibility to-day rests with men, both white and black. There is no question of waiting until the black man (or the white man, either, for that matter) is strong enough to bear so heavy a burden: there is no longer any choice. It would perhaps be something if we knew how to allay the neurotic reactions to which these difficulties are bound to give rise. They are probably due to a feeling of helplessness before the immensity of tasks which are yet not wholly clear.

NATIONAL INDEPENDENCE

THE historian, accustomed as he is to explaining great and complex events by relatively simple abstract causes, never hesitates to tackle the question of colonial nationalism, but the psychologist is shy of this delicate problem, for he feels obliged to decide either what is the exact place occupied in the personality by 'national sentiment' or what personal feelings correspond, in the individual psyche, to the nationalism of the group, and lend it their support.

The idea of a collective consciousness is hardly admissible, for it is really a contradiction in terms. The contradiction might perhaps be less glaring if we were to speak more loosely of a collective psyche. But we must not allow ourselves to be deceived by a metaphor; the collective psyche can only be apprehended through individuals; at most it is the group aspect of the individual psyche. When a writer like Keyserling states that the German nation is suffering from an inferiority complex dating back to the Thirty Years' War, we are prepared to accept his statement on one condition: that it be not impossible to perceive, theoretically, how this complex could have been passed on from generation to generation, how it originates in the child or how, in the adult, it is grafted on to an already existing inferiority complex of infantile origin, why it should take root at all, why, that is, the individual should prefer this 'national complex' to his own personal complex, and what satisfaction it is that he derives from it. We may also wonder whether the sense of inferiority resulting from the Thirty Years' War sprang directly from a national element in individual German psyches, or whether it was that the war gave rise to social conditions likely to breed a sense of inferiority without at first bringing into play strictly national elements in the psyche, and so on. Of course we are not obliged to go into such detail; we could, as Keyserling does, simply speak of an inferiority complex dating back to the Thirty Years' War and leave it at that, but we can only do so legitimately if we are sure that we could go into detail and give a full explanation; otherwise this sort of observation has very little value. Similarly we should, I think, consider what, psychologically, the Malagasies' demand for national independence represents. Doubtless we shall not be able to go very far, for the nationalists have naturally not come forward for analysis, but it is possible to make a certain number of useful observations.

In the first place, we are not dealing with a desire for independence as such, for that would have expressed itself in immediate claims for more freedom for the individual, whereas the champions of independence have, on the contrary, bound themselves by pledges and taken magical oaths of the most restrictive kind possible. This is no mere perverseness; it is not the first time that there has been a contradiction between the primary desire for a certain good and the collective ideal which has formed around the concept of that good thing. Men go to prison to defend liberty, die for a better life, unite to protect individualism. However, we ought perhaps to try to analyse it.

The man who goes to prison in defence of freedom is sacrificing the primary desire for actual freedom, freedom immediate and personal, to the more distant, secondary ideal of the good of the community. We may wonder whether it is possible to form a clear idea of the relationship between the ideal which is sacrificed and that which is pursued—the psychological relationship, of course, for answers have already long ago been given in the philosophical, moral, and political spheres. Or is it perhaps simply that freedom does not mean the same thing in the two cases?

An extreme right-wing supporter believes in order, but his behaviour is such as to sow disorder everywhere. A psychologist at once asks if his behaviour is not a protest, and if so against what aspect of his personal situation, if it is not the compensatory behaviour of an asocial being who pays lip-service to a social ideal, and so makes good in his professed beliefs what he failed to find in his family upbringing. If we knew the answers to these questions we should be well on the way to discovering specific and individual explanations for certain aspects of political 'collective thinking', always provided, of course, that the individual in question could be considered typical of his group. It is only in this way, however, that we should endeavour to explain the 'collective thinking' of the Malagasies in the matter of political claims.

The first thing to notice is that for the Malagasies independence is only a means; the goal is nationalism. The Malagasies do not want a national government in order to ensure their independence; they want sufficient independence to be able to have a national government. (A national government without independence would of course hardly warrant the name of government.) They do not expect to gain any specific advantages from this government, either material or political. And in particular they do not hope for greater personal freedom. When Europeans tell them they will gain nothing from independence, but rather the contrary, they are wasting their time; the Malagasies know it already.[1] With a Malagasy government in power there would be more arbitrariness, more corruption, more forced labour, heavier taxes, and so on. Political oppression would be greater, penalties would be more severe. All this they know, but it does not deter them.

The feelings driving them on are much less individualist and much more powerful than these deterrents—judging at least by their effects. The effects amounted to a rebellion, and a rebellion requires a vast output of energy. Whatever shady intrigues, secret pressures, selfish deals, or deliberate provocations may have precipitated the rebellion at that particular time, the fact is nevertheless that they were able to mobilize an immense reserve of psychic energy. The psychologist finds himself faced with the task of explaining how thousands of men could have courted death in conditions of combat unbelievably unfavourable to them. To bolster their courage they invented tales which they would never have put faith in for an instant in normal times. They joined battle without hope and persevered in it in spite of failure. And these were people generally supposed to be peace-loving and who are said to lack courage. The psychic energy brought into play must have been enormous. Where can it have come from?

The answer to that question is rather complicated, but one important element in it is the feeling of abandonment to which I have already referred. This feeling caused great disturbance in the minds of the Malagasies and touched off those guilt complexes which seem to be closely linked with it. At the same time, in their efforts to escape the horrors of abandonment the Malagasies endeavoured to re-establish typical dependence systems capable of satisfying their deepest needs. Finally, there are the phenomena of identification, which are difficult to investigate, but play a large part in questions of this kind.

[1] This kind of argument is a strong one to the French mind (it is somewhat anarchistic), and the French are always surprised when they meet people upon whom it makes no impression.

I shall be referring later on to the way in which the identification of a subject with a leader operates; there seems in this case to have been an identification of the individual with the group. In Europeans our acknowledgement of this identification appears to be offset by an equally conscious will to individualism. Nevertheless even the least patriotic of men, the least nationalistic, the least infected with inferiority, cannot avoid a certain degree of identification with the group to which he belongs; he is, after all, a member of it, so that even if he criticizes it or runs it down he is to some extent criticizing himself. The process of identification is no doubt necessary for the formation of a national spirit, and it may be that in Madagascar we have been witnessing the first signs of the occurrence of a process of this kind, which has up to now been unknown to the majority of Malagasies. There must clearly have been some crisis in the functioning of the security defences based on psychological dependence, an effort to restore this dependence, and a neurotic recoil from individualization, evidently combined with a bad conscience. (I shall later be quoting some passages from Dama Ntsoha which are very revealing in this respect.)

How did the crisis come about? How was it that a feeling of insecurity arose at the very time when, objectively speaking, there was no outside threat to security at all? The order which the Malagasies deliberately shattered [1] when they started the rebellion guaranteed them adequate means of subsistence, if not plenty. There were difficulties, admittedly—food was not always in good supply, clothing materials were scarce—but they were negligible compared with those which disorder invited and the catastrophes which actually ensued. In accordance with a new policy, they had just been granted greater liberties and fuller guarantees; they could no longer be forced to contribute their labour [2] and they were given protection against

[1] The Malagasies on the east coast, that is, for the Merina nationalists did not disturb public order.

[2] The European public knows very little about the requisitioning of colonial workers. A wartime measure authorized the Government to requisition workers for jobs for the public benefit (which came to mean almost exclusively the upkeep of roads). The indirect beneficiaries of this measure were the white colonials, for the Malagasies rushed to sign on with them on any conditions, so as to escape Government requisition. Consequently the plantations were overstaffed; the workers did very little and were paid even less, but everyone was satisfied. At the end of the war the Government abolished the order, and the plantations immediately lost all their 'free' labour just at the time when, as a result of improved transportation and a rise in world prices, the planters saw some fat years approaching.

The ideal situation for the colonial is that the administration should be severe enough to serve him as bogeyman and beater. (Generally it refrains from doing so, whence certain conflicts.) He himself would rather have *protégés* than *workers*; his 'clients' do arbitrary punishment. A Parisian socialist newspaper said that it was inconceivable that the Malagasies should have revolted against the suppression of forced labour and the *indigénat* system. Logically, of course, it seems absurd, but psychologically it cannot be dismissed so easily. The situation was intolerable to the Malagasies because, in spite of the objective security it offered them, it roused in them subjective feelings of abandonment and guilt. They felt abandoned because they could no longer be sure of authority, for the Europeans [1] were at loggerheads among themselves. People say that internal rifts weaken a nation in the face of an outside danger. The colonial situation strikingly refutes this dictum. The Europeans themselves were not much affected by their disputes, but the natives suffered considerably as a result, especially as the disputes were about them. Some Europeans told them they were free and congratulated them; others told them that this freedom was a snare and delusion and that no good would come of it. Half the Europeans encouraged the Malagasy to do as he pleased as a free man; the other half were more hostile to him than before—their hostility being the psychological counterpart of the paternalist attitude, as we have seen. It is important to appreciate the true emotional significance to the Malagasy of the bonds of dependence in order to understand his appalling feeling of desolation on seeing these bonds snapping all around him. Moreover, the feeling reawakened his childhood sense of guilt, for guilt and fear of being abandoned by the parents are closely linked at that age.

It is noteworthy that these feelings first expressed themselves in the form of delusions and veritable hallucinations, a fact which may throw some light on the descriptions we find in ancient records of the supernatural signs which accompanied periods of unrest and of the weird portents presaging great calamities. Fear crystallizes in the form of terrifying visions. In Madagascar a number of people claimed to have seen supernatural beings. Reports of a centaur in Vato-

---

not work regularly but are always on the spot, with their wives and children, ready to give 'a helping hand' for almost nothing. That is the ideal, of course, and things are not always like this in practice, but this system is fairly widespread and accounts for the poor quality, professionally, of these so-called workers.

It can also be seen why the suppression of the requisition order provoked serious conflict between the colonials and the Government.

[1] The Europeans in Madagascar to some extent, of course, but more especially white men in general, the white population all over the world, whom the Malagasies see as a single entity. Europeans' wars amongst themselves are very disquieting to dependent peoples.

mandry [1] spread terror among the people, and they shut themselves up in their houses. Similar occurrences were reported elsewhere, and there must have been many more which were never reported, for the Europeans did not attach much importance to them; they made light of the Malagasies' panics, and so failed to profit from their implicit warning. [2]

Further proof of the Malagasies' extreme susceptibility to feelings of guilt, which are always bound up with fear and insecurity, is their belief in the *tody*, according to which the desire to hurt someone else rebounds upon the person guilty of the desire by virtue of a magical *lex talionis*. The root from which the word *tody* [3] derives signifies return to the point of departure. Similar beliefs have doubtless been known in all countries; 'evil spirits' can be exorcised, and we talk of an 'immanent justice' which will punish 'where we have sinned'. But the exorcism of evil spirits requires a magical operation, and the idea of immanent justice is a consolation to those who are faced with obvious injustice, while the *tody*, which sees evil intentions as a kind of boomerang, dangerous to hurl because it will spring back unexpectedly, indicates an unconscious feeling of guilt, and is probably the simplest and most primitive expression of remorse.

The only alternative of remorse is resentment, accompanied by hatred and violence. Violence springs from guilt, and guilt from a feeling of abandonment. [4] The most stubborn of the rebels were former soldiers who had come back from Europe; I have already explained what sort of influence Europe may have had on such men. It must be added that for the majority of them the army had been a system of very close-knit and numerous bonds of dependence which replaced the family and social bonds. When these men suddenly found themselves demobilized, in spite of the precautions which had been taken and which for the European would have been enough to cushion the shock, they fell into the emotional state of the abandoned. Their psychological condition was in itself enough, therefore, to lead to feelings of hostility. It remains, however, to discover how these feelings came to be expressed in open hostility, and in par-

---

[1] Where, a few months later, the revolt was to break out with extreme violence.

[2] With regard to these panics, see E. Cailliet, *Essai sur la psychologie du Hova*, pp. 17–19.

[3] On the *tody*, see Cailliet, ibid. (from Andriamifidy: *Ny Hevitra Malagasy*, in *Ny Mpanolo Tsaina*, Antananarivo, 1905, p. 206). Compare the meanings of the roots of the words *ody* and *tody* and their derivatives, in P. Malzac's Malagasy dictionary.

[4] See Part III, Ch. IV.

ticular why they condensed around claims for national independence. The rebels had only the vaguest ideas about the meaning of independence, but they had very clear notions about what kinds of leaders they wanted; they knew them personally and referred to them by name. Political systems and constitutions meant nothing to them. They wanted these particular leaders in order to be able to restore the broken bonds of dependence which they saw no hope of re-establishing with the Europeans. They also wanted them in order to be able to identify themselves with them. And finally they wanted them in order to lay upon their shoulders—but not through hatred—their painful burden of guilt.

Immediately these leaders were arrested, Malagasies who had not taken part in the revolt, but who had nevertheless unconsciously felt rather guilty for having hoped that the nationalists would win, spontaneously demanded the exemplary punishment of the men whom up to then they had looked upon as their models and heroes, without even waiting for a verdict on their actual 'guilt'. They turned their gods into victims, their heroes into scapegoats, their saints into martyrs, in accordance with an absolutely classical psychological process. Had the French authorities been 'primitive' enough themselves, had they offered the Malagasy people their own leaders as expiatory victims (while washing their hands of the whole affair), we should have seen a repetition of those emotional phenomena which occurred in another colony some twenty centuries ago when another people tried to wash away its sins in the blood of its own lamb.

The Malagasy rebels, however, had no such sacrifice in their minds; they wanted only to be delivered of their feelings of guilt by the restoration of clear and firm bonds of dependence on the traditional pattern.

This, I think, is an appropriate point at which to mention the phenomena of identification with the leader. A subject always—and almost always unconsciously—identifies himself with an acclaimed and acknowledged leader. For a leader is never really recognized as such, in any country, unless the man-in-the-street has the feeling—it may be illusory, but that is immaterial—that he understands him, that he can predict what he is going to do, and that he himself would do exactly the same if he were in his place. Whatever qualities a government may have, it will please only that fraction of the population which has the same qualities. It will become popular only when the man-in-the-street has unconsciously identified himself with it and feels that its actions are prompted by feelings akin to his own. If he cannot achieve this identification, though it is easy enough in normal times, then he projects on to it all sorts of low motives and sees it as prompted in all its actions by malice, self-interest, bad faith, and imbecility. If this sort of thing can happen in Europe, where those who govern and those who are governed are of the same nationality and have personalities of similar structure, how much more likely is it to happen in a colonial situation. True, the colonial inhabitants are not very exacting as to the conditions for identification; they were prepared to treat as father and mother governors and administrators not always worthy of that honour; but people dominated by a need for dependence cannot identify themselves with leaders who, they feel—they may be wrong, but no matter—have abandoned them. They saw nothing generous in our proposal to loosen some of their bonds of dependence, at least in the conditions in which the proposal was made, namely, after a war which had made them doubt the power of their overlords, after sharp disputes over domestic policy, and in the midst of a conflict between stern but 'tried' colonialists and politicians who, while preaching liberty, did not commit themselves in any way, had nothing either to gain or lose and remained infinitely more 'apart' from the Malagasies than the most brutal European foreman.

When the French arrived fifty years ago, the Malagasies did not receive them indifferently in the way people might, say, accept a new employer or a new justice of the peace; their feelings were much warmer, and the French, responding in their fashion, unwittingly created a situation which, though satisfactory to them, was in fact based on a complete misunderstanding. Many changes have taken place since then. To-day the Malagasy wants to project upon us his shortcomings and his ill intentions; he wants to find other leaders with whom to identify himself. We can no longer comfort ourselves with the thought that we are leading our colonial protégés slowly but surely along the path of progress towards a remote but accessible ideal: that of civilization, assimilation, emancipation. . . . For the Malagasies say that they are still following this path, but with other leaders; they do not want us any more. They no longer reproach us for imposing our civilization upon them; they now accuse us of withholding it from them, of barring the path we opened up for them. It is a political reversal—of that there is no doubt—but the political is simply a reflection of the psychological reversal, for at bottom what the Malagasies want is indeed our civilization but not from us.

These aspirations of theirs formed the kernel of the 'nationalism' and 'patriotism' which backed the programme for national independence. The details of that programme [1] were borrowed and the ideology was left vague, but neither programme nor ideas were required to win adherents. When the leaders the people wanted demanded 'independence within the framework of the French Union' the Political Affairs and Police Departments thought themselves positively Machiavellian in allowing another party to be formed and to claim, with impunity, absolute and unconditional independence. In spite of these attractions, however, and in spite of the newspapers placed at its disposal, the party had no success, because its leaders were not the ones the people wanted. The Malagasies took very little interest in programmes as such; they did not see themselves as champions of freedom (typical Malagasies, that is, for there are some who approach political problems as we do) but as followers of certain specific leaders. These followers were not rebels; they were 'nationalists' and an armed revolt does not appear to have formed part of their plans. The rebels came from more backward tribes, but they adopted the same men as their leaders. Naturally this does not mean that those leaders sanctioned the revolt, but the connexion itself was enough for the Prosecution to maintain that they were responsible, without bothering to go into details.

When the disturbances first began, and although at that time no one knew very much at all about their political causes, the colonialists with one accord and without the slightest hesitation demanded the arrest of the Malagasy chiefs. Subsequently they demanded their execution without trial. There was some sort of minor conspiracy— which failed—to place absolute power in the hands of the military, so that they could be executed under martial law. (This little plot, like all plots, had other motives too, but it was the desire to secure the immediate 'punishment' of the leaders which gave it sufficient emotional force to influence public opinion and make it, not a mere conspiracy, but a genuine *movement* among the colonials.) The colonialists were not interested in real responsibility and guilt; they felt, they knew instinctively that their rivals in the hearts of the Malagasies were neither freedom nor independence but the actual

[1] It is these borrowings which give colonial movements having no real connexion with each other a superficial resemblance.

persons of the Malagasy leaders, whether or not these men had anything to do with unleashing the revolt.[1]

We shall be returning at a later stage to consider other aspects of these psychological facts. For the moment it is enough to note that nationalism, to the masses, was simply a means of restoring the ancient pattern of dependences. Those woven around the Europeans had not withstood the test of time and change.

[1] The trial of the leaders has taken place since these pages were written, but in conditions such that no acceptable proof of their guilt has been brought forward. Nothing has become clear, except that the investigation was mishandled from the start. This can be said because the chairman of the tribunal has admitted it in as much as he has ignored the preliminary examination. The judgement given has been accepted in official circles, especially in its political implications, as a remedial measure rather than as a sentence.

CHAPTER III

REGRESSION, STAGNATION, PROGRESSION

I HAVE shown how the crisis through which the Malagasy is at present passing is bound up with a disturbance of his feeling of security. In the Malagasy personality this feeling is conditioned primarily by the position of the child in the family and by the pattern of family attachments. It is disturbed when the possibility of transferring these attachments to other objects is in doubt because the social environment is undergoing change.

There is of course no logical connexion between the satisfaction of the need for security, which is purely subjective, and the actual situation of fact as regards security. Whether or not the Malagasy feels secure depends entirely on how he sees the objective conditions, and he usually sees them wrongly. This need hardly surprise us, for it is almost always the case in such matters. Obviously a personality constructed on the Western pattern and one constructed on that of dependence do not take the same subjective view of the same external conditions, but they are both equally likely, when the need for security is greatest, to throw themselves into wild activities and run the gravest risks rather than tolerate an imaginary insecurity. If that were not so, there would never be any wars or revolutions. Human beings have always been subject, it seems, to the evil counsellor, fear, to panics which make them put their heads straight in the lion's mouth. But different peoples do not all display these neurotic reactions in the same circumstances, which is why Europeans find it difficult to understand the Malagasies' need for security, even though it is essentially very similar to their own. They see the Malagasies' reactions as the stirrings of a half-tamed barbarism of the instincts, while at the same time, the contradiction notwithstanding, they like to consider them the product of some deliberate and evil plan, hypocritically worked out behind the screen of an inscrutable 'face'. No one thinks to question the naïve idea, which is widely held, that the colonial peoples are still 'barbarians' at heart, and that barbarism is simply a certain youthfulness of the natural instincts, nor do people think of examining the very vague theories on which such ideas are based.[1] As for the charge of deliberate machinations and hidden motives of evil intent, it may very well be true of certain individuals thoroughly infected with European psychology. But the mass of the people, who provide the psychic energy without which these schemes would remain mere intentions, are themselves the victims of more deeply-hidden psychological phenomena—for those who are subject to them understand them little better than those who only see their effects. Historian and judge alike attach great importance to plots and intrigues, but the psychologist knows that there may be a myriad plots and intrigues, but that they will be quite harmless unless they can draw upon some vast supply of emotional energy such as that which is released by a sudden feeling of insecurity.

In order to understand the nature and place of the feeling of security in the dependent personality we must first analyse it in ourselves. We, in fact, tend to repress, or at least ignore, what remains in us of our original dependence, and since we are not aware of it in ourselves, it is difficult for us to appreciate it in other people. We must first of all, therefore, find out what connexion there is between dependence and the need for security in the average European of to-day.

The European resorts to infantile dependence through an emotional regression when his sense of security is seriously threatened, as for instance when he is confronted with difficulties which he cannot or does not know how to overcome. Such difficulties give him a paralysing feeling of helplessness, a feeling he commonly experienced in childhood. Then it is that he resorts to magic or prayer or seeks refuge in the sheltering image of the mother or some mother-substitute. These are all subjective means of protection and must somehow be connected with each other. Apart from these occasions, when we are overwhelmed by a sense of our own impotence, we lay claim to protection of an entirely different kind and one to which we attach much greater, if not indeed sole value, maintaining that the others are accidental failures in correct adaptation, excusable lapses, or neurotic regressions. What we rely on, in fact,

[1] The idea is allied to *primitivism* and its origin in the 'id' (see Introduction). In fact, the 'barbaric' rising was quelled by force of arms and 'hypocritical' nationalism by means of law, while in the confusion the Malagasies were accused of every conceivable shortcoming.

is our technical skill, and we place all our faith in the laws of a nature careless of our plans and indifferent to our interests. It is in this respect that our attitude differs fundamentally from that of the 'non-civilized' individual. Our confidence, however, is not based on the success of our techniques, or rather their success would not of itself suffice to create this confidence, for all peoples, however backward, have acquired techniques which they regularly employ with equal success, and yet these successes have not persuaded them to adopt the same course as ourselves. Such successes would indeed create very little impression were it not for the fact that the personality of the European is almost entirely free from dependence. All plans and calculations based on technique, however sound, are always liable to be upset by the operation of chance, by the accidental and the unforeseen. The laws of nature in which we have such faith are really infallible only in laboratory conditions, carefully insulated from the uncertainty of the real world. The scientist can be sure of the future when it concerns the experiments he has set up in his own laboratory—but if someone knocks at the door he has no idea what may happen to him, and if he is subject to anxiety his faith in the laws of nature is no longer of any use to him. At that moment he needs a genuine moral virtue composed of courage, trust in luck, and self-confidence. Descartes, who was familiar with and perhaps over-estimated the power of scientific knowledge, gave this virtue a name which it has not retained: he called it generosity. He gave it so much of his attention that we are probably right in inferring that he himself had a great struggle against a feeling of insecurity, a struggle which has made him one of the foremost exponents—heroes, one might say—of the modern spirit. We may take him as an example of those who invented, instigated, and popularized that Western self-confidence of which I have been speaking. A study of Bacon or Auguste Comte or of many other men would probably be equally instructive, but Descartes is very typical and can help us considerably in understanding this question.

In spite of the fact that Descartes was a philosopher and that his biography is that of a man who lived behind a mask and offered no confidences, yet there is sufficient material for a brief analysis. We do not know when or where he discovered that irresolution is the worst of all evils; instead of this information he has left us only the heroic theory of the will which was able to give him confidence and resoluteness at the very moment when he had brought absolutely everything into doubt. We do know, however, why he needed to formulate such a theory and why he needed to create an image of the world from which the void, chance, and the Evil Genius had been excluded, a world in which a man with nothing but his own resources, provided he were resolved to do his best, had no need to fear the unforeseen consequences of his actions.

We know that Descartes's was a sickly childhood and that the doctors forecast an early death; this false diagnosis no doubt explains the confidence he later placed in the possibility of inventing a new system of medicine capable of prolonging human life almost indefinitely. His confidence, however, was also the reaction of a man who, having lost faith in the support of others, finds he must rely on himself alone. As a result of the doctors' verdict his parents virtually 'abandoned' him by sending him first to the country and then to college. He never knew his mother and was firmly convinced that she had died at his birth—he wrote as much to the Princess Elizabeth. It was not true, however; she died at the birth of another child which did not survive. His biographers only note this strange error in passing, but it shows just how much the mother-image was disturbed in his psyche. We may remember, too, his odd relations with women, for he was interested only in servant-girls and royal princesses and shunned the women of his own class, maintaining that he preferred philosophy to them! Later we find that after taking a vow he went on a pilgrimage to Our Lady of Loreto. But this pilgrimage appears to have resolved the remainder of his attachment to the mother-image, for very shortly afterwards he called such vows 'excesses'—pledges which curtail a man's freedom of action. He then turned directly (without *intercession*) to a God both abstract and free, the bulwark of science and the guarantee of human reason, a God who would ensure the progress of a solitary individual provided he were armed with a firm resolve. Thus Descartes reassured himself while teaching others a new form of confidence in a world from which he excluded or tried to exclude all maternal protection— a world in which a man could do without both the help and the authority of others.

This attitude is so typical of the Western spirit that any curious-minded person who sets out to study another civilization cannot help wondering, like Gobineau, at the beginning of his *Philosophies et Religions en Asie Centrale*, what effect a translation of the *Discourse on Method* would have on a mentality radically different from our own.

It is an excellent exercise to consider the possibility.[1] But in actual fact such a work would be quite incomprehensible to a completely different mentality; it would become meaningful only after the personality had undergone a total transformation. Descartes, as we have seen, overcame his feeling of insecurity by deliberately placing himself in a position of abandonment. In order to overcome anguish he plunged into the midst of anguish in a crumbling world where only he remained upright, sure of himself in the midst of error and universal deception. Appearances notwithstanding, no one achieves that result by 'demonstrative reasoning' alone; there must be other, psychological causes. For a personality which has preserved the original bonds intact it is not, as in Descartes, irresolution which is the worst of all evils, but abandonment. For such a person to adopt the Cartesian attitude some stratagem would be necessary; he might perhaps project the mother-image on to nature, or separate science which *isolates* from philosophy which *unites*. Pascal tried very hard to follow the same path as Descartes; he was equally if not more successful in the sphere of the natural sciences, but yet he failed to find a cure for his insecurity because he continued to struggle against abandonment.

Pascal, too, was a sickly child, but how fiercely he clung to his family! 'He could not bear to see his father and mother near each other,' says Marguerite Perier. 'He screamed and struggled with all his might. This went on for more than a year, during which his illness increased, and his condition became so serious that he was not expected to live.' And this was at the age of one year! With such a precocious Œdipus complex, how deeply he must have suffered at his mother's death when he was three. We are not told what happened at that time, but we know that he transferred the attachment in the first place to his sister. His need for human intercourse made him turn away from science because it offered so little opportunity for communication with other men and also because he believed that it was impossible to demonstrate everything by reason, for reason merely lit up a single point in the infinite while all the rest was terrifying darkness and silence. He tried in vain to adapt himself to the world, spurned diversion, and finally sought refuge in a God

[1] When I was in charge of the information service in Madagascar I myself thought of publishing a translation of the *Discourse on Method* into the *Vao-vao frantsay malagasy*. But it was a temptation I had to resist. Instead, I had Balzac's *The Country Doctor* translated; this was much more accessible to the Malagasies and was read with great interest.

having nothing in common with that of Descartes, for He permitted personal attachment and cured the hurt of abandonment. Whereas Descartes is the man of abandonment who has renounced maternal protection, Pascal is the child lost in the forest who goes searching for his mother everywhere. Yet all his life Pascal showed an ambivalent tendency both to seek and to scorn family tenderness and affection.

Descartes is an example of the typical occidental personality, confident in the face of an abandonment which he has converted into independence. Pascal, however, shows us how fearful are the obstacles which lie in the path of the man who seeks such liberation. Together they represent the essence of the modern temper, oscillating as it does between the most audacious rationalism and the most infantile superstition, for the typical occidental is caught between his desire (or the obligation) to break free from family attachments and the desire to renew and strengthen them. This becomes apparent whenever his security is seriously threatened. The soldier in battle, for instance, will rely on his *savoir-faire* to extricate himself from a tight spot and escape harm—and in so doing he is following Descartes —but he will probably also carry talismans and good-luck charms about with him and he will most certainly have photographs of his dear ones somewhere on his person; he says it is to beguile their absence, but that is not entirely true: it is not just a question of their absence, but that their pictures increase in value by reason of the danger he is in. If he is captured or wounded he brings them out and shows them; it might be said that he does it to gain pity or sympathy, but it is obviously primarily a gesture of self-protection. Countless instances could be cited to illustrate this contradiction in Western man, both confident orphan like Descartes and frightened child like Pascal, anxiously seeking a mother everywhere.

Modern society, however, emphatically favours the Cartesian attitude and holds that positive action is the only sure defence against insecurity. Anything else is mere superstition and therefore valueless or else of value only in 'some other world'. . . . This is a social imperative, not the product of reason or experience. In order to perceive how extraordinarily heroic such an attitude is we have but to put ourselves in the position of an 'uncivilized' person; he would feel terrified and impotent when confronted with all the dangers we are taught to scorn. It is no exaggeration to say that we encounter these dangers in the form of nightmares when we are asleep and therefore off-guard. In this sense we could say that the 'uncivilized' person must live in a continual nightmare if he has not escaped the feeling of abandonment and does not feel all around him the presence of the original protective powers. He lacks the strength which enables the occidental to leave his father and mother and go and live by himself, to pass through abandonment to an independence of which the non-civilized man has no conception and which he would reject with horror if he could imagine it.

Raoul Allier, in his book *The Mind of the Savage*, writes (p. 217):

> 'We should define the former (the civilized individual) as a human being who, while not incapable of any belief in magic, is not dominated by it, but is able to reflect, deliberate and draw conclusions as though it were non-existent; and the latter (the uncivilised man) as the human being in whom the belief in magic determines the essentials of his inner life.'

Thus Raoul Allier, like Lévy-Bruhl in his Oxford lecture, allows a small area of common ground between the civilized and the non-civilized and lays the emphasis on the *intellectual* development of the former. But the non-civilized man is equally capable of reasoning and drawing conclusions as if magic did not exist, so long as his sense of security is not threatened—though that is rarely the case. The civilized man, contrariwise, will be governed by magic in one form or another if his feeling of insecurity increases beyond certain limits. It would be more accurate to remove the stress from purely intellectual development and to say that the civilized person decrees (and adheres to the decree so far as he possibly can) that positive action, in spite of the obstacles it may encounter, is the only effective course, and he maintains that such dangers as may persist after such action has been taken are negligible—at any rate while they are not actually present. Moreover, when he gives in to magic he does it with a bad conscience. The non-civilized person knows no such decree. He admits the effectiveness of positive action when no danger is near, but his only protection from danger, even when it is imaginary, is the security he knew as a child, and that leads him straight to magic. Nor has he any bad conscience in resorting to magic; rather the contrary, for he is placing his trust in the collective wisdom, in a doctrine approved by the group. This makes it clear why the native we are trying to civilize may become subject to panic fears which are to all appearances inexplicable. These panics have been commented on by many observers, including Cailliet (*Essai sur la psychologie du Hova*, pp. 99–104), where he describes them among the Merina. But we must also note, in contrast, the equally astonishing fact that these fears are calmed the moment superstitious practices are set in motion, even among people who might be thought to be fairly well colonized or civilized.

After the 'rebels' had attacked Antelomita, some twenty miles from Antananarivo, in the middle of the Merina country, there was found among the dead a Protestant minister, a Malagasy, and clenched between his teeth was a bit of wood on a string—the *ody-basy*, a charm which is supposed to protect the wearer against rifle-fire. It is placed in the mouth in the moment of danger. This incident, which the reader may find it hard to credit, aroused very little comment when it was publicized in the Antananarivo newspapers of the time. But a Merina Protestant minister, however ill-educated, can hardly be called a 'primitive', and he must have had plenty of time in which to reflect upon magical beliefs. Whatever conclusions his reflections may have led him to, however, it is clear that at the moment of real danger he slipped back at once to the level of the least developed Malagasies. On discovering such facts as these, Europeans in Madagascar, unaware of their own superstitious tendencies, immediately use them as an argument in support of their purely racialist convictions.

Nevertheless there are many colonial natives who are sufficiently far advanced to have abandoned magic, at least in appearance, but they have not been induced to do so by scientific proof, or at any rate not by that alone. How, for instance, could we 'prove' to a man that he should stop wearing charms against crocodiles? By telling him that a man who wore one had been eaten? Not at all, for that would 'prove' nothing to him; he would always say that the man must have been in a state of sin, no matter what the sin may have been. Charms are laid aside only when anxiety has been relieved. Europeans have helped allay the Malagasy's anxiety not by assisting him directly in the reconstruction of his personality along better lines, but by making him feel that objective danger has been removed. His view of the world has changed and the presence of Europeans has made his world seem a safer place. The child is comforted when the father takes it by the hand, even though the external danger is no whit diminished by his presence, as, for instance, in a thunderstorm, against which the father's hand is clearly powerless. But the father's very calmness is itself calming, and no physical experiments, however convincing, can produce this sort of result. I shall later be discussing the educative value, in certain psychological conditions, of the experimental approach; but isolated samples have no more effect on the mind of the native than conjurors' magic has on ours. We have also countered the 'primitives'' magic indirectly, by reorganizing the social environment; we have introduced a new way of being in order and having a quiet conscience through our systems of buying and selling, paying taxes, declaring births and deaths, and so on. Even the imported religion, which, as I have explained, has become an almost entirely social affair, offers comfort and reassurance. What it amounts to is this, that a man who has a piece of paper in his hand—a title-deed, a tax-receipt, a certificate of confession, or any other—feels he can safely lay magic aside for a while, as an obsessional might temporarily forget his pierced farthing or his lucky horse-shoe because he has acquired a doctor's prescription. The assurance thus gained naturally serves to diminish anxiety in situations where a piece of paper is of no help at all, as in the fear of crocodiles or ghosts.

This explanation may seem very bold, because it has not been given much consideration before, but what other theory will explain such a host of paradoxical facts? Some years ago I climbed Mount Ambondrombe. This mountain is said to be the meeting-place of the dead from all over the island, who can be heard beating their drums there at night. To the Malagasies it is forbidden ground and they never go there, for, they say, if one should stumble upon the Magic Lake one would die. Yet the Betsileo-Tanala who came with us as porters showed no anxiety at all; when questioned about this, they said that they had been recruited officially and that we had with us *taratasy-fanjakana*—Government papers. It was not that these documents were believed to possess magical properties; their value was of a different kind: they put their holders outside the range of magic. How was it that mere papers could make these men feel safe in venturing on to a ghost-haunted mountain? It was because such papers were properly reassuring in other spheres.

It cannot be said, therefore, that there has been any genuine mental progress. When the Malagasy has reason to doubt the administration and its papers he immediately falls back on magic; in 1947 the very same Betsileo-Tanala were in the front rank of the rebels shouting 'Rano, rano' to turn the rain of bullets into water.

I shall be giving more detailed consideration at a later stage to the problems involved in the acquisition and development of the experimental spirit, but I should like to draw the reader's attention in passing to the fetishistic character of our porters' attitude. There was a time when to have peace of mind it was necessary for them to be at home among their friends and relatives, to have living evidence of protection. Nowadays they are satisfied with whatever evidence they can carry about with them. The result is in every sense a certain liberation of the individual: [1] with papers he feels more free to move about and, having papers, he is freed from the fears he has projected on to the unknown territory. Thus through their liberating effect the new administrative methods have been more beneficial to the Malagasy than one might at first have supposed.

It may well be that the method employed by the French Government was after all the best; by organizing and administering things and relations it appears that in the end one transforms persons. But this reformation has been slower and more susceptible to reversal than we had hoped. And since administration in Madagascar, like anywhere else, tends to become more and more mechanical and impersonal the net result is that, paradoxically, we are trying to modify personalities by operating on the periphery, by remaining at the greatest distance and avoiding all real human contact. This of course will not be of great assistance.

[1] All religions have the same liberating effect. Forces at first strictly local are mobilized in the form of fetishes, and once mobilized they can be interiorized.

CHAPTER IV

ADMINISTRATION AND PSYCHOLOGY

I HAVE tried to show how far administrative routine can provide a secure framework for the lives of the Malagasies. Native civil servants find their place in the administration reassuring, not because of the advantages it offers them in the way of salary and a pension, but because they feel safely supported by a complex network of dependences within a system which is fairly rigid. As for the Malagasies who are not civil servants, the administration can liberate them to a certain extent by introducing a new way of having a quiet conscience, of being in order, very different from the old ways, which are, however, contaminated by it as I have shown. Thus, in giving the Malagasy a birth certificate, an identity card, and sundry other documents, the administration has gone a fair way to providing him with the material for a personality of a kind quite different from the one he originally possessed. These papers and regulations are far more individualizing than the old ties between the members of the group. Dependence can thereby be transferred to a remote, abstract, and almost imaginary object, the *Fanjakana* (the Government), and transference weakens its hold, thus allowing the personality some room for development.

It might, however, be worth our while to give the Malagasy's attitude to administrative authority closer attention in order to find out in what ways it differs from our own.

We Europeans accept the principle that the purpose of all regulations is to satisfy a certain ideal of justice. If administrations very often appear to us to have lost sight of this ideal it is a failure to which we may resign ourselves but not without thoroughly deploring it. Failure results from a deterioration of aims which culminates in the growth of a bureaucracy, a system which none can approve without reservations. When a Goethe attributes greater value to order than to justice we are deeply shocked, for he is attacking what in us is an imperious claim, our famous 'thirst for justice', to which we attach great importance and which we might even be prepared to call sacred.

The Malagasy is unaware of any such claim, not because he is incapable of demanding his rights or of seeing that justice is done him, but because he does not feel that regulations, litigation, or even law itself have placed obstacles between his aspirations and his ideal. The attitude of Alceste, which rouses in us a sympathetic if naïve response, would be well-nigh incomprehensible to the Malagasy, for a reason not far to seek: Alceste repudiates the place assigned to him in a system of relationships; he wants absolute justice, independent of law, proceedings, and precedents. His is a strictly individualist claim and before he could make it he must first have been conscious of his own individual value as opposed to that of the group. The Malagasy has never travelled along these paths, into which, indeed, one must be impelled by inferiority.

To the Malagasy administration is, ultimately, what the individual administrator conceives it to be, and the latter assumes that the motive force behind all human activity is egoism. At best, then, regulations are a means of diverting egoism for the sake of the general good, while at worst they are a means of hobbling and paralysing the egoistic administree through setting a series of formidable obstacles in his path. The administration is in fact able to exercise a somewhat sadistic authority—and with a clear conscience.

But the Malagasy does not think it reveals a low estimate of humanity to say that all human actions are prompted by egoism; he has not made social prohibitions part of his own conscience and, unlike the majority of us, including Gonzalo, he hardly ever dreams of a society composed of men of goodwill among whom regulations are unnecessary. Even the most cynical European must at some time have entertained such a vision and it is very likely that his cynicism is the result of his having been obliged to reject it. The Malagasy has never formed such an ideal; he unhesitatingly accepts the most bureaucratic concept of social organization and with such good faith that there has been an extraordinary flourishing of everything administrative in Madagascar. Moreover, not only does he accept administration readily but he even extends its use into fields where it does not belong—to home life, for instance, where a father, under the influence of what he has learned of our methods, will end by running his family in accordance with more or less explicit rules.[1] It would

[1] See *Revue de Madagascar*, special number, January 1945, pp. 40–41.

be wrong, however, to suppose that the privileged position accorded the administrative temper in Madagascar was the result of a deliberate effort of expansion on the part of the Government services themselves. On the contrary, the administration has been rather carried away by the readiness with which the Malagasy has accepted it: it appeared to fill a want. We may wonder why this is so.

For the Malagasy, laws are divided into two main categories, customs (*fomba*) and decrees (*didy*). From a metaphysical viewpoint like that of Kant the decrees of the city and the laws of nature finally coincide in the end they serve. The Malagasy has no idea of the possibility of such a unity. To him the *fomba* are nature: the forms of the plants, the instincts of the animals, unchanging habits, customs, and long-established social practices are all indiscriminately called *fomba*. Decrees emanate from authorities, from parents, from ancestors, from the vague supernatural powers which constitute fate. A decree may embody an order to change the customs. If the authority is reliable, they should be changed, though such a course is fraught with danger, for any break in custom gives rise to a feeling of insecurity and therefore guilt. In the ordinary way the *fomba* should be respected in the execution of decrees, but the *fomba* cannot provide against all eventualities, and some 'suppleness' and skilful navigation are consequently required for the Malagasy to obey both the *fomba* and the decrees at the same time.

The exact position of the Malagasy is therefore difficult to grasp, for on the one hand he bows before all forms of administration, while on the other he attaches primary importance to the *fomba*. The fact is that he has tried to add the two principles together, to superimpose them one on the other, not suspecting that they might be incompatible. He has been encouraged in this attitude by the colonizers, who were determined to respect the *fomba*, and so drew up their regulations in such a way as to cut across them as little as possible. It will be easier to understand the Malagasy's concept of orders and administration if we consider his picture of the ideal leader. His ideal leader is a projection of the image of the father who rules in the name of the dead—a much more powerful image than that of the father who rules by virtue of his paternal authority. The good leader issues no unnecessary orders. He is an example. He is looked up to and he spreads confidence. He respects the *fomba* and they are respected by everyone else. He is peaceful of heart and the country enjoys peace. His needs are satisfied and no one is in need. He listens carefully to all opinions and has none of his own. He decides and settles questions when there is no other way out; then everyone else obeys because there is no other way out. This picture of the leader as guardian of peace and order through respect for all the *fomba* handed down from the dead is worth considering, because it enables us to understand the Malagasy's behaviour and his attitude to life.

Naturally, Malagasies who are more advanced, less fixed in the social framework, or more conscious of inferiority have quite different attitudes, full of grudges and complaints, so that their concept of the leader is much nearer our own. But even with them the traditional image is not far removed.

In developing according to its own laws, the European administration has inevitably altered the country little by little and has therefore come into conflict with the customs. If anything goes wrong, the Malagasy is not prepared to believe that it is due to faulty organization or to errors in the setting up of the machinery. He is unshakably convinced that it is the result of tampering with the customs, and he feels guilty because he has allowed them to be changed. If the Rice Office has all but caused a famine, advanced Malagasies know perfectly well that it is the consequence of embezzlement, black marketeering, and a host of blunders; indeed, they have probably been astute enough to draw some dubious profit therefrom themselves. But the average Malagasy is certain that there is no rice in the pot because the *fomba* have been meddled with. He has never felt it necessary to consider how and by what means the offence induces the punishment; [1] indeed, it would be difficult for anyone but an economist to grasp the sequence of cause and effect in this instance. What Europeans find it difficult to understand, however, is that the Malagasy will never refuse to obey an order point-blank; if he cannot get round it by 'suppleness' he will obey even if it means violating the *fomba*; but from that moment on any untoward event which may occur will appear to him to be the punishment he has earned. Thus the administration is presented with the possibility of modifying the *fomba* actually with the co-operation of the Malagasies themselves, provided that no unfortunate consequences ensue, even

---

[1] It is that of the *tody* which I mentioned earlier, the automatic return of evil upon the doer. Even if the Malagasies say they no longer believe in the *tody*, they act as if they do. Moreover there is the extraordinary proverb: 'There is no *tody*; it is simply the evil a man does which returns.' We can see from this proverb how difficult it is to give up the idea of the *tody*.

accidentally. The porters who accompanied me to Mount Ambond-rombe under the safe-conduct of the *taratasy fanjakana* would have deserted me without compunction had I fallen ill or been seriously hurt: they would have seen such a misadventure as punishment for my reckless violation of the *fomba*.

When the more or less unevolved Malagasy calls the white rulers gods (*Zanahary*) and when the 'colonized' Malagasy calls them father and mother (*Ray aman'dReny*) it is neither naïvety nor flattery, but a reaction of defence against anxiety. The white men are in control and there is no escaping their orders. If the Malagasy can persuade himself that they exercise divine power he has less reason to be afraid. But the white man fails to understand the magnitude of the trans-ference of which he is the object; if he realized it he would, as a white man, feel the weight of the burden he had assumed. Even the Reverend Father Vincent Cotte allows himself to be deceived (*Une tribu malgache*, p. 59):

> 'One should not take too much account of certain verbal flourishes or exaggerations which the Malagasies are given to. For instance, they will say to a European: you are a god, *anao Zanahary*, which is some-times deliberate flattery with a hope of gain, and is not likely to deceive the least modest of Europeans. Our poets have very often said similar things.'

There are no doubt flatterers among the Malagasies, but in this instance they would be echoing a real sentiment and not inventing one. All peoples nowadays, and not only colonial peoples, always try to lay upon the shoulders of their governments or rulers the burden which used to rest lightly enough on the shoulders of fate. If we were to remember how easily such transfers are converted from positive to negative we should be less likely to dismiss them as mere flowers of rhetoric, for the confidence which the Malagasy places in us is not always justified by the facts. In abandoning his *fomba* the Malagasy is amputating some portion of his personality, and he cannot make good the loss with *taratasy fanjakana*, however ex-aggerated a value he may have placed on these official documents in the early stages.

The Malagasy, then, has no sense of justice as we know it, is ready to conform to any and every regulation, but likely at the first mishap to feel guilty because he has abandoned the traditional *fomba*, and in-clined to accord authority excessive respect because that in some way assuages his feeling of guilt. He is absolutely incapable of individual and open resistance to any abstract system which is threatening to encroach upon his rightful liberties. All those little protests and objections which Courteline carefully observed, and caricatured, and which are met with daily, though in a less picturesque form, throughout European Government services, even that mere grumpiness at ticket-offices which affords the ego some satisfaction, and the continual disobedience in little things which is a gesture of protest which many a European finds necessary—all this is completely unknown to the colonial native. He will never, for instance, seek to 'register a complaint', but will try to gain satisfaction through personal contact, 'influence' or gifts—traditional with him—or even downright corruption, without the slightest prickings of conscience.

There are people in Europe who behave very much like the Malagasies; they are usually 'well-brought-up' people and law-abiding enough, but they seek unjust privileges through 'influence'. In the end they lose all sense of justice and contemporary morality condemns them. Courteline's grumbler belongs to a different class: he is one of the little men and has a marked inferiority complex. He is blamed for his bad manners and despised because his aggressiveness is a reaction of impotence. The Malagasy does not feel that he gives cause for blame; feeling neither inferior nor superior but yet wholly dependent, he plays an elaborate game with the administration and can see no reason for acting in any other way. The colonial administration finds him fertile soil for its own development, issues more and more regulations, and lends itself to 'suppleness' to a dangerous degree by taking account, unofficially of course, of personal situations and relationships, particularly at the lower levels of the hierarchy. Malagasy chiefs of cantons, for instance, are capable of enforcing the rules with the strictest precision and even pedantry, while at the same time allowing themselves to be influenced by personal relationships, social position, and the small but frequent gifts which they accept without the slightest feeling of dishonesty.

But the Malagasy's compliant attitude should not deceive us; he cannot adopt it without transferring to us certain very powerful sentiments. The lack of safety-valves may build up hidden pressures over a long period, but though the reactions may be inhibited and held in check, they will not thereby be obliterated. They will provide a reserve of energy which can escape only in outbursts of brutal violence. Moreover, the Malagasy himself is unaware of the existence of these pressures. He simply becomes more and more submissive and obedient until the unforeseeable moment arrives when he finds he must disobey—rebel violently against authority—and his feelings at that moment are like those of a parricide.

My interpretation will appear perfectly acceptable to anyone familiar with this kind of psychological research, but certain colonial experts will no doubt find my conclusions somewhat surprising and will probably put them down as figments of my imagination. I should therefore like to include as a sort of appendix to this chapter three further observations which will serve to support them.

1. The point I have tried to bring out is that the Malagasy in course of colonization transfers to his colonizer feelings of dependence the prototype of which is to be found in the affective bond between father and son. In the European these attachments are usually sublimated or liquidated in the course of growth, but in the Malagasy they persist without any marked change and are preserved in the structure of society and in the cult of the dead. This theory of mine is, moreover, fairly well borne out by the observations of investigators using quite different methods: Emile Cailliet, for instance, in his *Essai sur la psychologie du Hova*, published in 1924, shows the Malagasy constantly wavering between the ancestor and the 'foreigner'—that is, the white man—in his choice of a guide. This is what he says (p. 180):

'At first the ancestor rules with absolute authority. He is the life-giving force, the ousted and jealous father; he is loved and feared, and also worshipped. . . .

'Then suddenly the Malagasy finds himself confronted with a scheme of life which cuts sharply across his own; all is novelty and enchantment to him . . . he plunges eagerly into a way of life which has for him the peculiar attraction of the forbidden. At first it is a craze, an exaggerated fashion. Young people leave for Europe inadequately prepared; they throw themselves body and soul into European culture and glut themselves with ill-digested ideas. When they return to their own country, they cause alarm and dismay. People do not understand them but feel that they have acquired the power of the white man. The *vazaha* in the country are not taken in by this half-knowledge, and the newly-civilized man who was fêted abroad is suddenly degraded. Seeing that the Europeans are not taking him seriously, he withdraws into himself. It is then that the ancestor, who has been on the watch for just such an opportunity, resumes his rights. Thou shalt be my prophet and I shall be thy god.

'Hence those people of strange psychology whom we come across nowadays (1924) among the Merina; they behave like ancestors, have the manners of foreigners, and serve an outmoded custom. Should the foreigner at this moment become harsh, a whole crop of national heroes would arise.

'Thus there is no constant development, but an oscillation between the two levels, in a series of conflicts between ancestor and foreigner, and this will continue until a way has been found to pass from the one to the other. . . .

'A favourable juncture of circumstances is required before the movements deep within a people can become manifest, but these national awakenings are simply the symptoms of a deep and continuous conflict which crystallises alternately around the ancestor and the foreigner. Thus even when the foreigner appears to be triumphant, the ancestor is nevertheless still lurking there, invisible, on the battlefield, awaiting his hour of revenge. . . .'

It is hardly surprising that at the time when it was published this document did not attract all the attention it deserved, for the political situation at the time gave no indication of the grave reversal of the transference which has since taken place. Moreover, though Emile Cailliet revealed a quite extraordinary psychological intuition, such that he discovered the key to Malagasy behaviour although he had no means of analysing it, his discovery remained for that very reason too intuitive. It was not easily communicable, and his description is hardly convincing. His readers could—and probably did—take this passage to be mere rhetoric. Yet it contains all the essentials of the situation, and he was the first to grasp them: the transference of a group of sentiments from their first object, the ancestor, to the stranger (Cailliet calls it crystallization); the tendency to oscillate from one to the other; the sense of guilt (the attraction of the forbidden). He also noted abandonment: the Malagasy 'withdraws into himself'.

What errors there are in the description are also due to its too intuitive character. As I have already said, understanding other people is primarily a matter of arranging one's own thoughts and images in one's mind in a particular manner. Every portrait is also a 'portrait of the artist'. Errors in the detail must thus be explained by analysing the colonial mind rather than the 'mentality' of the Malagasy. Why is the Malagasy at ease in Europe in spite of his half-knowledge and suddenly degraded in his own country? Why is he fêted in Europe but not taken seriously in Madagascar? Cailliet did not think to ask himself why the colonials made such great demands in the matter of knowledge, or he would have been bound to see that knowledge or half-knowledge had nothing to do with things. Also, it is not when the foreigner is harsh that the Malagasy reverts to his traditional protectors, the ancestors, but when he begins to doubt the foreigner's strength and capacity to protect, for it is then that he feels he is in danger. Moreover, these psychological processes are at work in all Malagasies and not only among those who have been to Europe or have undergone strong European influence.

Nevertheless, Cailliet's impassioned intuition—despite the impression he gives that he was in some way troubled by the thought of the Malagasy's emancipating himself—took him, in one step, far further than the detachment and objectivity of other observers who described all that they saw of the Malagasy's customs and came to the conclusion that he was unfathomable.

2. My theory, then, is not so original that it cannot be seen as a formulation of intuitions I share with other observers who have studied the same people but used quite different methods.

Now, by way of verification, what results do we get when the methods I have followed are applied to a somewhat different subject? These methods were invented by Freud, and we may see the conclusions he reached when he used them to interpret facts observed by Frazer. The facts concern the way in which certain 'savage' peoples behave towards their rulers of the same race (see *Taboo*, Chapter I, 'The Burden of Royalty', p. 7):

'. . . The idea that early kingdoms are despotisms in which the people exist only for the sovereign, is wholly inapplicable to the monarchies we are considering. On the contrary, the sovereign in them exists only for his subjects; his life is only valuable so long as he discharges the duties of his position by ordering the course of nature for his people's benefit. So soon as he fails to do so, the care, the devotion, the religious homage which they had hitherto lavished on him cease and are changed into hatred and contempt; he is dismissed ignominiously and may be thankful if he escapes with his life. Worshipped as a god one day, he is killed as a criminal the next.'

An ethnologist knows at once how and why adoration turns to hatred. Indeed it is not even necessary to leave Europe in order to find examples of comparable emotional reversals. In an ironical moment Aldous Huxley suggested that a new form of anthropology should be instituted, to be called 'anthropology at home'. But this science already exists; it is in fact none other than the psychological analysis of the unconscious. Its originator, Freud, in his book *Totem and Taboo*, referred to the passage just quoted from Frazer and showed how an analysis of the neurotic thinking of 'civilized' persons can help us understand what is called 'primitive' thinking.

> 'The model upon which paranoiacs base their delusions of persecution is the relation of a child to his father. A son's picture of his father is habitually clothed with excessive powers of this kind, and it is found that distrust of the father is intimately linked with admiration for him. When a paranoiac turns the figure of one of his associates into a "persecutor", he is raising him to the rank of a father: he is putting him into a position in which he can blame him for all misfortunes. Thus this . . . analogy between savages and neurotics gives us a glimpse of the truth that much of a savage's attitude to his ruler is derived from a child's infantile attitude to his father.' [1]

We must not understand Freud to mean that the 'savage' is a paranoiac or that 'primitive' thinking is pathological. What he is trying to show in this passage is that pathological and 'primitive' behaviour have a common denominator, namely, infantile behaviour, which survives, though in very different circumstances, both in the 'primitive' and in the psychopath. The difference lies in the fact that in the former case this survival is fostered and encouraged by a whole social system which comfortably prolongs the infantile situation.

It would of course have been possible to reveal the Malagasy's psychology by placing the two passages, from Cailliet and Freud, side by side. I chose another method, laying great stress, particularly at the beginning, on our position as white men in the context of the colonial situation. It therefore became necessary to prove all over again what Freud, who invented the analytical method, sets forth in black and white in a few brief lines. The effort will not have been wasted, however, if it has enabled us to avoid the mistakes which are made, and which Cailliet, for instance, made, precisely because of the colonial situation.

3. For a final check we need the testimony of a Malagasy. Naturally this is very difficult to obtain, for any such document would necessarily have to be interpreted. We could use Dama Ntsoha's description of the difficulties he had to contend with, but Dama Ntsoha is a semi-Europeanized Malagasy and therefore not sufficiently

---

[1] *Totem and Taboo*, English translation by James Strachey, p. 50.

typical. Here, instead, is a translation of a *tsimihety* popular song, and consequently an absolutely typical text. It is a *sova*, a humorous poem describing the arrival of the white man. It shows how easily the father-*imago* came to be identified with the first colonizers.

Sova momba ny Vazaha

Poem describing the white men

I shall tell how the foreigners conquered this land:
They came of a sudden from the sea, these strange and unknown beings,
Shod in iron and metal-garbed,
With buttons ranged low on their bellies,
Their whiskers were red as pepper,
Their eyes were grey as cats' eyes.
They jabbered in their ships and chattered in their boats.
We understood not a word.
How all these things astonish me.

A book arrived from Bourbon,
A paper from 'Tananarivo.
'Let loose the slaves,' said the strangers.
'Lying and frauds,' said the Hova.
'Tho' the earth burst asunder and the sky be rent
We shall not liberate the slaves.'
They sent five hundred thousand horse,
Two thousand soldiers followed
From across the boundless seas.

'I shall go away,' said the Queen Ranavalona.
'Where will you go?' asked the Prime Minister.
'I shall go to the top of Ikongo—its peak is protected by cactus—
Where the long breech-loading guns will be useless,
And their shot bullets perish amid the rocks
That bristle with points like a shell.
They will need sledge-hammers to smash a way through
And they won't reach the top in a week's march.'

But nothing could stop the strangers
Who came ashore at Majunga
And went straight to 'Tananarivo
Led by a Koranely.
Women and children trembled,
Queen Ranavalona too.
The Hova had no time to gather their garments.

Now the country the strangers conquered is at peace.
There are no more outlaws and the slaves have been freed.
The blue-eyed strangers are mighty indeed.[1]

The sprightliness of this simple poem does not prevent it yielding useful information under analysis. We may note, first, the insistence on and exaggeration of those traits which made the Europeans appear almost supernatural beings. It is perhaps the first occurrence of the epic tone in Malagasy poetry. Beings are created capable of supporting the transference of certain very powerful sentiments without any residue of adherence to the traditional images of authority. Another point to be noticed is that although the new masters appear mighty and terrible, this is taken as an occasion not for fear but for joyous exultation, for their strength reassures the Malagasy. As he has violated the ancient customs, his new masters must be truly masterful or his burden of guilt will be too great. We may also observe the awakening and subsequent resolving of the Œdipus complex: the mother (here the Queen), her children (the people) and even the maternal uncle, the father's natural rival (the Prime Minister), all submit to the new paternal image whose potency is symbolized by the long rifles. In point of fact the Lebel rifles were a good deal shorter than the various types of rifle used by the Malagasies. 'Koranely' is both a corruption of the word colonel, and also a Malagasy word meaning a supernatural being. The outlaws are those who rebel against authority; the poet rejoices because there are no more rebels: in other words, he feels safe because he does not feel guilty. The slaves are freed; that means that the old order has been overturned. Psychologically it would be a mistake to suppose that the author of the song was capable of appreciating this liberation for what it really was—namely, a liberal reform, as we are tempted to do through imputing our own feelings to him. In order to see things in that way he would have to identify himself in his unconscious with a slave. No Malagasy, even had he ever been a slave, would ever dare to rejoice at being freed, nor even to feel a secret joy such as would make him grateful towards his liberators. The liberators have overthrown the customs—for better or worse as far as the slaves are concerned, for there is no question of their interests in our sense of the word—and since they are responsible they have, in the Malagasies' view, committed themselves. They are therefore to be counted upon,

[1] *Bulletin de l'Académie malgache*, 1913, Vol. XI, p. 129.

and all kinds of demands may be made upon them because they have taken the place of the fathers [1] and should provide every protection. The new master would be entirely mistaken, therefore, if he were to think that all he need do is await the expected gratitude for the good he has done. For he has done no good; he has simply introduced a change for which he bears on his shoulders the fearful responsibility: the Malagasy is pleased to see that his shoulders are so broad.

[1] In this *tsimihety* song, the white man evidently also replaces the ancient *Hova* masters, and the situation would be clearer if we had a parallel Merina text. . . . But this complication does not alter the essential point. Europeans have often based risky political speculations on the idea of the *gratitude* felt toward us by the various peoples whom we have *liberated* from the domination of the *Hova*. These speculations have naturally been belied by events.

CHAPTER V

WHAT CAN BE DONE?

WE cannot draw political conclusions or deduce a method of administration from psychological analyses; they simply do not warrant such use. An analysis is, as it were, a chart of a stretch of land, showing the easements, the sites of former dwellings, and the various workings, prosperous or otherwise. Such a map would play very little part in determining the plans an architect might draw after looking at it, for he might make use of what was there already or do away with it altogether, and his plans would vary, depending on whether he wanted to build a model prison, say, or lay out a children's park. The information on the map would be useful in either case.

It will naturally occur to anyone reading this book to ask what is to be done about things, but he should not expect to find the answer in these pages. He will find neither methods nor programmes, but only a more accurate formulation of the question, and that from the psychological point of view only. Policy, in the sense of a plan of action, requiring the use of the power of the State to induce changes in human societies, necessarily springs from a choice, a decision, which is neither metaphysically free nor psychologically determinable. The same is true of individuals.

When he was asked what was the best way of bringing up children in the light of psychoanalysis Freud once said: whatever you do is wrong. Such an answer may seem surprising to-day, when child psychology has made such rapid strides, but its pessimism did not seem exaggerated at the time, especially from a man whose job it was to perceive all the difficulties and weigh all the risks involved in interfering, and even less when it was a matter of giving advice only. When people ask what practical use can be made of psychology in the field of colonial policy and administration, one is tempted to repeat Freud's reply, while hoping that just as Freud's pessimism proved unjustified in the light of the success of his followers' experiments, so in this case, too, future progress will enable us to see the problem more clearly.

In the meanwhile, although we cannot tell what harm we may un-wittingly do in spite of our good intentions, we can be quite certain that we shall not be blameless nor shall we avoid all risks by doing nothing. Some educators, influenced by Freud's remark, reduced their interference to a minimum, but they did not for all that avoid doing some harm.

It is of course somewhat arbitrary to compare educational with colonial problems: the colonial peoples are fully adult, and those who think of them as overgrown children may be accused of harbouring paternalist motives or at any rate an unconscious paternalist attitude. Such a charge would not be without foundation, but it is not worth our while discussing it; we must start from the situation of fact and that has an element of paternalism in it. We have long been in the habit of speaking of the colonial peoples as being under our guardian-ship, and the present troubles are largely due to their struggles for emancipation. The reason for this situation lies deep in the nature of human relations as they exist in a colonial situation. Europeans did not bring paternalism into the country along with alcohol and small-pox; it grew on the spot out of the inter-racial psychological situa-tion which developed and the relations which formed between the two different types of personality. To imagine that it is possible to take direct steps to combat the paternalist behaviour of colonial Europeans while the situation persists is to adopt a purely moralistic attitude, refusing to admit the facts and indulging in futile idealism. Whatever we do, we must accept the present situation, for in any case our relations with the colonial peoples are the result of past history and not of the application of rules or the performance of a contract. It is a fairly simple matter to alter a contract, but it is well-nigh impossible to forecast what effect this alteration will have on the course of events.

Sometimes a harsh parent suddenly realizes what harm he is doing by his excessive severity; he may then decide to be more lenient, or even not to interfere at all. But if so he will in a way be acting even more positively than before, for his change of attitude will provoke unexpected reactions in the child. This fact may well explain why hatred of the authorities is most marked just when they appear to be full of goodwill!

The situation of abandonment which would result from a sudden and complete emancipation of the colonial territories might well be considered the necessary starting-point for a process which would in time lead to real progress. The argument is tenable, but we must see its implications. Our present relations with the colonial peoples have become very disagreeable, the more so as we have become more sensitive about them. We could break them off, but we certainly ought not to do so just for the sake of our conscience and our sensitivity, for it is difficult to say whether by so doing we should really be improving the situation of the people we abandon or, in Künkel's term, betray. That, clearly, is a problem which goes beyond the scope of psychology proper. All I can do is to point it out and delineate it clearly. On the one hand there is the attitude, which we may call colonialism, which bases the authority of the European on a superiority either felt as a right or affirmed as a fact, according as it is explained by the idea of race or by that of a difference in the degree of civilization. This attitude has grave drawbacks. But the opposite attitude, which favours pure and simple abandonment, however we may seek to justify it (either selfishly, by saying that we should leave alone a problem which demands too great an effort of us, or generously, by saying that all men are by nature free), is not necessarily the right one simply because it is the contrary of a wrong one. It may well be, as frequently happens, that some third attitude, less sharply defined than the other two, is to be preferred.

This third attitude can be defined in advance, however, only in terms of intention. We are in the midst of a historical process; we are entering upon it blindfold, and it would be very naïve to think that we could compel history to follow a preconceived plan. In that connexion the present hesitation of political theoreticians before the facts of the colonial situation should be considered a great step forward. Doctrines have been preached in the past and have crumbled under the pressure of facts, but their psychological effects have remained, and it will be a long time before every trace of them is wiped out. Fortunately it is very difficult to-day to patch up the holes in the doctrinal fabric, and so there is a chance that we may at length begin to deal with the real problems as they become perceptible through the cracks in ideology.

As I have said, psychology cannot help us formulate a colonial policy any more, say, than studying a disease can help a man design a hospital or draw up rules for its administration. The reader will at times no doubt be tempted to draw moral or political conclusions from my psychoanalytical observations. He may, for instance, find in them arguments for condemning all colonization out of hand [1]—or, equally, for condemning a liberal attitude! But these are not legitimate conclusions; they are comparable with the arguments a reformer and a reactionary might draw from a study of neuroses for the damning of modern civilization. The only conclusion that can legitimately be drawn from my analyses in the realm of general attitudes is that many things are amiss in a colonial situation and that for reasons far more complex than is generally supposed. Also, many of the remedies which have been suggested are simply reactions, insufficiently thought out, and there is no guarantee that they will afford any appreciable benefit. Such conclusions, however, are hardly original; they would be reached equally by an analysis of many other types of situation (marriage, the family, economic relations, &c.).

It only remains, therefore, for the man who is in a position to do so to shoulder his responsibilities in the name of his moral and political ideals, and not try to escape them by saying that he is bound by the facts of the situation. Of course that is true, just as it is true that the situation exists and must be 'taken into account'. A feeling of helplessness before the actual situation and a tendency to formulate utopian and unrealistic schemes usually go together, as psychology shows, and this is so in the political as in other spheres. But I am concerned only with the psychological situation, a proper understanding of which could, it is true, give rise to observations of a practical nature. Is it possible, for instance, to do anything to bring about a better inter-racial understanding (which is not the same thing as an agreement, for people may agree upon some limited project on condition that they are not obliged to give their reasons)? In the problem I used as an example, that of the bringing up of children, it will readily be admitted that whatever one's favourite educational system, the most important thing to do is to save children from the neurotic reactions of people round them. A colonial situation tends to encourage this kind of reaction. In the case of education the problem is difficult and the difficulty is often shifted, for in some instances, in order to help one child, it is necessary to re-educate two grown-ups. But in the colonial situation, even if that is so, it is easier to influence some thousands of Europeans than it is to influence several million natives, especially as the latter can be reached only

[1] It might, for instance, be concluded that *colonization should never have taken place*; but this sort of conclusion is valueless.

through the former. Moreover, the European population is still relatively unsettled and changes periodically for the most part, so that some sort of psychological plan would be possible so long as it remained fairly modest in scope and envisaged results only in the long run.

As I have already shown, the colonial vocation, which ensures the continued recruitment of officials and other colonials, is far from being a guarantee of psychological aptitude. A minimum of guidance is so eminently desirable in this respect that it will assuredly be given in the years to come, perhaps in response to the request of the colonial peoples themselves, although we cannot be sure that it will be wholly of the right kind at the start or that sufficient attention will be given to affective psychology. Means for investigating the affectivity of a subject already exist, and such investigations would take hardly more time than the various vaccinations which are compulsory nowadays. But they could not be introduced before the psychological difficulties inherent in the colonial situation had been systematically examined, and that would presuppose the possibility of a study being made of the psychological development of the different human elements, white and black, making up the colonial population. A colonial administration is likely to feel that it has no use for psychological documentation of this kind, just as in the early days of flying, pilots thought they could do without meteorological information in which they had no confidence: indeed, it was very difficult to persuade the colonial government to take meteorology seriously, but to-day everybody agrees that many lives would have been lost without it. Nevertheless their number would have been smaller than is the number of those actually lost as a result of psychological errors so great that people will one day be astonished that they could ever have been committed. For the present, however, we have no guarantee against the periodical recurrence of the same mistakes.

It is to be feared, however, that when at length the importance of psychological research is recognized, psychological studies may be continually vitiated by the desire to apply them with interested motives in mind. So that it would perhaps be better for the authorities to remain in ignorance and for disinterested research to continue.

It would, besides, be rather naïve to try to pass straight from a general study of the kind I have just made to immediate and specific application. There is as yet no adequate theoretical basis for such an application and the atmosphere is certainly not favourable. More-over, there would probably not be enough people in the colonial territories capable of even a superficial understanding of the real nature of the psychological problems.

Schools which train young people for a colonial career should include in their schedules a thorough course in really modern psychology. Whatever gaps there may be, at the start of his career, in a young administrator's knowledge of history or political economy, the consequences will be far less serious than those which may result from a psychologically unsound attitude. If he forms a mistaken idea of his own prestige and authority in the eyes of colonial peoples, the consequences may be grave indeed. Neither the fine analyses of Lévy-Bruhl and Frazer, nor the very latest theories will be of any avail then.[1] On the other hand, however, an administrator tends to think that psychological studies should magically reveal the workings of the mental machinery of the people he administers, so as to lighten his task. There is nothing to be done once this attitude has been adopted. The only *useful* psychology is one which will enable the administrator to understand himself in relation to the native; it is also the most difficult sort of psychology and cannot be learned from books. . . .

There was a time when Europe was easily able to provide the sort of colonial who was capable of guiding native peoples. Indeed, it was the existence of this type of man which made colonization possible. He was the *vazaha* of the *tsihimety* song I quoted above—the n.c.o. with the huge moustaches who did not quibble and gained authority by virtue of his courage, rough justice, and simple good-humour. This type is no longer met with in Madagascar except for a few isolated specimens who have become more or less caricatural in the course of time; they are the relics of a former age, and no further useful service can be expected of them.

It is not by chance that this heroic and picturesque type of colonial has disappeared. On the contrary, his very disappearance is a sign of the change which has come about imperceptibly but relentlessly in the course of the last fifty years, and that change, as I have indicated, has some connexion with the decline of paternal authority in Western societies.

The typical colonials of to-day are neither so colourful nor do they enjoy such prestige as did their predecessors. They are in a state of

[1] Cf. G. Hardy, *Revue de psychologie des peuples*, July 1947, p. 237.

degradation or transition; they are Crusoes or Prosperos beginning to have doubts about themselves. They feel inferior before the paternal images of the heroes of colonization whose memory they never cease to recall, though in vain, like the Epigoni, strengthened but paralysed by the memory of their great forefathers. From the purely psychological point of view it would seem desirable to relieve them of this crushing burden of recollection which serves no useful purpose and indeed prevents any progress. It is desirable, too, in order to release those qualities in the psyche of occidental man which will allow inter-racial harmony to develop. It would be pointless to try to depict in advance the sort of white man who will worthily represent our civilization among the peoples we still call colonial. Relations between white men and these peoples are obviously about to undergo a total change and the concept of colonization in its present form has clearly very little longer to live.

Probably the most useful thing we can do at present is to take note of all the possibilities for change; they are less fixed than one might suppose, and nothing is absolutely inevitable. The real obstacles, however, are still those which Shakespeare indicated in the minds of Caliban and Prospero, and it may be that they are so much a part of human nature as we know it that there is no point in our studying them. In that case the only genuinely collective psychotherapy is what is known as politics.[1]

But even if that were so, those isolated individuals who learned by means of analysis to study themselves in the context of a colonial situation might prove to be an important agent of change. I am not thinking of a collective catharsis, for the presence in a group of even a very few persons with a different type of personality would probably be enough to modify the group as a whole It is difficult as yet to say exactly what form this possible modification would take.

Self-government

As I have said, it is not permissible to use psychological findings either to construct a colonial policy or to condemn all colonial

[1] Certain it is, in any case, that a good political training could make up for the lack of a psychological training, for political development can alter the whole structure of the personality. Indeed, it is hardly necessary to stress so obvious a point, since this has always up to now been the way in which personalities have been transformed. In presenting the psychological as against the political point of view, I am not in any way suggesting that the one should be substituted for the other!

policies even though psychology can point out their inherent weaknesses. If they are to be condemned, it must be in the name of
principles of another kind. To revert to an example I have already
used, who is better equipped than a psychoanalyst to appreciate the
drawbacks of marriage? Yet when we criticize marriage as an
institution we cannot do so in the name of psychoanalysis. We
must find other arguments. Nevertheless anyone setting out to
remedy the defects in the marriage system would do well first of all
to go to the psychoanalysts for information. Afterwards he will
probably be in a better position to see where the difficulties lie.

Every colonial doctrine is based, explicitly or implicitly, on the
situation as it exists and claims to remedy ills which must first be
described with whatever means are available for such description.
It might therefore reasonably be expected that a fresh description
would have an effect on doctrinal concepts. This is a somewhat
cloudy and confused region, but evidently it is open to the
psychologist up to a certain point.

Any psychologist who thus considers the present situation is not
likely to place much hope in reforms inspired by political tradition,
not that such reforms may not have some value in themselves or may
not afford considerable benefits, but that they are not a remedy for
the essential evils of the situation. It would be mere justice, for
instance, from the human, moral, and political points of view to
grant the right of suffrage to all adult natives. But the effects of
introducing such a reform will be very different in different psychological circumstances. It has been noted, for instance, that a reform
of this kind was introduced in Madagascar at such an ill-chosen
moment and in such unfortunate circumstances that it led to a
psychological regression, a reversal of the transference, and an outburst of hostility arising from a sense of guilt—to say nothing of
its no less disastrous repercussions on the psychology of the majority
of the European colonials. It is psychology's job to find out the
reason for these effects and not to pass judgement on the reform
which in other circumstances might well have had a successful outcome. Once it is realized that the results of political measures may be
good or bad according to the psychological circumstances, it will
readily be seen that these circumstances merit careful study.

It is the psychological factor which accounts for our impression
that the effects of politically-inspired reforms are never direct but
always indirect, and somehow accidental; in fact they are the result

of processes which the reformer never takes into consideration and indeed usually ignores. Moreover, a psychologist cannot help seeing the reforms which a European politician might consider introducing into colonial administration as a means whereby he hopes to salve his own conscience rather than a means of helping the colonial peoples out of their difficulties. The urge to reform certainly does credit to the man who feels it very strongly. Furthermore, as the colonial situation is one where two psychologies meet, it can be improved only if all psychological needs, and that includes those of the Europeans, are met to the greatest extent possible. This is true even if the European's needs spring from a sense of guilt, the consequences of which would be far more harmful if it were not assuaged by his impulse to institute reforms which he feels are generous. But this generosity would, of course, be more real if the reformers' efforts were so directed as to ensure a definite improvement in the situation and not merely an impact, the immediate effects of which are problematical and its long-term effects wholly unpredictable.

It may be assumed, not only as a legitimate deduction from present tendencies, but also as a goal in many respects very desirable, that administrative responsibility will fall increasingly upon the shoulders of the indigenous peoples themselves. This does not mean, however, that we can escape our own responsibilities, for we shall continue to play a large part in the native's thoughts. He will study us, imitate us, love us, and hate us, even when he has become, *de jure* and *de facto*, master of his own fate, rather in the way a young man who has started out on his own still retains in his mind a father-image or a mother-image with which he finds it far more difficult to come to terms than he does with his real parents who have set him free! The comparison is a poor one, however. The European will in fact play a far more important part than that, and will continue to exercise a real influence even in a 'colony' which has become independent and where he is simply a guest. It is perfectly obvious, however, that in present circumstances a political reform of that magnitude—complete self-government—would be no solution to the psychological problems, for neither colonizer nor 'colonizee' would be able to adjust to it: we might as well ask Caliban and Prospero to meet on an equal footing, expect Prospero to behave as Caliban's guest or Caliban to treat him like one. In fact a change of status would not of itself help to improve human relations, or rather, if a change of status could be effected, it would be the proof that a decisive improvement in these relations had taken place. It is the goal we should bear in mind, but it is not a sufficient means of attaining that goal. On the contrary, it would, as I have shown, provoke unfortunate psychological reactions. It is in the light of these considerations that we should attempt to see the question of granting self-government to the 'dependent' peoples.

There is a sociological law which admits of no exception that all peoples, even the most ignorant and backward, are capable of governing and administering themselves, provided, of course, that they are left to choose their own methods. But although most 'civilized' persons are, for very sound moral reasons, in favour of granting self-government to overseas peoples, they more or less assume—again for sound moral reasons—that this 'self'-government will obey certain rules. If the once-subject peoples were to revert to political systems of which we disapproved we should feel uncomfortably responsible for letting this regression take place. However, the 'civilized' world is unlikely to be able to detach its interest entirely from this aspect of the question, while at the same time there is little doubt but that the 'liberated' peoples will be constantly aware of this, as it were, moral trusteeship which the West is exercising over them, and so relations between the 'civilized' countries and the others will take a fresh turn. They will neither be severed nor fixed once for all.

It is perhaps not very generous to say to someone: you are free provided you do what I tell you. But, as we have seen, 'civilized' people are not prepared to forego all conditions. However, bearing in mind on the one hand the lessons of psychoanalysis and on the other the illusion which will no doubt arise that all these problems can be solved at one go and in accordance with certain abstract principles, we may perhaps try to set down the conditions for a correct solution. The solution is not implicit in a statement of the problem, but we may find we have part of the answer if we postulate that any form of self-government would be acceptable which was built upon those ideological and psychological foundations we call democratic. If this were an arbitrary assumption dictated by political preference I should be going beyond the limits of this study, but that is not the case; this is indeed a psychological question, for the acquisition of a more democratic outlook is part and parcel of emancipation from psychological dependence and the attainment of an independent personality. Naturally this process can be speeded up by a change of status, electoral reforms, and so on, but it will not result from them automatically, and moreover if they are badly implemented they may tend to discredit the democratic ideal they serve. Unfortunately they are sometimes deliberately mismanaged at the executive level for this very purpose. . . .

In any democratic institution it is assumed that people are capable of deciding for themselves and of taking responsibility for their decisions. The average Malagasy, however, does not decide for himself and has very little sense of responsibility. In a democracy the minority yields to the majority opinion. The majority is not tyrannical; it tolerates opposing views. It may not take any notice of them, but it cannot suppress them. Opposition is always in the open. Political struggles are likely and may even be acrimonious, but they will never end in violence. The Malagasy is incapable of this kind of opposition. He cannot bear being in a minority position and will immediately go over to the majority, like a flatterer servilely adopting the master's views. If he continues the struggle it will be by underhand methods, as if opposition must for him always be clandestine. If it comes out into the daylight it will be open conflict, with a rupture and revolution. Moreover, the Malagasy is held in bondage by innumerable ties of dependence, and the servant dare not contradict his master nor the poor man contradict the rich. If he opposes he will feel like a rebel and will fall prey to feelings of guilt and an inner horror which will drive him to acts of violence.

This, then, is the position we start from; it would be foolish not to face it squarely. We should be right to conclude that a democratic mentality will not develop of itself, but we ought also to note that in endeavouring to promote its growth we shall not only be liberating the Malagasy politically; we shall be contributing, too, to his psychological liberation. I believe that such liberation is possible. If it were not, our position as colonizers would be very difficult to defend. It is already contradictory enough to be wanting to *impose* liberty.

At the present time when we give a Malagasy a ballot-paper he is impelled by his unconscious dependence to pay homage to his overlord, the Government, even though the Government tells him officially that he is perfectly entitled to vote against it. But there are some liberated Malagasies and they stand for open opposition to the Government. The elector thus finds himself in a dilemma which it is probably difficult for us to appreciate. It becomes comprehensible only when we realize how different a place the image of authority occupies in his personality and in our own. As events have shown, the Malagasy is capable of rising in rebellion the moment the authority he knows encourages him to hold an independent opinion or to pursue an independent line of action! That is not to say, of course, that the reforms could not have been introduced without any disturbance at all; they were badly timed and badly presented. Many of the Europeans responsible for putting them into force were obviously reluctant to do so and the Malagasies could not help being aware of that. All this, however, simply shows what precautions must be taken in order to prevent the occurrence of certain reactions of a kind very different from any we should be likely to experience. The Malagasies felt they had been abandoned. They suspected us of setting a trap for them. They were sure—though it seems absurd to us—that they were in great danger.

But we must beware of drawing from our examination of the situation the too convenient conclusion that we ought after all to retain in our own hands sufficient authority to reassure the average Malagasy! In any case the more advanced Malagasies have already passed beyond this stage. They complicate the issue, for if they are not completely cut off from their people by a total Europeanization they will serve as guides and models and the people will become dependent on *them*, with the result that their psychological advance will be precisely nil. The problem must therefore be tackled from the bottom and not from the top: the people as a whole, and not just the élite, must be helped forward and they must go forward alone and not in the wake of guides, for that would but perpetuate their psychological dependence. When clearly stated, the facts certainly seem to pose a problem which it will be very difficult to solve. But the problem is not insoluble; there is one possible way of approaching it, provided we do not expect miraculous results immediately, and that is through reviving the ancient institution of the *fokon'olona*, the village councils. It is not just a matter of turning the clock back but of restoring a tradition which the Malagasy will find it easy to accept and understand, in order to use it as a spring-board for a fresh advance. I would point out that this reversion to the traditional is of no value in itself; its interest lies solely in the possibilities it opens up if certain prior conditions are fulfilled.

The Fokon'olona

The *fokon'olona*, a traditional Malagasy institution, do not at first sight seem very unusual. They are simply village councils, or in the towns, district councils. There is very little that can be said about them as social or political organizations. But that is to take a purely superficial view; as soon as one looks beneath one finds a vast field rich in the social psychology of the Malagasies. I shall confine myself to a brief sketch in order to show how the *fokon'olona* could form a solid basis for all that we hope to construct and what is their real value in terms of an emotional framework for the individual.

Before the arrival of the Europeans, the *fokon'olona* were flourishing throughout the Imerina country, and they have never completely died out; they have simply lost their importance. Nothing would be easier than to revive them and they could even be implanted—with suitable modifications—outside the Imerina country. It was in the *fokon'olona* that the villagers used to settle all their own affairs; nowadays the Administration does it for them. If the Administration were to stand aside for a while, the village councils would at once regain their old importance and resume their former functions. Of course it must not be imagined that they would thereupon become a democratic institution, for that they never were. They would be more like a family gathering where the young and the poor relations have practically no voice in matters. The notables—men on whom the rest could project the father-image—would very soon take the lead. No real opposition would make its appearance. The weak would be exploited by the strong and it would not occur to them to complain because of the psychological comfort they would gain from the strength and firmness of the bonds of dependence thus assured them.

Reconstitution of the councils would, then, represent a distinct regression. The regression is desirable, however, for a number of reasons, but mainly because it offers the only possible basis from which we could make an advance. If we try to skip this first stage, on the grounds that it is a step backwards and not a step forwards, we shall find ourselves building on sand. So we must simply put up with it.

We must put up with it, if only because reform must be induced without active intervention on our part. We cannot ourselves resurrect the *fokon'olona*, for our influence, however discreetly camouflaged it might be, would immediately attract the Malagasies' feelings towards us, as in the day of direct administration, with an ambivalence not hard to imagine. It will be quite simple, however, for us to let them revive of their own accord. The reader may then ask whether there is any real hope of a fresh advance being made once the *fokon'olona* are reconstituted, whether there is any guarantee of a successful psychosociological development. I think so. Putting the picture first in the most optimistic light, and leaving aside for the moment the deeper emotional difficulties, we may say that the village will necessarily, in the course of things, gradually learn to manage its own affairs and bear responsibility for them. It will levy taxes, distribute a budget proportionate to its needs and resources, keep order and administer justice; it will negotiate the placement of its manpower with private individuals or with the Government. In other words, it will engage in a whole series of activities which will in themselves be educative. Responsibility will be unevenly divided, of course, and will for the most part be delegated to the notables. But the more extensive the responsibilities entrusted to the *fokon'olona* the more the notables will have to reckon with the rest of the community (*ny amban'ny vohitra*), however diffident it may be. Economic questions will be particularly useful in this kind of education. The taste for profit is psychologically one of the most straightforward human traits; it is easy to see whether a just distribution has been made and profits and losses fairly shared. Plans made for the purpose of gain represent a psychological advance in relation to the mere hopes and desires they replace. And it is in business, after all, that the rules of the game are most widely proclaimed and recognized— even among the shrewdest businessmen. It would be quite simple, therefore, for the *fokon'olona* to become a producers' and consumers' co-operative, responsible for the distribution of imported foodstuffs and for the execution of production plans for the village as a whole. There would undoubtedly be many injustices in its various operations, but we could seek to remedy them only indirectly, through training and education, although the influence of these, albeit slow in producing results, would in the end prove quite substantial. Whatever happens, we cannot impose justice. And we can put up with this situation because, although aware of the injustices, we need not feel responsible for them. What we might perhaps do is to establish some authority higher than the *fokon'olona*, Franco-Malagasy courts, say, to which in certain circumstances the villagers might appeal. But we must always remember that if we trespass on the preserves of the *fokon'olona*, their authority will crumble, and reform will get under way only if we maintain their authority intact.

That, then, is the way in which things may proceed if all goes well. The courses of action open to us are few indeed, and this is probably the only one which will not lead to severe disappointment. The first advance which can be achieved by this means is the transference of the feeling of dependence from the individual to the group as a whole, and this is a necessary step on the road to liberation. But of course we have no guarantee that the transference will not be made to other paternal images, and that would put a stop to all progress. But even so, economic activity would continue to play a useful part. The average Malagasy is not at present capable of working regularly for a wage, nor could he work for an employer not prepared to permit and endure the transference to himself of feelings of dependence, but he could work under the orders and supervision of the *fokon'olona* and receive his share of the profits therefrom. Naturally the problem is less simple than I have made it appear—for even if the difficulties which may arise between indigenous workers and employers are not discussed directly between the two parties but through the intermediary of the *fokon'olona* council, the representatives of the *fokon'olona*—the notables—will certainly have to undertake direct negotiations, but of course their position will be rather different from that of a labourer or foreman on the employer's pay-roll, and that will be enough to make the situation easier.

I shall now try to show what psychological preconditions will be necessary for the social and political development to be launched in the way I have indicated. We have very little information to guide us—which is understandable, after all, for we are trying to penetrate a future which, though not far removed, depends largely on accidental circumstances. The two documents I am going to quote have both the advantage and the disadvantage of emanating from the same Malagasy author. It is a disadvantage in so far as the writer can hardly be considered typical: a truly typical Malagasy would vouchsafe no comment on such a question. It is an advantage, on the other hand, because the second document was written three years after the first, and the author's attitude changed in the interval in a most significant manner; the change clearly shows what serious psychological obstacles he had to grapple with in the interim. The solutions he suggests are his own and, unrealistic though they may be, we can be certain that they are the answer to inner problems which were real enough. And these are the very problems which Malagasies in general will encounter, though in a less distinct and conscious form, and which they will find it equally difficult to overcome.

The writer is a Malagasy 'intellectual' who signs himself Dama Ntsoha, obviously a pseudonym. He writes both for his compatriots and for Europeans, his articles being published in the two languages.

At the end of the war it was felt that for various reasons it would be advisable to introduce a system of indirect administration, leaving the communities, that is to say, really to run their own affairs, levy taxes, allocate jobs, administer justice, and so on. This reorganization must be proving difficult to effect, for though agreed on in principle long ago it is taking practical shape only very slowly and has really hardly begun. But Dama Ntsoha was prompted to write his first article as early as 1945, immediately after the publication of the official plans and promises.[1]

In spite of its title, *New Times*, the pamphlet advocated a pure and simple return to the ancient customs. The author does not deny that; on the very first page he says, 'Let us cull the fruits of the past, and weigh their worth.' 'What a miracle,' he cries, 'the white world of the West has suffered a change of heart to-day and that is the great news of these new times. They tell us that all men are brothers . . .' Consequently, 'The Malagasies see spreading before them the happy prospect of being able to resume their normal course of development which has been interrupted by fifty years of blank despair.' He goes on to describe what he calls 'the fundamental principle of Malagasy social life'—the *fokon'olona*. 'The *fokon'olona*', he says, 'typified by the gathering of the notables, is a government of wise and just *ray aman'dreny*.' The expression *ray aman'dreny* actually means father *and* mother, but it is used here to designate an authority clearly paternalist in form, for it is not delegated by the community as a whole: it belongs to the notables (the *ray aman'dreny*) as of right. Dama Ntsoha says specifically: 'The government will model itself on the family', and in order that there shall be no mistaking him he declares that the inhabitants will be ranked according to wealth, that a feudal type of hierarchy will be restored throughout the country

---

[1] Dama Ntsoha, *Les Temps Nouveaux*, Imprimerie Antananarive, 2 *bis*, rue Galliéni, Antananarivo, November 1945.

but that at every level authority will be in the hands of groups of notables and not in those of individuals. And he concludes, significantly, 'The feast of the bath, the *fandroana*, will be restored, so that hearts may be exalted in union in the eating together of the sacrificial dish of the *Jaka*, token of true love.' To any Malagasy the feast of the bath can mean only one thing, the feast of the Queen's bath, and the *Jaka* must be understood as a play on words: the first meaning it suggests is the fruit of the Jack-tree, but in the Malagasy tongue *jaka* is the root of a verb which means to reign, and *mpanjaka* means king and queen.

This, then, was how in 1945 Dama Ntsoha greeted the new times and the declaration that all men are brothers; he unashamedly recommended a return to a feudal type of social organization. Although he himself had no experience of it, at least he remembered that it was in the Malagasy tradition. After 1945, however, he must have realized that he was on the wrong road. Although the reconstitution of the *fokon'olona* was still no more than a vague intention, it was clear that the authorities were determined that they should be democratic, with elected leaders and no 'ranks according to wealth'. Dama Ntsoha was utterly bewildered, not because he felt either his interests or his authority threatened, for he was as it were merely a commentator and had no personal stake in the matter, but because it had become apparent that although the white rulers were giving up part of their authority they were going to prevent the Malagasies seeking immediate refuge in the psychological protection offered by the traditional images of the leader. In other words, they were to be cast into a state of abandonment in which each man would have to bear the full weight of responsibility for his own personality, his own opinions, and his own decisions. Such a state would inevitably lead to anguish. So, three years later, Dama Ntsoha wrote a second pamphlet entitled 'Malagasy democracy'.[1] His bewilderment is apparent even in his style: whereas the first pamphlet was succinct, clear and quite well written, the second is full of eccentricities which suggest that the author is no longer able to handle the French language.[2] In it he offers a mystical form of communal life, in which there is no separateness, but a fusion of individualities one into another. Psychologically, this new regression is perfectly under-

---

[1] Dama Ntsoha, *La Démocratie malgache. Fokon'olona. Ny fitondra-mbahoaka, fomba gasy*, Imprimerie Ny Fananatenana, 66, rue Galliéni, Antananarivo, 24 pp.
[2] Nor Malagasy either, for that matter; there is the same awkwardness in it.

standable: the author, denied a return to a paternal type of authority, falls back on a more archaic, imaginary world, in which there is a hint of a matriarchy. He pursues the concept to its extreme, moreover, for he even goes so far as to call up the image of a return to the maternal womb, in other words, a seeking in death of the final satisfaction of his enormous need for communion. In the latter pamphlet there is no reference to the notables or the *ray aman'dreny*, no stratification of society according to wealth, nothing suggesting the paternalist family structure current in Madagascar, nor any mention of the old royal feasts. Evidently they all went together and together they were thrown overboard. But the affective need for a communal life persisted, deep down, and the later work should be seen as the anguished cry of this need. The later work obviously cannot reflect as faithfully as did the earlier one the views prevailing among Malagasies in general at the time; the author is now wrestling as best he can with his own dismay. He is inventing explanations in the way a writer might invent a fantasy, but his inventions and his delusions are an indication of needs he shares with almost all Malagasies, the only difference being that the latter are not yet conscious of them because they do not yet realize the emotional danger they are in. The vision Dama Ntsoha describes is, as it were, a dressing indicating an *imaginary* wound—the conflict in the affective bases of his personality.

In the later work, in place of the *fokon'olona* there is the community itself, and its members are on an equal footing. The author thinks he has adopted the official democratic ideal by declaring that all men are free and no one is to issue orders. He sees this as the development of 'a remarkable feeling of unity'. And he goes on: 'A man's essential nature is something he shares with all men; so each is one with all and a man can only be truly himself when he has lost himself in the all. . . .' This remark may seem commonplace enough, but it is illuminated by what follows: 'This bond of love will not be confined to the living; it will be even stronger with those who have passed beyond. Union will then have attained the highest peak of perfection; all will be one in the indissoluble unity of the *tsy misara' mianakavy* (the communal fusion he calls the "Primordial Unity")'.[1] This unity, he says, which 'helps us bear our present earthly existence, is ephemeral indeed compared with the ineffable union which is that of real existence in the Ultimate Reality'.

[1] Fritz Künkel's *Urwir*, evidently, but transposed into death!

I shall not dwell on the borrowings from Buddhism upon which the author bases his construct, claiming—fancifully, of course—that such was the religion of the ancient Malagasies. What he is doing in fact is to seek refuge in an ancient—though imaginary—tradition, in order to escape from a real tradition which he conceives to be of more recent origin.

The strange fusion he seeks can hardly be identified with Nirvana; it is something much nearer the cult of the dead ancestors. It would probably be more accurate to describe it as the reaction of someone who feels he has lost the strength to live as an individual, because he has had to renounce the father-image together with the patriarchal, or at any rate paternalist order of things which reflect this image in the outer world. Instead, he seeks refuge in a pre-natal world, in a return to the mother's womb—that is, the world of the dead. There is little doubt that for Dama Ntsoha the father-image stood protectively between himself and death, just as the *ray aman'dreny*, the paternalist authorities, were placed by him symbolically between the village and the tombs. Of this there is, if not proof, at least evidence, on page 11 of the pamphlet, where Dama Ntsoha describes the cult of the dead as he imagines it to have been among the ancient Malagasies. Nowadays the rites are performed by the father, who represents the ancestors, but this is how the author describes the cult:

'People lived all their lives in continuous awareness of the eternal beyond; they were in constant communion with the ancestors whose dwelling, the tomb, was right there in front of the house in the inner courtyard.'

And the reason for all his extraordinary distortions of Malagasy history is apparent in the conclusion:

'The Malagasy system of democracy reached this high degree of perfection right at the outset, offering the possibility of a human life rich in every virtue, and more, the value that came from the union of earthly life with the life beyond. The Malagasies of old were not earth-bound; their gaze was fixed on the haunting world of Eternal Existence where in some way which can neither be thought of nor expressed, all would be joined in one single whole.'

Dama Ntsoha's 'beyond' was not, in fact, very far: it was, as he says, right there in the courtyard before the house, in the tomb, whence it offered protection against the feeling of abandonment.

We may observe that this feeling recurs whenever Dama Ntsoha tries to describe individualism. He is under the impression that the Malagasies have become 'rabid individualists' (there is no need for me to point out how little inclined to individualism the Malagasies really are). 'They have,' he says, 'undergone a most unfortunate disintegration as a result of which every man is obliged to bear alone the whole burden of care for his own person.' As a means of combating this alleged individualism and this disintegration, the author recommends certain practical measures which he has borrowed from Europe, such as the development of co-operatives and even for some things, nationalization, of which he has not, however, a very clear idea. But he adds that these remedies will be effective only if they are backed by a belief in the mystic unity of the world of the dead, in what he calls the Eternal Existence.

There have been visions other than that of the eternal life: there has, for instance, been that of the land of Canaan, flowing with milk and honey, that of Paradise Lost, a vision which has not always been prohibited by the father-image, or again, that of the Land of Cockaigne. Dama Ntsoha's idea of the organization of the communities which will be formed from the fusion of the individualities of all their members is very similar; there will, he says, be 'neither authorities, nor police, nor taxes nor the slightest trace of officialdom. Everything will be arranged and regulated with the greatest ease in the world through the super-human wisdom of love'. (In order to appreciate how far Dama Ntsoha has come, we need to go back to the 1945 pamphlet and read what he says there about taxation, prison-organization, road-building, the need for 'clear and accurate records of the import-export trade', the setting up of a Bank of Madagascar, and so on). The differences in the later work, which reads like a recantation, give us a better understanding of the contrast between paternalist dominance with its organizing power and the right of payment which goes along with this form of authority (*auctor*, after all, bears the sense in Latin of 'father'), and the maternal abundance of nature, who provides for all without effort like the mother remembered from infancy. Now we see by what paths in the unconscious Shakespeare was led to include in *The Tempest*, alongside Prospero the paternalist, Gonzalo the utopist, dreaming of the Land of Cockaigne.

Thus Dama Ntsoha provides us with an example of affective psychology applied to the problem of the organization of community life. We have seen how heroically he tried to face the prospect of a situation of abandonment and how he failed to do so even in imagination and on paper, except at the price of a regression which led him back beyond weaning right to a pre-natal world.

There are a number of useful lessons to be drawn from this experience of Dama Ntsoha's. First, no colonial administration, however much aware of this problem, can take account of it in practice in any way which would be at all helpful. Nor could we reproach it on that account without raising a protest against all administration in the name of the individual human being, and in this case virtually in the name of anarchy. For inevitably the problem changes in nature as it changes in scope: the underlying needs of the human personality may well be expressed in terms of political claims, but they are changed thereby, though not necessarily degraded. The Malagasies probably do not yet know how to translate their real needs into political language, but they will undoubtedly learn to do so in time, whether we help them or not.

There is another aspect to this question, however: neither the administration nor the Europeans in general always fully appreciate the painful sincerity and moral heroism with which Malagasies like Dama Ntsoha have tried to face up to their difficulties. Europeans like Cailliet, from whom I have quoted, tend to treat such Malagasies as no more than half-civilized people who have ill digested the education we have given them, as pseudo-intellectuals whose lucubrations are devoid of interest. Such an attitude is not only uncharitable; it is wholly unacceptable. A Malagasy like Dama Ntsoha is an authentic product of our activity and influence. We cannot disinherit him on the grounds that he does not sufficiently resemble us. We could, of course, have Europeanized him completely and made him write exactly like a colonial administrator; we could then have counted him to our credit as a success. But instead we were content to plunge him into a state of confusion beyond our imagining, and left him to find his own way out. If the paths he tries seem absurd to us, that is because we fail to see quite how lost he is. He has become what he is through reacting to our presence; neither the administration nor the Europeans really know what this reaction means, for they are still thinking in terms of assimilation, even though they say they have given it up as an objective. In the future, however, we shall have to deal more and more with Malagasies who have this new kind of personality, for it is we who cause them to develop. We may recall Cailliet's description, in 1924, of 'those people of strange psychology whom we come across nowadays among the Merina; they behave like ancestors, have the manners of foreigners and serve an outmoded custom', and he added, without apparent logic, that there would emerge from them 'a crop of national heroes'. But the inference is perfectly logical and Cailliet's intuition was quite sound.

It is unwise, therefore, for experts in Malagasy affairs to ignore the 'semi-evolved' Malagasies and to concentrate instead on elucidating the statements of Adrianampoinimerina, now more than a century old, simply because they do not give them that disagreeable impression that modern Malagasies do, of aping Europeans. We must also try to understand the 'lucubrations' of our 'colonizees' in their confusion, for they fully warrant it. Psychiatrists of earlier days used to try to cure delusions by an appeal to common-sense, and when that failed they lost their temper with such stupidity and resorted to the strait-jacket. We should take care lest our colonial attitude should one day appear equally hasty and ill-judged.

There is much in what Dama Ntsoha has to say and we should remember Cailliet's words; from 'strange psychology' to 'national hero'. . . . *Up to now* the Malagasies have moved forward by leaning on ourselves, by making use of the image they have formed of us to protect themselves against the fearful feeling of abandonment. Now we want them to take responsibility into their own hands without falling back on the protective images of the past. They are no doubt capable of doing it, but we cannot rightly appreciate the efforts they are making unless we are fully aware of the difficulties they are bound to encounter.

CHAPTER VI

THE EXPERIMENTAL SPIRIT

THERE is a link between the democratic spirit and the experimental spirit as we know it; both spring from the same source in the 'civilized' personality. The movement which led Europeans away from the Aristotelian tradition carried them forward towards the democratic and the experimental simultaneously.

Sociologists have observed that, lacking this scientific sense, which would at first sight seem so easy to acquire, a non-civilized person refuses to acknowledge as facts things which happen under his very eyes in what we would call the natural course of events. It was their astonishment at this impenetrability which led the sociologists early in their investigations to attribute to backward groups a pre-logical mentality incapable of assimilation to our own. They even went so far as to declare that this mentality was characterized by disregard for the principle of non-contradiction, which philosophers consider to be the basis of all logical thinking.

Nowadays we know that this interpretation was false, and the sociologists themselves have admitted it. To take a famous example, when the Bororo Indians maintained that they were parrots—*arara*—they made a statement we found unacceptable; but the reason lay not in the form of the statement or the logical structure of their thinking—for we, too, say: ice is water, or: water is hydrogen and oxygen, which is equally contradictory in *form*—but in the difference between their attitude to experience and our own. We base our assertions on a certain type of experience which may be called positive or technical, whereas the Bororo Indian bases his on his experience of dreams or totemic dances, and trusts blindly to tradition.

It was Lévy-Bruhl who first postulated as a working hypothesis the heterogeneity of the various types of conceptual thinking. Between 1910 and 1922 he no doubt gained—and certainly gave—the impression that his hypothesis was confirmed by the observations brought back by various travellers. After 1922, however, his approach became more subtle and finally he came to admit that the peculiar characteristics of 'primitive' thinking resided, not in its logical structure, but in the experience on which it was based. He conceived the idea of a *mystical experience* peculiar to backward peoples, an experience differing fundamentally from our own by virtue of this mystical element; reference to this theory is made in the lecture on the Primitive Mentality which he delivered in Oxford in 1931.[1]

But careful examination of the facts will show that this idea of mystical experience has little value as an explanation. When a Malagasy dreams about a dead ancestor his 'experience' is one which could equally well happen to ourselves. The experience will disturb us, too, to an extent depending on our emotional state at the time. But however disturbing it may be, the average European will usually manage to persuade himself not to believe it, whereas the average Malagasy *always* believes his dreams. So, then, the difference lies less in the nature of the experience than in the state of what classical psychology calls the beliefs. True, it is very difficult for anyone equipped only with the methods of this classical psychology to find out much about the real nature of the beliefs, for it always tries to attach them either to knowledge or to free will. It was because he tacitly admitted the postulates of classical psychology that Lévy-Bruhl was led to seek an explanation of the 'primitives'' beliefs in each of the two components of knowledge in turn: first, logical structure (he talked of pre-logic) and secondly, experience (he called it mystical). He thought it unnecessary—and rightly so—to consider the third hypothesis of this psychology and look for the operation of the will. Once these suppositions are set aside, however, it is possible to find a new way of analysing the primitive's attitude to experience without resorting either to the idea of pre-logic or to that of mysticism.

The philosophers, forgetting how much stress pre-scientific

[1] Lévy-Bruhl's position can be summed up, without risk of over-simplification, by saying that he tacitly accepted an empiricism which reduced knowledge to sensations and the tautological principle of identity; to this positive knowledge he tried to add, in contrast, a mode of thinking of an entirely different kind, to which he gave the name of mystical (his successors called it *mythical*).

This position is untenable, because whatever is presented as empirical data, the *things* must be accepted and the appearances rejected. The philosophers would have us do this on the basis of certain lists or forms which, under whatever name they are disguised, are evidently mere embellishments of Plato's Ideas or Aristotle's categories.

What I am trying to show in what follows is that the structure of reality—that is, the way in which we organize appearances in order to apprehend the things themselves is determined by the structure of our own personalities, or, by the way in which we have arranged our fears and desires in relation to the social environment.

philosophy had laid on the ambiguity and deceptiveness of everyday experience, came to exaggerate the importance of the impact of that experience on the mind. Modern science was the result, not of a change in the nature of experience but of a change in the attitude of the observer. Before this change came about—and it was a change affecting the whole structure of the personality—man had learned not to heed, or to heed as little as possible, the daily lessons of the world of sense-perception, and these lessons had not by themselves the power to command his attention. It is hardly surprising, then, that we should find among peoples who are very far from being, in any sense of the word, primitive, peoples who cannot even be called backward and of whom all we can say is that they have only recently been touched by Western civilization—it is hardly surprising that we should find this same imperviousness to experience even among their more Europeanized members. Certain Merina doctors, for instance, though trained in our methods, still believe in magic. (Of course it is not impossible to imagine a European believing in magic too, but in that case he would be very far from typical, whereas the Malagasy in so behaving is doing no more than the majority of his fellows.) The fact is that the scientific education we give the Malagasies may very well be superimposed on their ancient beliefs without contradicting them. When a man's beliefs are based on a recital of imaginary facts it is perfectly easy for him to add on scientific truths as part of the whole folklore; they tend to enrich and to some extent to *confirm* instead of invalidating it, as we are all too prone to believe.[1] The success of scientific demonstrations, of which Maurice Leenhardt gives us some striking examples in *Do Kamo*, clearly shows that peoples who are prepared to adopt our civilization are prepared to accept some of our truths, too, and even to abandon some of their errors (though not on any important point). They are the more ready to do it, moreover, in so far as they see no reason why they should give up their attitude as a whole, however much 'contrary to experience' it may appear to us to be.

There must be some obstacle in the human psyche which prevents the development of the experimental spirit. It does not prevent new truths being admitted, even if they are the product of scientific experiment, so long as they can be added on to the corpus of old-established beliefs, but it is firmly opposed to the adoption of an

---

[1] We can see all around us how progress in the physical sciences can strengthen certain occultist convictions rather than discredit them. . . .

attitude whereby every belief is examined in the light of experience. Even among Europeans the great majority are still unable to adopt this attitude in its entirety, and it is even doubtful whether it can truly be regarded as an ideal. But that it is an ideal which the European entertains with regard to that part of the field of knowledge with which he is most familiar there is no denying. When, in the pursuit of this ideal, we come up against the unconscious obstacle we tend to mistake its nature and to explain it away as laziness, lack of intelligence, or sheer habit—as some deficiency—which the force of logic, the impact of experience or even the moral obligation to learn will overcome. But the psychologist wonders why habit, laziness, or lack of intelligence stood in the way and where the obligation comes from.

In the history of Western knowledge, elegance and profundity, the aristocratic attributes of thought, have always been on the side of the rationalists, and so mathematicians and astronomers have always been in a privileged position. The empiricists have always been opposers, heretics, sceptics. Every means has been employed to discourage scientific curiosity: to stick to the *words* and leave the *things* alone has been considered the right attitude. To look and examine carefully has been thought to show a lack of respect and proper humility—an impious attitude.

The reader will no doubt be reminded of prohibitions in the sexual sphere, for seeing, touching, and knowing are desires with very definite objects in the young child. But this is not an easy matter to elucidate, for the obstacles to the development of sexual knowledge are certainly no greater in non-civilized than in civilized persons—rather the contrary, in fact. But it is precisely the intensification of prohibitions in modern societies which has led to the recent outbursts of experimental curiosity as a gesture of protest and self-assertion. People mistrust tradition as they would untruthful parents, and only believe what they can see for themselves. This agrees with what I have said in Chapter VI about the importance of the acceptance of abandonment in the development of the personality. I am not mentioning this matter here for its own sake, however, but only in order to show that backward peoples, though they lack neither logic nor intelligence, and though nature offers them as many lessons as she bestows on anyone else, are unable to move forward because they have not yet freed their personalities from an obstacle which we have succeeded in surmounting. Before we could do so, however, we had to pass through religious and social upheavals such that our personalities emerged with an entirely new structure. Auguste Comte's Law of the Three Stages is not acceptable as such because Comte, believing that the emotions were not brought directly into play, saw development only as a succession of different systems of conceptual thinking. In reality the sociological stages of mankind are essentially the product of changes in the structure of the personality as a whole; they cannot be described simply in relation to the various dogmas or ideologies (even if they are 'positive') which human intelligence has contrived from time to time.

The experimental spirit presupposes a certain attitude to reality. A realist would say that the scientific mind strips reality of all that is inessential and seizes it in its purity. But we do not know what reality is, essentially, and it would be better to say that it is we who strip and purify ourselves, for then at least we should be confronted with a reality which is what it is and nothing else—self-sufficient, constant in its behaviour, to be relied on so long as we take account of its laws and not in so far as we fear, flatter, adjure, threaten, or worship it. There is a clear connexion between the concept held of reality and the structure of the personality which holds it. The scientific man forms an image in which he sees himself as independent, self-sufficient, and obedient to the laws of reason and not to those of irrational sentiment. It may well be objected that this is not a portrait of his real personality but his ideal of himself. Nevertheless it is true that as, in experience, nature is divided up into self-sufficient parts, each of which in isolation reveals the working of the universal laws, so the experimentalist sees the human group divided up and himself as self-sufficient in his isolation and in harmony with the universal laws of reason without the intermediary of God or the ancestors and without acceptance of dependence on family, society, or any sort of authority. Thence arises an equality of value between all men, a principle of liberty inherent in each individual, and a Universal Reason whose projection to the realm of the infinite shows that it is simply parallel to individual reasons and not the centre from which they spring.

Thus, whatever obstacle it is that hinders the development of the experimental spirit, it is the same as that which the personality encounters when it endeavours to escape dependence. A study of the history of experimental method from this angle would no doubt reveal how this obstacle was gradually removed from the psyche of

Western man. Nor is there any conflict between my explanation and
the theory that it was their social structure which prevented past
civilizations developing scientific techniques and undertaking experimental research—the fact that they were based on slavery, or con-
quest, or mercantilism, or that the mechanical arts carried no prestige
in them. On the contrary, my analysis could help us to understand
how it is that the structure of a society can hinder the development of
the experimental attitude—for the social structure itself cannot prevent an alchemist, a research worker, or a curious-minded person
interrogating nature if he has the time—but the imprint of that
structure on his personality may prevent him obtaining positive
information from his interrogation. Positive science would have
encountered many more difficulties at the outset if mathematics, the
science of reason and socially acceptable, had not given it indirect
assistance. In ancient times Archimedes introduced experiment
covertly into the mathematical citadel, but the obstacles were such
that his example was not followed for some two thousand years.

There is, I believe, no way other than this of explaining both the
difficulties which the experimental attitude once encountered in
Europe and those which it is encountering to-day in the backward
countries. D. Westermann, in his book, *Noirs et Blancs en Afrique*,
says that the idea of an event occurring as a result of inner necessity or
natural law is wholly foreign to the negro because his thoughts and
his imagination depend primarily on his sense-impressions; behind
each event he sees 'the one who caused it'; if a tree or a person dies it
is because someone, ghostly or human, made them die; personal will
is substituted for inner necessity or natural causes. . . . But the facts
the author relates refute the explanation he offers. If the negro
attributes the most obvious occurrences to some invisible personal
cause, it cannot be because his thinking is too much the product of
sense-impressions. The author must have conceived such an explanation because he felt an unconscious urge to deplore the exercise of the
senses, in accordance with a tradition which goes back to Plato and
which runs completely counter to experience. The explanation contains a moral judgement. I shall not risk analysing the psychology of
the African negro, about whom I know nothing, but if it is true that
he personifies causes, the reason should be sought in some attachment to persons—an attachment which might conceivably be comparable with the dependence complex as I have described it.

I have said that the impact of experience is not of itself enough to transform the personality; but some pressure is exerted all the same, and even the most 'primitive' man cannot be wholly insensible to a genuine experience. He is not able to draw from it the inferences we should draw, but it is not without effect on him. The rebels who believed that the *ody basy* would protect them from bullets belonged to groups which had not been much affected by colonization. At first they put their disappointments down to the poor quality of the *ody* and they blamed their sorcerers.[1] But the frequency of their failure—of course, as always, there were times when chance created an appearance of success—finally shook their faith. There is a story told, though I have not been able to verify it, that a group of sorcerers who had faith in the power of their *ody* openly defied the rifle-fire and were killed. For the witnesses that should have been a decisive test and conclusive proof that the bullets were more powerful than the *ody*. But one piece of evidence is not enough to alter the whole mentality while the structure of the personality remains the same. The episode was far from being what the European might imagine it, a crucial experience deciding the issue once for all between magic and science. It was simply a trial of strength between the *ody* and the rifle. Respect for the rifle might have grown, but there can be no real question of mental progress. If, then, the pressure of experience can affect the personality, it will be only after a great period of time, and probably only then if the personality has been disturbed by some other means and is already in a state of change. This is the case, in fact, with peoples who are already thoroughly 'colonized'; with them it should be possible to use the scientific approach as a powerful and effective adjunct to the evolutionary process. One must be cautious, however, in making any such forecast; until a short while ago not one European in Madagascar would have believed that even the most backward tribes were capable of marching into fire armed only with a blind faith in the power of the *ody*. The rebels included a number of men—servants of Europeans, old soldiers, bearers, and so on—who were familiar with rifles from their own experience and would never ordinarily have placed any confidence in the *ody*. The ease with which they underwent a total regression came as a complete surprise.

In occidental societies there are still some archaic personalities:

---

[1] Colonials tend to take the sorcerers for agitators; it is more likely, however, that they were sought out by the rebels who felt a need for guidance and protection against the anguish of their guilt.

they are usually attracted into politics [1]—which is one of the reasons for the troubles of our present civilization. These archaic and infantile personalities set out to influence public opinion, to win confidence, to compose differences, to split the opposition, and so on. In other words, they play upon the emotions of the masses and have no interest in the technical means of reaching real solutions—or only in so far as public opinion requires it of them. More highly developed personalities, however—those less adept at these political gymnastics—see society as one of the things which can be experimented with, and men, though bound by certain very definite laws, as free and independent outside those laws. A worker, for instance, may be bound to his employer by his contract, but outside the circumstances laid down in that contract they are perfectly free to ignore each other, in absolute independence and equality. *The characteristics of the scientific approach to reality are in fact the same as those of democratic society and of the highly-developed personality*: it might be interesting to find out how the processes of introjection, projection, and identification contribute to these parallels. In the other direction, it is easy to show that for those who have not reached a high degree of development of the personality, objects, like persons, are seen in terms of dependence. Indeed, 'everything depends on everything else' might well be considered a definition of magic.

It is clear, then, that the Malagasy worker is not at present capable of being bound to his employer by definite rules, and for the rest, independent. His dependence is as complete as that of the child on his parents (they owe it to him to provide him with everything he needs and he owes everything to them, and yet is not responsible in any degree. Even law, as we know, stops at the threshold of the home. The father was once all-powerful, and even now the law can be invoked only in exceptional circumstances. For the rest, it is confined, or very nearly, to checking the accounts and seeing that the obligations of guardianship have been fulfilled.). Employers who are aware of this situation take advantage of it. Those who are

[1] A. Hesnard writes in *Freud dans la société d'après-guerre* (p. 92): 'The day will come when the masses will understand that these chiefs who have risen pathologically from their midst are all, in spite of their prestige in another age, abnormal people, barbarians thrown up regressively in the course of the progressive development and liberation of society.'

I believe that these regressions are caused by the existence in one part of the population of a more or less repressed need for dependence and in another part of a need for domination, which can be satisfied only by identification with a leader. They show how recent and fragile, even among the civilized, are the liberation and reconstruction of the personality on experimental, democratic foundations.

not, however kind and generous they may be, find their workers leaving them 'for no reason at all', and showing resentment towards them, what is more.

The relationship between one man and another can be such that there is no emotional reaction to that other; he is neither to be loved nor feared, neither cajoled nor threatened; some authority can be exercised over him but only in certain conditions; he, too, can exercise a certain authority but again only within limits. *Once the capacity to enter into such a relationship with men and things has been acquired, the dependence complex can be dissolved and the way is open for the attainment of a free and independent personality, a scientific approach to reality and a democratic society.*

If these are to be our goals, what are the best means by which we can reach them? Should we encourage economic activity, or political sparring in defence of party interests, or should we foster the practice of techniques based on the lessons of experience? Or would it, perhaps, be better to develop all these activities simultaneously, since they are, as it were, sectors on a common front?

The European worker is trained in two schools: the one, that of apprenticeship, makes him independent of the world of things and enables him to escape from bondage to them through consciousness of his technical skills; the other, that of the family, first places him within a system of personal dependences and then teaches him how to free himself from them. Colonial society, however, gives the dependent person nothing but his dependence. When confronted with reality he has no feeling of liberation; his tools and his technical knowledge give him no sense of mastery—tools are simply an extension of the master's orders, technique just a set of rules to be obeyed; his hands are still the hands of a slave.

There is no doubt that mass-production and over-specialization could create an analogous situation in the West, and enslave the worker, but there would remain one paramount difference: the occidental would always feel the pull of liberty; he would thirst for justice. These demands of his are psychologically linked with his feeling of inferiority. Inferiority is the price he pays for his aspirations and ambitions and his will to power, all of which are excluded from the purview of the dependent being. The latter, with no urge to anything beyond everyday life, and wrapped in emotional comfort, represents a stable and homogeneous phase in human development— or so it appeared a few years ago, and might perhaps even to-day to someone from Mars. We Europeans, however, have cast the seeds of our own restlessness into this tranquil world. We offer palliatives at the same time, it is true, and among them the democratic ideal and the scientific spirit. But the European colonial is himself more powerfully affected than the native by the new situation and he soon loses the qualities he acquired in Europe; he tends to give up the democratic attitude for paternalism and his faith in experience for Prospero's magic. This reversal is a direct consequence of the difficulty of the task assumed; it is a reaction from failure in the endeavour to create a type of inter-racial relationship which the European colonial found it too difficult to sustain.

CHAPTER VII

THE UNITY OF MANKIND

IN his essay, *The Relation of the Ego to the Unconscious*, C. G. Jung says: 'Viewed from a relatively safe distance, say from Central Africa or Tibet, it would almost seem as though this fragment of humanity (Europe) had projected upon peoples still sound in their instincts an unconscious "mental derangement".' This sentence takes us straight to the heart of the matter; for it is true that by and large our image of these peoples is simply a reflection of our own inner difficulties. Thus, 'colonial problems' stem from conflicts within European civilization itself, and the racialist reactions of the white man to the black are the product of elements already present in his psyche.

We must beware, however, of seizing upon this topographical distinction between internal and external in order to explain offences by finding a moral substratum for them and thus 'situating' responsibility. We ought to be able to manipulate the idea of an inter-racial situation without its crumbling the moment we begin analysing it because of that over-moralistic attitude the 'civilized' man is too prone to adopt. Of course if we were to adopt such an attitude in perfect honesty it would compel us to withdraw within ourselves and to try to conquer ourselves rather than fortune and to change our desires rather than world order. It is doubtful, however, whether this process would materially improve the situation, for it would probably make us avoid inter-human relationships and put our heads in the sand—or become hermits like Descartes—whereas it should be possible for us to overcome the risks and dangers of such situations without either running away or refusing to be drawn into them.

Nevertheless in order to be able to analyse these situations in *psychological* terms we should, I think, have to adopt some sort of metaphorical topography because we should need to know where the different traits of behaviour we wanted to understand 'came from'. But so many theoretical difficulties would arise—the meaning of causality, for instance, and the need to strip this vague notion of all its associations with another and if possible even vaguer notion, that of responsibility—that it would be an almost hopeless task.

Fortunately, however, our real problem is somewhat different. It is not really necessary for us to find a psychological explanation for the facts of colonization; what we need to know is why we perceive these facts in a distorted fashion. After all, psychology can teach us very little about accurate perception; but it alone can explain the deceptions to which the senses are subject (there would have been no Gestalt psychology had it not been for the study of the *relief* of flat images). Psychology cannot tell us much about sound reasoning, but it alone can make sense of a delirium. Similarly, only psychology can explain how and why a colonial situation so easily deteriorates into one of error and illusion, and this is precisely the job psychoanalysis should perform in the study of such situations.

Psychologically, then, errors of perception in colonial matters may well be, as Jung suggests, the result of the projection on to the object of some defect which is properly attributable to the subject. But the projection is not quite as he describes it. He thinks of people not yet influenced by European civilization as being 'still sound in their instincts', and that is a form of primitivism. The belief in primitivism, as I explained earlier, takes two opposite forms; on the one hand there are those who, like Jung, think that this youthfulness of the instincts represents health and normality, and on the other those who see it as barbarousness and brutality. And these are more or less the two opposite attitudes men take of Nature, though there is no objective justification for either; the choice is decided for each man by the attitude he spontaneously adopts towards his own nature, or rather towards that confused picture he has in his imagination of his own instincts, of his own *id*. The Jungian attitude is in effect a search for a lost innocence, for a return to the happy intimacy of mother and child—and it produces an equally false picture of 'savage' man as the opposite attitude. It is also equally likely to end in failure; Prospero's relationship with Ariel, for instance, was as *unreal* as his relationship with Caliban. What we project on to the colonial inhabitant, in fact, is not our 'mental derangement', but our most elementary and deeply-hidden fears and desires, the primal Good and Evil, not as a philosopher might see them, but rather as they might appear to a child in a dream, or as Shakespeare and Daniel Defoe saw them.

Every human face appears enigmatic to us at first. An analysis of the rules of politeness of different countries would show this. It can also be seen from the way a small child, when confronted with an unknown face with no particular expression on it, will hesitate anxiously for a while and then suddenly either smile or burst into tears. Although we cannot vouch for what is going on in his mind at that moment, it seems probable that the face becomes meaningful *to him* just then and that he *makes* it either friendly or unfriendly, so to speak, from inside himself.

That, no doubt, is the beginning of all misunderstandings between human beings; it has been described in four lines by an author who was evidently much preoccupied with such questions, since he invented the double character of Jekyll and Hyde. In a romance called *The Pavilion on the Links*, Stevenson's hero tells how he first met the woman he was later to marry. It is night-time; the hero is in hiding and the young woman comes along carrying a lantern: 'She was extremely pale; but in the light of the lantern her face was so marred by strong and changing shadows, that she might equally well have been as ugly as sin or as beautiful as I afterwards found her to be.'

In the same way the face of the 'savage' or the 'black man' rouses in us at first this anxious hesitation, and makes us doubt ourselves. We do not want it said that, like children, we are frightened of the faces we have ourselves made terrifying, so we prefer to maintain that this unpleasant thing stirring to life in ourselves is due to something evil in the black man before us or to some quality inherent in his race or tribe. Naturally, once we begin to doubt ourselves when confronted with a human being of a type so different from our own, all kinds of things become possible. Sometimes, before this highly revealing mirror, the white man comes to see himself as he really is, which is what happened to Robert Louis Stevenson and perhaps to Rimbaud. It may explain the story of Lord Jim. But very few men are capable, when they are at length obliged to acknowledge the existence of other people, of recognizing in themselves what they never suspected was there, without an outburst of the fear, hatred, or harshness they had directed towards an aspect of themselves which in very truth they had wanted to ignore. On waking to the real situation they will find themselves pursuing a type of colonial life which may lie anywhere between evangelism and sheer brutality, depending on the way they dealt with this internal threat— with an inflexible will or with scorn, ignoring it or reconciling themselves to it.

When Stevenson was just about to land on a Pacific island, a woman passenger asked him how the natives were dressed. All he said was that they did not wear trousers. This joke was more cruel than he supposed, for the feelings it called up—feelings whose existence was perhaps already betrayed by the question—could not but have been extremely painful at that time to anyone brought up in a certain moral atmosphere. It is probably true to say that all the savagery attributed to Oceania is due rather to this kind of feeling than to any peculiarity of the islands' natural inhabitants.

Nowadays this illusion is expressed in other ways, but it remains the same in its essential nature. Nor is it specifically colonial: it can be found almost anywhere, for it is only too human. Cases are known in mental pathology, for instance—indeed, they are met with in everyday life—where a woman will project all her (imaginary) vices on to her bitch [1] and make the wretched animal the very incarnation of impurity; she will then send it to the vet for an injection, thereby hoping to recover her own lost innocence. The psychological mechanism is that of human sacrifice. Now the colonial situation offers us expiatory victims at little cost. It also brings these mechanisms into play in the European, particularly during periods of emotional disturbance, through the ambiguity of the faces confronting him, the anxiety roused in him by his encounter with unfamiliar customs, the sense of insecurity which naturally results from expatriation and finally, through the operation of the unconscious forces which are powerfully at work in him and which were originally responsible for his leaving Europe.

We can explore the retinas of our own eyes by looking at a piece of white paper; if we look at a black man we shall perhaps find out something about our own unconscious—not that the white man's image of the black man tells us anything about his own inner self, though it indicates that part of him which he has not been able to accept: it reveals his secret self, not as he is, but rather as he fears he may be. The negro, then, is the white man's fear of himself. This fear may have been well camouflaged, and its sudden appearance is all the more of a shock for its having gone unrecognized in other circumstances. The rift between man and man which racialism indicates, with all its confused emotional force, thus reflects an inner conflict in which we are divided against ourselves.

[1] A case of this kind is described in detail in *La Jalousie amoureuse*, by Professor Lagache. I have myself recorded a case of a Mulatto woman who kept a female monkey as her screen! This was at the same time a caricatural display of racialism.

This shows us what part is played by the psychological explanation. Corresponding to the abstract concept of humanity seen as a biological species, there is an abstract concept of the individual who is considered to be unified by the metaphysical 'I think'. But whatever the formula employed, this purely theoretical unification of the individual necessarily leaves out of account all emotional conflicts. Similarly if humanity is seen as an abstract unity it can, theoretically, be rent only by an external clash, and not by some essential inner conflict. Any study in this field will be falsified from the start if it tacitly admits these abstract concepts, for it will then be of the 'broad principle' school, which treats real conflicts as chance occurrences outside the scope of its theories, and such a procedure can only give free rein to the most troublesome and irresponsible forces.

These concepts of the abstract unity of man as species and as individual are nothing but idealist constructs, whatever other names they may be given. They are simply fiats of the mind and, like all such, are liable to be flouted by everyday facts. We can only begin to perceive how in practice the individual or mankind could be unified by examining actual concrete situations; and we should probably find that the two unifications demanded roughly the same conditions. Psychology requires us to undertake this concrete examination, for it would be very risky to try to construct an anthropological or an ethnographical system which was not to be wholly academic, while leaving aside as merely accidental all those human conflicts which are to be found in the individual and in the world at large.

The above considerations are valid for all inter-human situations, of which the colonial situation is, as it were, a caricature, because it magnifies all the elements. They explain colonial racialism, interracial suspicion and hatred and the urge to exercise absolute authority; they explain, too, the submissiveness of the colonial native and his occasional outbreaks, his docility, which is something different from our discipline, and his nationalism which is different from ours.

There is, however, one aspect of colonization which these observations do not seem to explain, and that is the fact of economic exploitation, which is characterized by the maintenance of a very low standard of living. Owing to a system which allows a colony to have a 'prosperous' economy although none of the profits can be realized in the country, the average Malagasy is rather poorer to-day than he was in the time of Galliéni, which is enough to explain his indifference to the methods we use and the efforts we deploy to 'develop' his country.

Economic questions are certainly very important; they may not absolutely determine the future of the colonial peoples, but that future will undoubtedly depend on them to a very great extent. I ought therefore to explain why they are given so little space in this book. It is because economic explanations are too general in their application to account very accurately for the facts of colonization: economic exploitation occurs wherever political and social conditions favour it, in the colonies as elsewhere. In the colonies, however, its character changes and it becomes colonial exploitation. But economic concepts cannot explain this change. It can be explained, however, if we take account of the colonial situation as I have analysed it—that is, as a special type of inter-human relationship. As I said earlier: to say that the negro is unhappy because he is exploited is undoubtedly true, but it is an incomplete truth unless we add that he is exploited because he is a negro. And the whole truth, probably, is that the colonial situation created by the encounter between white and coloured men is exploited by economic forces which in themselves have nothing to do with the colonies, except in so far as the latter constitute a remote and, for those concerned, abstract source of profit. A deaf man, after all, can make a living by exploiting concert-halls without understanding or needing to understand why the public is so ready to part with its money. Similarly, those who exploit a colonial situation do not know and do not wish to know the real reasons why they can get rich so quickly in this way. The way they influence 'colonial policy' to serve their own interests, ruining colonials as well as natives as often as not, shows that for them the colonies are just a business like any other, in which every man tries to perpetuate the conditions which are advantageous to him and resists changes which will 'cost money'. Their overriding interest is profit and they are not spontaneously racialist; they become so only upon the persuasion of their account books, rather as our deaf man might develop a weakness for Mozart if the Mozart concerts produced the best returns. Now, it so happens that once a colonial situation has been established, it can be exploited very profitably, and that accounts for one form of colonialism, a form which may do a great deal of harm. The real colonialist, however, is part and parcel of the colonial situation itself; he it is who alters that situation and renders it exploitable, though he himself may derive little enough profit from it.

If we were to take any example of colonial economy and to set the exploiters on one side and the exploited on the other, we should find that the population was not evenly divided into blacks and whites. We should also find that the whites whose profits are only middling are more fanatical racialists than those who get rich, that it is easier for people to get rich if they confine their interest to the purely business aspect of their activity and refrain from any racial discrimination, and that if this attitude is very rare it is not because the colonialists do not realize this fact but because they hold impassioned views. Europeans have been known to leave Europe in order to make a fortune in Madagascar and, having made their fortune and returned to Europe, to have experienced such nostalgia that they have gone back to Madagascar even though they had sold everything up. Others, on the other hand, have been ruined and their businesses have collapsed and yet they have stayed on in Madagascar because they 'could not afford' to return to Europe. What keeps the real colonial tied to the colonial situation, then, is not primarily profit, whatever he himself may think. If he has lazy slaves instead of efficient workers it is because he does not particularly want the latter; he derives greater satisfaction from keeping his slaves. Naturally he would prefer it if his slaves worked *like* employees, but he will not sacrifice the satisfaction of being absolute master: he would rather forego the profit.

Those are the factors which give the economy its *colonial* character; they explain why the native is exploited in a different way from the white man. The white colonial, moreover, is clearly conscious that he, too, is being exploited, though more anonymously, by Europe. He is aware that up to a certain point he is one, *economically*, with the native, but he cannot admit this, or the psychological satisfactions which are more precious to him than gold would vanish overnight.

It should thus be clear what makes a colonial situation so easy to exploit: it is the fact that the inhabitants of the colony, the blacks and the whites, are divided amongst themselves and that there is no possibility of concord between them; the fact that the natives are denied their rights, not because this pays, but simply because they are natives; the fact that the standard of living is kept low because the native will put up with it just because he is a native. . . .

In spite of the paramount importance of economic conditions, therefore, they will not explain why colonial exploitation is different from exploitation pure and simple, why the native is a slave and not a proletarian, why the colonial is father-and-mother and not employer, for when we seek to discover what those who take the trouble to perpetuate such a situation gain from it, we find that it is not greater profit, but satisfactions the value of which cannot be entered in the books.

There was once a law in Ethiopia according to which a creditor might attach his debtor to him by means of a chain. Thus they were both in exactly the same situation, but in this situation the debtor was to be pitied, whereas the creditor, on the other hand, gained some satisfaction. This illustrates, in its pure state, the satisfaction of the master who owns a slave. And even though it concerns a creditor, no economist can explain it. Economics can tell us how a man can dominate other men in order to acquire greater wealth, but it has very little to say about a man who uses his economic superiority simply for the pleasure of enslaving another man. It is essential, however, to take this sort of pleasure into account in any attempt to understand what is colonial about a colonial situation.

There is, moreover, considerable danger in adhering too closely to the economic explanation, for it implies that colonization would have been a good thing if it had been economically honest, if lust for gain had not falsified the accounts, if the colonizers had been economically disinterested. But there have been cases of this kind, instances where small tribes were colonized, at least for a time, by men interested not primarily in profit but in converting or evangelizing.[1] Their 'honesty', however, did not prevent them creating ill-starred inter-human situations. Honesty of their kind in fact is not enough to bring about the unification of mankind through the unification of the human being. This is an attainable ideal, and humanity has already made visible progress towards it, through wars, revolutions, and conflicts of all kinds. The mistakes and failures of colonial policy may simply be some of the painful steps we are taking along this road.

[1] In certain Pacific islands it was not economic exploitation which decimated, or even exterminated the population, but our moral attitude, the conscientiousness with which we condemned beliefs and customs which were in fact the life-blood of the native peoples.

Dependence and civilization

While trying to explain the nature of the phenomena of inter-racial psychology as they appear in a colonial situation, where they are exaggerated as a result of the great difference in the degree of development of the two civilizations, I have found myself, without intending it, describing the human personality and its development. I have not been trying to prove a theory or maintain a thesis, but simply to present things in a new light.

I have tried to show how, in the development of the personality, the personal emerges from the collective and becomes distinct from it by accreting to the individual. It never detaches itself completely, however, for it was formed in the collective and always retains, in some form or other, some residue of the original attachments.[1] These attachments are biologically necessary, moreover, at least for a time, because of the naturally dependent situation of the young child. The personality first begins to develop in the dependent world of childhood and the adult's social relationships or, more simply, his relations with other adults, are determined more or less directly by the later history of the original attachments—by their conservation or their transformation.

This proposition appears to be valid for animal psychology, too, for it is a fact that the only animals which can truly be tamed are those species whose young are for a time dependent on the mother or the parental couple, and they are confined almost exclusively to mammals and birds. The rest can only be trained. I think it can be accepted that taming is simply the artificial prolongation of the childhood bonds of dependence, and that human sociability has the same biological origin.

During the long periods of stability through which the so-called 'primitive' civilizations have passed, no problem arises; society is so organized that the bonds of dependence remain unbroken and indeed they form the basis of the personalities typical of such civilizations. Abandonment is inconceivable; the social structure necessarily affords everyone a place, and no one can live without the emotional comfort derived from an unequivocal attachment to it, no matter how society is organized. The individual can only be encouraged

[1] These attachments are not exactly the first expressions of the *libido* in relation to the world of things; they are something deeper, the *libido* itself, rather, in its search for expression.

to move outside the familiar framework with the aid of magical substitution-phenomena; the substitutes, real or imaginary, are invested with the power of protecting the isolated individual.

The evolving civilizations of the West are radically different from those in that the typical occidental succeeds in integrating abandonment into his personality. Integration is made possible by the introjection of the parental images, and it in turn makes possible the placing of confidence in techniques guaranteed by positive laws and verified by experience. But this result has been achieved only after a prolonged crisis, or rather a series of crises separated by intervals of calm. The structure of the typical personality underwent radical changes in the course of those crises—changes in which religious ideas played an important part. As a result, the occidental of to-day can face situations he would not have dared to contemplate some centuries ago—not without anguish of course, but at least with an anguish he is able to master. He feels that he and all his civilization have been launched towards some chance goal which he cannot yet glimpse or guess at because evolution itself must create it. At the same time he feels more and more master of his fate and claims responsibility for it. Events have very often cruelly belied this feeling, but it is still the only possible basis for our personalities, or so we think, and it may be that we are not entirely deceiving ourselves. Certain it is, however, that no man reaches such a situation by simply following his instincts or his natural tendencies, or even the voice of reason. He must first have seen himself, however dimly, in history. Obviously we cannot expect peoples who are less far advanced along this road to place themselves in the same situation, not because they are insufficiently educated or lack the requisite technical equipment, but because their personalities have not yet acquired the necessary defences against the anguish of abandonment. Even the occidental personality sometimes finds its defences inadequate.

The need for attachments is perhaps one of the hereditary characteristics of mankind. Our society does not encourage such attachments but neither does it wholly discourage them, and we feel both compelled to sever our childhood bonds and guilty when we have severed them. We waver between the desire for a society, quite different from our own, in which the attachments will be preserved with the maximum of emotional comfort and stability, and the desire for complete individuation where the individual is radically independent and relies wholly on his courage, technical skill, and inventive powers. When the child suffers because he feels that the ties between himself and his parents are threatened and at the same time feels guilty because after all it is he who wants to break them, he reacts to the situation by dreaming of a world where there are no real bonds, a world which is entirely his and into which he can project the images of his unconscious, to which he is attached in the way which is to him the most satisfying. Now, it is this imaginary world which is, strictly speaking, the only 'primitive world' and it serves, so to speak, as the model of all other worlds. The dream-world in the child's mind exists side by side with the world of reality; it penetrates that world and organizes it emotionally and gradually it comes to coincide with it more or less exactly. During the transitional period the real world is felt to be full of angels, demons, and other mythical beings. It is this 'primitive' image of the world which we have in mind when we become explorers, ethnographers, or colonials and go amongst societies which seem to us to be less real than our own.

If the desire to break every attachment could be realized, it would lead to a sort of savage emancipation [1] of the adult of a kind seen only among certain species of animals. The completely detached person, however, remains a more or less ascetic ideal which has never been more than remotely approached. It is realized in a way, however, by the substitution of depersonalized links for the original attachments—the anonymous neighbour whom charity bids us love, the pin-up girl who can take the place of any man's *anima*, a regimental number towards which our duties have become purely abstract—all these, there is no doubt, are still persons, but only just enough to enable us to form unreal relationships with them, like Prospero's with Ariel or Crusoe's with Friday. They are embodiments of the primitive *socius*, who tends to become very nearly the pure individual. At the same time there has developed a concept of matter according to which all its parts are interchangeable. Persons and things have thereby been set free in a neutral space, and it is no coincidence that there has been a simultaneous rejection on the one hand of the hierarchical concept of things—high and low, appointed places, and so on—and on the other of authority, whether that of Aristotle or that of a king by divine right. This characteristic

[1] The use of the word 'savage', which I find necessary here, shows how we think of savagery as a solitary return to instinct after the childhood period of social life. Thus Defoe's myth explored all forms of savagery.

feature of Western civilization has given man a greater power of altering things and human groups than any the magicians could have dreamed of. The price he pays is acceptance of abandonment.

Modern society is determined in part by the childhood image of the primitive world: the undifferentiated crowd, as it has often been said (even by Descartes in a now famous letter),[1] affords the same emotional solitude as the desert island, and the same opportunities for projecting the images of the unconscious—the film-star and other such figures taking the place of Ariel and Friday. Nor is there any lack of other figures to represent Caliban or the Cannibals. Archaic societies are quite different; they are still governed by a sort of paternal authority, an authority which, however, in the final analysis, no one really exercises, for it has become formalized in the customs or lies hidden in the tombs.

As the *socius* becomes more and more impersonal, so rules of conduct become more and more abstract and almost, though not quite, as imperative as rules of law. Professed beliefs are judged in relation to dogmas, whereas in archaic societies beliefs are modes of being: they are customs, that is to say, but customs which are intimately bound up with the personality, or even part of it. It is unthinkable, therefore, to change them in the way opinions are changed: they can be changed only through a crisis, during which the old structure crumbles to make way for something new. We Europeans tend to think that a man can change his customs (which we are apt to identify with prejudices) by a simple act of will, because we do not imagine that the highest moral processes of the personality are much affected by such a change. But archaic personalities have no moral touchstone higher than the customs. They may modify them in appearance, to the point of persuading us to believe—and even themselves of believing—that they have abandoned them altogether, but so long as the basic structure remains they cannot truly be given up. The position of the archaic personality rather resembles that of the obsessional neurotic: the sick man can relinquish his habits only at the price of unbearable anguish. However, there is nothing pathological in the archaic civilizations; on the contrary, they are in fact very stable.

In our world the ideal of interchangeability has led to the development of deep and more or less repressed personalities with unsuspected originalities lying right outside the field of comparison.

[1] To Balzac, on 5 May 1631.

They may give rise to change and progress or to neuroses. Archaic personalities, however, exist only by virtue of the well-defined place they occupy in an unchanging whole, and it is that place which is instrumental in the first instance in giving them their form. They cannot contemplate leaving that place for another, except on very rare occasions, and that only with the help of magical ceremonies powerful enough to loosen the affective bonds. In such instances there results a sort of adaptation of the individual to his environment which the occidental can understand because he still remembers his lost dependence, which he may unconsciously regret all his life. But he has accepted abandonment and has learned to live in a sort of emotional vacuum, where yearnings towards perfection, the absolute and the infinite may take root and flourish. These yearnings have long been the core of an ideal which the civilizations of the West have cherished, whence are derived alike their success and their discontents.

BIBLIOGRAPHY

The following is a list of books and articles about the customs or the mentality of the Malagasies—or about the way in which Europeans have reacted to those customs and that mentality.

Allier (Raoul): *The Mind of the Savage.*

Augagneur: *Erreurs et brutalités coloniales* (Colonial Mistakes and Cruelties).

Aujas (L.): *Rites du sacrifice à Madagascar* (Sacrificial Rites in Madagascar).

Andriantsilaniarivo and Abraham (Ch.-E.): 'La Littérature Malgache' (Malagasy Literature), in *'Revue de Madagascar'*, July 1946.

Andriamifidy: 'Ny Hevitra Malagasy', in *Ny Mpanolo Tsaina*, 1905, p. 206, Antananarivo, 1905.

Barnaud: *Mon voyage à Madagascar* (My Journey to Madagascar), Paris, 1895.

Benevent (Ch.): 'La conception de la mort chez les Malgaches' (The Malagasies' Concept of Death), in *Revue de Madagascar*, September 1901.

Benyovsky: *Memoirs and Travels.*

Berthier (H.): *Notes sur les coutemes du peuple Malgache* (Notes on the Customs of the Malagasy People), Antananarivo, 1933.

Birkeli: *Les Vazimba de la Côte Ouest* (The Vazimba of the West Coast).

Boiteau (P.): 'La structure sociale' (The Social Structure), in *Revue de Madagascar*, January 1945, p. 39.

Boiteau (P.): 'La situation matérielle et morale des travailleurs Malgaches' (The Material and Moral Position of Malagasy Workers), *Esprit*, February 1948, p. 240.

Boudry (Robert): 'Le problème Malgache' (The Malagasy Problem), in *Esprit*, February 1948, p. 240.

Buet (Ch.): *Six mois à Madagascar* (Six Months in Madagascar), Paris, 1895.

Callet (Rev. Father): 'Tantaran'ny Andriana,' in *Bulletin de l'Académie Malgache*, 1913, vol. XII, pp. 21 f.

Callet (Rev. Father): 'Tantara,' ibid., 1919, pp. 92 f.

Cailliet (E.): *Essai sur la psychologie du Hova* (Essay on the Psychology of the Hova), Paris, 1924.

Cailliet (E.): *La foi des ancêtres* (Ancestor-worship), Paris, 1930.

Cameron (J.): *Recollection of Mission Life in Madagascar*, Antananarivo, 1874.

Camo (Pierre): *Madagascar*, 1928.

Carol (J.): *Chez les Hova* (Among the Hova), 1898.

'Chansons tsimihety' (Tsimihety Songs), in *Bulletin de l'Académie Malgache*, 1913, vol. XI.

Clark (H. E.): 'The Ancient Idolatry of the Hova', in *Antananarivo Annual*, 1885, p. 78.

'Convention de Fokon'olona à Tananarive en 1884 (Une)', in *Bulletin de l'Académie Malgache*, 1908, vol. III, p. 66.

Coppalle (A.): Voyage dans l'intérieur de Madagascar en 1825' (Journey in the Interior of Madagascar in 1825), in *Bulletin de l'Académie Malgache*, 1910, vol. VII, p. 25.

Cotte (Rev. Father Vincent): *Regardons vivre une tribu Malgache* (Let us See How a Malagasy Tribe Lives), Paris, 1947.

Council of the Republic: *Proceedings* of 18 and 24 July, 1947.

Cousins (W. E.) and Parret (J.): *Ny Ohabolon' ny Ntaolo*, Antananarivo, 1885.

Dalhe: *Specimens of Madagascar Folklore*, Antananarivo, 1887.

Dandouau: 'Ody et Fanafody', in *Bulletin de l'Académie Malgache*, 1913, vol. XI, p. 151.

Decary: *L'Androy*.

Deteil: 'Les Fokon'olona', in *Revue de Madagascar*, January 1933.

Demaison: *Un voyage moderne* (A Modern Voyage).

Deschamps: 'Pamosavi Antaisaka', in *Revue de Madagascar*, July 1935.

Deschamps: 'Les Antaisaka', in *Bulletin de l'Académie Malgache*, first series, vol. IV.

Drury (Robert): *Madagascar or Robert Drury's Journal, during Fifteen Years' Captivity on that Island*, 1729.

Dubois: *Aquarelles Malgaches* (Malagasy Watercolours).

Dubois: *La connaissance des mentalites malgaches* (Knowing the Malagasy Mentality), Paris, 1931.

Dubois: *Monographie du Betsileo* (Monograph on the Betsileo).

Esmé (Jean d'): *Les Barbares* (The Barbarians), 1925.

Esmé (Jean d'): *L'Ile Rouge* (The Red Isle), 1928.

Faublée: *Ethnographie de Madagascar*.

Faublée: 'Les types et les sociétiés Malgaches' (Malagasy Types and Societies), in *Encyclopédie de l'Empire Français, Madagascar*, vol. I, p. 63, Paris, 1947.

Flacourt (Et. de): *Histoire de la Grande Ile de Madagascar* (History of the Island of Madagascar), Paris, 1658.

Flinbert (Elian J.): *Le livre de la sagesse Malgache* (The Book of Malagasy Wisdom).

Fomba Malagasy, Antananarivo, 1920.

Fontoynont (Dr.): 'Kabary Merina des Funérailles', in *Revue de Madagascar*, April 1935.

Fontoynont (Dr.): 'Le folklore et les coutumes' (Folklore and Customs), in *Encyclopédie de l'Empire Français, Madagascar*, vol. I, p. 87 (with a bibliography).

Gennep (van): *Tabou et Totémisme à Madagascar*, Paris, 1904.

Grandidier (A.): *Les voyages de Mayeur*.

Griffith (R.): *Children of Madagascar*.

Hardy (G.): 'La psychologie des populations coloniales' (The Psychology of Colonial Peoples), in *Revue de la psychologie des peuples*, Le Havre, July 1947.

Hessling: 'La criminalité en Imérina', in *Revue de Madagascar*, 1904.

Ivry (H.): 'Le mouvement national Malgache', in *Esprit*, February 1948.

Jaubert (J.): *Pour une agriculture collective indigène* (In Favour of a Native Collective Agriculture), in *Revue de Madagascar*, January 1945.

Julien (G.): *Institutions politiques et sociales de Madagascar* (The Political and Social Institutions of Madagascar), 1904.

Julien (G.): *Ibotoala*, 1923.

July (A.): *La question des enfants métis* (The Problem of Half-caste Children), in *Revue de Madagascar*, July 1905.

Lallier de Coudray: 'Du rôle des administrateurs dans une colonie neuve' (The Function of Administrators in a New Colony), in *Revue de Madagascar*, June 1902.

Laurence (Jean): *Ranora*, 1932.

Laurence (Jean): *Rakotomavo*, 1935.

La Vaissière: *Vingt ans à Madagascar* (Twenty Years in Madagascar), 1885.

Lavau (G.): *Rites funéraires malgaches* (Malagasy Funeral Ceremonies), in *Revue de Madagascar*, January 1934.

Leblond (M. and A.): *Les sortilèges* (Sorcery), 1905.

Leblond (M. and A.): *Fétiches*, 1925.

Leroux (Lina): *L'Envers du rêve colonial* (The Other Side of the Colonial Dream), 1936.

Lessay (Jean): 'A Tananarive, deux sociétiés se cotoient sans se connaître' (In Antananarivo, two societies live side by side and do not know each other), in *Le Monde*, 15 May, 1948.

Lhande (Rev. Father): *Notre épopée missionaire: Madagascar* (Our Missionary Epic, Madagascar).

Linton: *The Tanala*.

Locamus (P.): *Mes trois voyages à Madagascar* (My Three Journeys to Madagascar), Diégo-Suarez, 1909.

Mager: *La vie à Madagascar* (Life in Madagascar).

Malzac: *Histoire du royaume hova* (History of the Hova Kingdom).

Mannoni (O.): 'La personnalité malgache, Ebauche d'une analyse des structures' (Tentative Analysis of the Structure of the Malagasy Personality), in *Revue de psychologie des peuples*, July 1948.

Mannoni (O.): 'Colonisation et psychanalyse' (Colonization and psychoanalysis), in *Chemins du monde*, vol. V, October 1948.

Mannoni (O.): 'L'Enseignement' (Education), in *Encyclopédie coloniale, Madagascar*.

Mannoni (O.): 'Andrianampoinimerina', in *Revue de Madagascar*, July 1936.

Merleau-Ponty (Dr.): 'La circoncision chez les Sihanaka' (Circumcision among the Sihanaka), in *Notes, Reconnaissances et Explorations*, 1897, p. 349.

Modain (G.): 'Condition sociale de la femme Hova' (Social Situation of the Hova Woman), in *Bulletin de l'Académie Malgache*, 1904, vol. III, p. 66.

Mondain (G.): *Consciences malgaches*, 1906.

Mondain (G.): *Des idées religieuses de Hova avant l'introduction du christianisme* (Religious Ideas of the Hova before the Introduction of Christianity), Cahors, 1904.

Mondain (G.): *Raketaka*, Paris, 1925.

National Assembly: *Proceedings* of 6–9 May, 1947, 6 June, 1947, 1 August, 1947 (Official Gazette).

Olsen: 'Histoire des Zafindiamanana', in *Bulletin de l'Académie Malgache*, 1929, p. 37.

Paulhan (Jean): *Les Hain-Teny merina*, Paris, 1913.

Ponds (Roger): 'Lettre de Madagascar. Passé, présence et avenir de la France' (Letter from Madagascar. Past, Present, and Future of France), in *La Tribune des Nations*, 6 February, 1948.

Rabearivelo (J.-J.): 'La poésie malgache', in *Revue d'Afrique*, August–September 1933.

Rabemananjara: *Les dieux Malgaches* (The Malagasy Gods; Tragedy in French Verse), Paris, 1947.

Rasamuel: *Kabary ampanambadiana* (Discussion of Marriage), translated by Colançon, in *Bulletin de l'Académie Malgache*, 1928, vol. I.

Réallon (Henriett-H.): 'Trois âges dans l'histoire de l'Imérina' (Three Epochs in the History of the Imerina), in *Revue de Madagascar*, January 1937.

Renel (Ch.): *Ancêtres et dieux* (Ancestors and Gods), 1920.

Renel (Ch.): *La race inconnue* (The Unknown Race), 1909.

Renel (Ch.): *La coutume des ancêtres* (The Custom of the Ancestors), 1913.

Renel (Ch.): 'Les amulettes Malgaches' (Malagasy Charms), in *Revue de Madagascar*, 1920, and *Bulletin de l'Académie Malgache*, 1915.

Russillon: *Le Vintana* (Fate), 1914.

Russillon: 'Le Sikidy', in *Bulletin de l'Académie Malgache*, 1908, vol. VI, p. 113.

Russillon: *Paganisme*.

Russillon: *Un culte dynastique avec évocation des morts. Le tromba* (A Dynastic Cult and Raising of the Dead; the Tromba).

Savaron: *Mes souvenirs* (My Recollections).

Standing (H. J.): 'Les fady malgaches', in *Bulletin de l'Académie Malgache*, 1904, p. 105.

Siriex (P.-H.): 'Les Affaires malgaches', in *Revue de Madagascar*, 1945, special number, p. 31.

'Situation politique de Madagascar', in *La Documentation Française*, fascicle no. 713, 29 August, 1947.

INDEX

Ann Arbor Paperbacks